*Buddhism*

*& the*

*Twelve Steps*

# DAILY REFLECTIONS

*Buddhism*

*& the*

*Twelve Steps*

DAILY REFLECTIONS

THOUGHTS ON DHARMA AND RECOVERY

BY KEVIN GRIFFIN

ONE BREATH BOOKS

*Buddhism & the Twelve Steps:* DAILY REFLECTIONS
Copyright 2021 by Kevin Griffin

First Edition, January 2021
One Breath Books
ISBN 978-0-9996789-1-6

# Preface

In this book I include several quotes from my other books.
Here are those book titles:

*One Breath at a Time: Buddhism and the Twelve Steps*
*A Burning Desire: Dharma God and the Path of Recovery*
Buddhism and the Twelve Steps Workbook
*Recovering Joy: A Mindful Life after Addiction*
*Living Kindness: Buddhist Teachings for a Troubled World*

To see a table of contents of *Daily Reflections* with the title of each day's topic, go to my website:
www.kevingriffin.net/reflections-TOC

# Introduction

Daily reflection is at the heart of both Buddhist practice and Twelve Step programs. With the Buddhist emphasis on staying in the present moment and the Twelve Step admonition to take things "one day at a time," the importance of not getting lost in the past or future is clear. Our life is only lived here and now. This collection of teachings and practices is meant to help you start each day with a clear focus on your spiritual condition.

The book is organized in a "Step of the Month" format but with a lot of room for general reflection. While the book is designed as a daily reader, it can also be used as a Step study. If you want to focus on a particular Step, you can go to that month and read those pages.

Most months also include several meditation practices so that you can use the book as a guide in developing a variety of approaches to meditation.

I hope these teachings will inspire, as well as inform you on your path of recovery.

# January: Step One

*"We admitted we were powerless over [alcohol, our addiction, food, sex, gambling, gaming, the Internet, etc.], that our lives had become unmanageable."*

# January 1

*"Keep Coming Back"*

Our dharma practice and our recovery program each rest on the foundations of intention and commitment. One day at a time and one breath at a time, we keep coming back to the present moment and to our wish to be free.

Sometimes the first day of a new year is our first day in recovery or marks a return from relapse. Barring those extremes, like the end of the previous year, it's a time for reflection and commitment: we consider what we've learned from the past year and commit to where we want to go in the coming year. In this first week, we will focus on various aspects of our recovery program, our meditation practice, and some core Buddhist teachings to deepen these reflections.

Whether you are a newcomer or have many years of recovery, today is a day to re-commit to your recovery program. In what ways have you let it lapse in the past year? What are you willing to commit to for the coming year?

As a meditator, whether you are new to practice or an old hand, today is a day to re-commit to your practice. In what ways have you let it lapse in the past year? What are you willing to commit to for the coming year?

In recovery, we commit to regular attendance at meetings or some kind of support gatherings; we vow to live a life of integrity; we share our experience with others who are struggling; and we continue to seek to grow spiritually.

In Buddhism, we commit to daily meditation and yearly retreats (more on retreats later); we vow to live a life of integrity; we give of ourselves through acts of compassion and service; and we seek wisdom and clarity through, study, practice, and reflection.

Today reflect on these commitments, where you are fulfilling them and where you could benefit from increased effort.

# January 2

### *"Keep Coming Back…to the Breath"*

There are many tools we can use for meditation. The breath is one of the simplest and most effective. We are always breathing, so the breath is always readily available. The breath is a "neutral" experience, not particularly pleasant or unpleasant, so it doesn't trigger any special feelings.

Right now, feel how your body is breathing. Where can you feel your breath? Your chest? Your belly? Your nose? How about your back? Anywhere else?

Just by feeling the breath, you are bringing your mind into the present moment. Allow your breath to relax you, and as you do, pick one of these points in the body to focus on more closely: the nostrils or the belly. Breath at the nostrils is felt as the touch of air coming and going. This can be perceived at first as a simple one-two, in-out, but with time we can start to notice more and more subtle elements of sensations. Breath at the belly is felt as the movement, rising and falling. This, too, can be a simple one-two, but with time is revealed to be a complex series of sensations.

When you meditate you can close your eyes, or if you're not comfortable with the eyes closed, simply lower the gaze and take the attention out of the field of sight. As you relax, start to pay attention to the sensations of breath. Whenever you notice that your mind has wandered, gently bring it back to the feeling of breathing. Try to do this exercise with a sense of curiosity and kindness, not fighting to do it "right."

At the end of five minutes, notice how you feel. It's important to see how just being still and quiet for a few minutes has a positive effect on our body and mind.

Today make a commitment to sit for at least five minutes everyday this week. Over time you can increase the length of your sittings.

# January 3

### *"Powerless"*

"We are powerless over the disease of alcoholism [and addiction] and the effects of alcohol [and other substances], but we are not powerless over whether we pick up a drink [or drug] or not." *One Breath at a Time*, p. 16

There is sometimes confusion over the meaning of being "powerless" in Step One. It doesn't mean we are helpless victims. It doesn't mean we have no agency in our lives. It's an acknowledgment of our lack of control over a certain realm, namely our addictive relationship to a substance or behavior. It doesn't mean we are powerless over everything else in the world.

Nonetheless, the reflection on powerlessness is a helpful one for keeping perspective. Trying to control that which we have no control over or battling with immoveable forces simply creates more frustration, pain, and suffering in our lives. We must learn to recognize when no amount of effort can change a difficult or painful situation, and mindfully accept things as they are.

Rather than talking about powerlessness, it might be more helpful to say we can't control everything. We couldn't control our behavior, whether substance- or process-related. This recognition is the start of the Steps and of true recovery. Without this surrender, there will always be a part of us that thinks we might be able to go back to "controlled" using. This is one of the most dangerous thoughts an addict can have.

Today, notice the moments of tension when you are trying to change or control things that aren't under your power. In each of those moments, see what it would mean to let go.

# January 4

*"Wanting recovery"*

What makes for successful recovery? It seems that every approach, whether Twelve Step or something else, claims that its method is the best. However, given the relapse rate among all addicts, it's hard to make that claim. In fact, no method has been shown to have even a 50% success rate, much less 100%.

Some people may make a great deal of effort and still relapse, while others seem to breeze along without doing a lot of work. So, if it isn't the method or amount of effort someone makes, what is it?

One Twelve Step saying is, "The people who make it are the ones who want it, not the ones who need it." This means that it is the quality of our wanting that determines our success. The lures for relapse are many, with opportunities all around us. Unless we are fully committed—unless we really want it—the likelihood that we'll fall back into addiction is strong.

So, how does someone get to a place of wanting recovery? Typically, it's hitting bottom that triggers our desire to escape suffering. When this happens we realize that there's no way out, that all our strategies to control our using have failed. This is perhaps the greatest motivator for recovery.

To further strengthen our motivation, we might ask ourselves what we really want from life. Do we want love? Purpose? Respect? Security? When we consider how to get these things, we realize that active addiction will always stand in the way, and hobble any chance at finding them. Remembering what we really want from life can be a great motivator for staying in recovery.

Today reflect on your level of commitment to recovery. What are your motivations for staying clean and sober?

# January 5

*"Hitting bottom"*

What does it mean to hit bottom? For different people, there can be vastly different definitions. We see people living on the street, strung out, broke, their bodies falling apart, their lives going nowhere, yet still resisting giving up drinking and using. Other people wake up with a hangover in their penthouse and decide it's time to make a change.

Each of us has to find our own bottom. And mindfulness can help.

Mindfulness makes us more aware of everything—including our pain and how it arises. When we start to pay attention in this way, we become sensitized; we feel our feelings more distinctly and more immediately. As we begin to experience the relief of letting go, we become less willing to live with unnecessary pain or discomfort.

We start to see more clearly the connection between our thoughts, feelings, and behaviors, and our pain and suffering. We see how clinging to anger, resentment, pleasure, or anything else is inherently unsatisfying. We hit bottom and want to let go.

Mindfulness makes us more sensitive to our bottom, in a sense, raising our bottom. We become less willing to tolerate unnecessary pain.

Today reflect on whether there is a bottom you still need to reach around your addiction or any other source of pain in your life. Are you willing to explore that with mindfulness and compassion?

# January 6

*"The First Noble Truth"*

The Buddha's First Noble Truth says that there is inevitable pain in life, and that we can never arrive at a place of permanent satisfaction. It is resistance to this Truth that is behind our addiction. Addicts want to find a way to create constant pleasure or at least avoid pain at all costs.

Step One is the admission that such a wish can never be achieved, that we have to find another way of dealing with life's challenges than painting them over with drugs and alcohol.

In some sense, addiction is a kind of immaturity, a childish expectation that nothing should ever go wrong, that pain or difficulties in life are a mistake, and that we can always avoid such problems. But the truth is, we can't avoid life's challenges.

A spiritual path is one that gives us the strength and wisdom to not only weather life's tough times, but to learn and grow from them. When we fight with or run from such challenges, we only create more problems and agitation in our lives. Buddhism and recovery both encourage us to see that these difficulties are a natural part of life, not an aberration. They both give us tools to deal with the ups and downs, while maintaining balance and peace in our lives.

Make it a regular part of your program and practice to acknowledge the difficulties in your life. Accept that they are a natural part of life's unfolding, not mistakes or flaws.

Today reflect on any challenge you might be avoiding or denying. How could you hold it more wisely?

# January 7

*"Powerless over thoughts"*

When we first sit down to meditate, we might have the idea that the technique we are being taught will stop our thoughts. So, when people learn mindfulness meditation and discover their mind wandering, they often have the idea that they are doing it wrong or that they aren't trying hard enough. The truth is, we aren't in control of our thoughts. Yes, with a lot of meditation practice we may have moments when our thoughts get quiet, but ultimately we can't turn them off. We are powerless over our thoughts.

At first we might be dismayed by this insight, but in fact it can be quite freeing. The struggle to stop thinking is not unlike the struggle to stop drinking and using; both can be frustrating and fruitless. When we admit we are powerless over our thoughts, we begin the vital shift in strategy from control to acceptance and investigation. Ironically, with this shift the thoughts become less troubling.

Fundamentally, what we are doing in mindfulness meditation is *changing our relationship* to our thoughts. Instead of believing and acting on every thought and impulse, we are observing and exploring our thoughts. This change involves seeing both the content and process of thoughts: what am I thinking and how does it play out?

Today in your meditation notice how thoughts arise without your effort or intention. See how, despite your effort at intervention, they persist. Notice how, no matter how many times you come back to the breath, eventually the mind wanders off again. Breathe, soften, and let the thoughts go.

# January 8

*"Mindfulness and Denial"*

Our years of active addiction went unchecked because we were stuck in denial, the refusal to acknowledge the truth of our problem. We sought to blame others or our own "unique" challenges for the continuing pain, failures, and confusion in our lives. Even when we blamed ourselves, we never saw that our addictive behavior was the root of the problem. We'd rather wallow in self-pity than take responsibility for our lives, for our feelings, for our relationships, and for our actions.

With Step One's admission, we come out of denial. That admission is founded in mindfulness, the clear awareness of what is happening. We finally see and fully accept the connection between our addiction and the suffering in our lives, the cause-and-effect relationship. We see the tangle of thoughts and feelings that led to an overwhelming craving. And we see how painful and unsatisfying it was to try to satisfy that craving. It's in this mindful attention that we finally overcome the denial and fully accept the nature of our problem.

It's not easy to face and accept our pain, but it is through this process of kind attention that we come through our struggles and find our way to clarity and freedom.

Today reflect on whether you have fully accepted the nature of your addiction. Have you brought mindfulness to the layers of your pain? Until we fully recognize this pain, we won't let go of denial.

# January 9

*"Surrender and Unmanageability"*

"No one wants to surrender. The word itself implies failure and vanquishment on the field of battle. But, as we enter the process we often find that it's the battle itself—with drugs and alcohol, with the world, with ourselves—which has crippled us in many ways, so surrender becomes preferable to going on fighting.

"Surrender is a traditional element of every spiritual journey. Before we can begin to realize our potential, we must break out of limiting concepts of who and what we are and what we think is possible. This may mean giving up long held beliefs and comfortable behavior patterns. Cynicism or fantasizing; fear or control; anger or grief: many of us clung to these patterns and others. As we began to surrender, we saw that we would have to let go of these destructive habits of mind before we could move toward freedom." *One Breath at a Time*, Part One, p. 3

We're only ready to give up, to surrender, when we've hit bottom and seen that our strategies for control would never work, and "that our lives had become unmanageable." In a sense, powerlessness is a reflection of our internal state, and unmanageability is external, seeing that our lives are collapsing around us. While the internal and external might not match up—perhaps one or the other doesn't seem out of control—the overall picture is one of a downward spiral. It is in seeing this clearly that surrender comes.

For most of us it was a long road getting to this point, but once we arrive, there is a sense of a great weight being lifted from our shoulders. No longer must we hold the world together alone; we aren't in charge of managing everything. The battle is over.

Today reflect on the ways your life is or was unmanageable. Have you surrendered to that truth? Try to get in touch with the joy of letting go and give up fighting.

# January 10

*"Breathing in, breathing out"*

At first when we try to practice mindfulness of breathing, called *Anapanasati*, in the Pali language, it can be difficult to even know what we are paying attention to. The sensations of breath are often subtle and difficult to distinguish. Here is one way to begin to feel the breath:

Put your attention at your nostrils, at the tip of the nose, and notice the difference between the sensations when you are inhaling and exhaling. While neither of these two feelings might be distinct by itself, usually when we notice their contrast, we start to tune in.

What sensations do you feel? What distinctions do you feel between the in-breath and out-breath? Notice the varying pressure and temperature.

It's also helpful to say the words "In, out," silently to yourself with each in-breath and out-breath. This can help the mind stay focused.

Something to watch out for is the tendency to try to control the breath in this exercise. Don't try to breathe in any special way. Don't try to slow or deepen the breath, just let the body breathe naturally. Mindfulness is about *observing* the experience, not trying to create any special experience.

At first mindfulness of breath can feel unnatural. Sometimes people get self-conscious about breathing because they've never thought about it before. You could get a little anxious or the breath could seem to get shorter or longer. If you stick with the process, all of this will pass. Breathing is the most natural thing in the world. All you have to do is sit back and watch with relaxed interest.

Today, start to stretch the length of your meditation to ten minutes or longer. Extending your meditation allows more calm and clarity to develop.

# January 11

*"Relapse"*

Relapse is part of the process of recovery. Whether in repeated failures to establish recovery or a slip after many years, most of us have experienced this falling back. How we respond to relapse is a vital part of the process. A typical response is, "Well, I blew it, so I might as well keep drinking [using, acting out, etc]." This reaction comes out of the sense of failure and despair that triggered the relapse in the first place. Clearly, such an attitude isn't going to help.

The first thing we have to do with a relapse is bring compassion and forgiveness to ourselves. It's painful to relapse, and that pain deserves our care, not punishment. We know that addiction is a tough condition to live with and that many before us have slipped, so forgiveness is appropriate. It's just a recognition that we are human and as such, flawed. We must forgive ourselves for our humanness.

Meditation gives us a kind of microcosm through which to view relapse. Every time the mind wanders, we are "relapsing." When we notice this, we don't beat ourselves up, but instead we come back to the breath and start over. Whether one day at a time or one breath at a time, recovery and spiritual growth are always about addressing the present moment situation, not judging or berating ourselves over our mistakes.

If we aren't berating ourselves, relapse can become an opportunity to evaluate our recovery—or lack thereof. With humility, we can learn a great deal from a relapse. What mistakes did we make? Where did we come up short in our efforts? What beliefs and attitudes were behind the relapse? How were we not taking care of ourselves? What were the triggers?

Today reflect on where your life will go if you continue in your addiction versus maintaining recovery. Make a commitment to do the things that will help you stay clean and sober.

# January 12

*"Fear of Change"*

One of the things that blocks us from recovery is our fear of change. The idea of living without getting high might seem joyless. Especially for alcoholics, our social life is often tied up with drinking. What will we do for friends? And if we're physically addicted, the fear of withdrawal can stop us in our tracks. This has been our life for so long that it can be difficult to imagine any other way of living. Only when the pain gets strong enough do we become willing to take the risk of change.

If we want to get clean and sober, we have to be willing to give up everything. We can't hang out with our drinking/drugging buddies; we can't lie, cheat, and steal; we can't avoid responsibility or run from life; and we can't avoid our feelings. Underneath our wish to recover there needs to be the willingness to change. We've come to the end of a failed strategy, and, as it says in the AA Big Book, "Half measures availed us nothing." We simply can't hold something in reserve, some escape clause. We need to be ready to give it all up.

In order to have the strength to do this, we have to first acknowledge and truly accept that there's nothing there for us in our addiction anymore. This is why a First Step Inventory can be so helpful. When we see clearly how bad it was, the pointlessness and uselessness of our addiction, we become ready to do whatever needs to be done.

Today reflect on whether you have completely accepted the failure of your addiction as a strategy for living. Is there any way you are holding back? What are you afraid to lose?

# January 13

*"Not helpless"*

The term powerless confuses and alienates people who think it means being a helpless victim. But that's not what Step One is saying. It's talking about our relationship to our addiction and to substances. We are powerless over the effects of drugs and alcohol, and over our response to those effects. Certainly we have the power to make choices, whether to use or act out or not, but once we engage in the addictive behavior, we do seem to lose control. The force of craving gets triggered, and with intoxication our capacity to resist is weakened. Now we are swept up in an energy that we don't control—over which we are powerless. That's why avoiding the behavior all together is so important. Nonetheless, the Buddha was clear that we are responsible for our actions, not victims of karma or destiny.

Addiction is powerful; so is craving. We can't stop their arising. However, we can respond to them skillfully. Mindfulness is the key tool to help in this process. Without awareness, without mindfulness, we just continue to react to our feelings, to act on unseen impulses. Before we've even thought about it, the drink is in our hands, the joint is at our lips, the pastry is in our mouths. Mindfulness helps us to see the craving, or even the first inklings of craving, before it becomes an obsession. Once we see the craving, we can take steps to undermine or weaken it.

This is where our program and practice kick in. We call someone, go to a meeting or a sitting, go to the gym, or simply breathe and let go. We can only counter the power of addiction with a strong intention and mindfulness.

Today reflect on what resources you are using for your recovery. What positive powers are you drawing on?

# January 14

### *"Thirst: the Second Noble Truth"*

Once the Buddha lays down the Truth of Suffering, he says that its cause, the Second Noble Truth, is craving. The word in Pali is *tanha*, which literally means "thirst." So, suffering is caused by thirst. Ironic if you are an alcoholic.

In Western Buddhism, we usually go on to expand that idea to mean craving of any kind, as well as clinging. For addicts, of course, this makes perfect sense. We're well aware how our craving and clinging caused us (and others) suffering. Our whole process of recovery is about overcoming destructive desires. These desires also imply our negative desires--our aversion, anger, resentment, and fear.

The Buddha doesn't stop at identifying these obviously destructive desires as the cause of suffering. By giving us the tool of mindfulness, he helps us to uncover the more subtle forms of craving that can infest the mind. As we sit and try to follow the breath, we're bombarded with thoughts and feelings that continuously pull us away from the present moment. When examined, we see that these distractions all have the common attribute of craving: craving for the future; craving for pleasure, success, or comfort; craving simply to be entertained; craving to avoid pain; craving to be superior to others; and craving to be recognized, to be known.

In this way, we are gently guided onto the path of letting go. We may begin this path by letting go of a harmful addiction, but if we continue to explore our hearts and minds, we realize that even subtle forms of craving cause suffering. We become motivated to let go in deeper and deeper ways, to let go of ego striving, pleasure seeking, bias, judgment, resentment, fear, and lust. Not that these feelings won't ever arise again, but we are no longer controlled by them.

Today begin to pay attention to more subtle forms of craving and aversion. See if you can let go of them moment by moment.

# January 15

## *"Right View"*

The first step on the Buddha's Noble Eightfold Path is Right View. This means we see the world clearly, we see the truth, and we understand how things work. The essence of Right View is understanding the Four Noble Truths, how suffering arises and how it ends. This then connects to an understanding of the Law of Karma, cause and effect.

For the addict in recovery, it's pretty clear how our craving (cause) led to addiction (effect). We see that our behavior was responsible for our suffering. No longer do we blame others, no longer do we see ourselves as victims, or as just unlucky. We take responsibility for our lives.

The "moment of clarity" often referred to in the Twelve Step world is a moment of Right View. Suddenly we see how deluded we've been; we see the truth clearly. Right View then is applying this same clarity to all the moments of our life, seeking to find the truth behind every thought, every feeling, every interaction, and every situation. We look for the truth in our relationships, in our jobs, and in the world around us. No area of life is discounted as not holding some truth if we look for it.

Today, look for the truth in all these aspects of your life. Look inside to see how you are still creating suffering for yourself. And look outside with compassion, kindness, and discernment.

# January 16

## *"Denial"*

The Twelve Step term for not having Right View is denial. This keeps us from even beginning to deal with our addiction because we won't even admit that it exists.

Dealing with the problem often seems to come down to a debate—with ourselves and with others—about how we identify ourselves. The question "Am I an addict?" (or an alcoholic) becomes a stumbling block, as though how we name our problem were the key issue.

Here's another way to think about it: When you are using, you have problems, but you can't solve them. When you are clean, you still have problems, but now you have ways to deal with them, one day at a time. This isn't a matter of identity or naming your condition. Rather it is going straight at the issue in a practical way. Denial isn't avoiding calling yourself an addict, it's avoiding dealing with the problem of addiction.

There are many ways we stay in denial. Maybe your life seems okay on the outside—job, family, friends. So, you can't be an alcoholic because alcoholics are homeless bums begging for change on the street corner. No, they are not.

Lots of people drink and use, we tell ourselves. We are "normal" (even if we tend to be drinking and using more than everyone else). If we socialize with other addicts, this is true—we are normal addicts.

Another form of denial is if you are a "controlled" drinker or drug user. You don't drink in the morning, you don't blackout, you don't drive drunk. Okay, but, again, is your drinking and drugging improving your life or just giving you a temporary escape from things you don't want to deal with, like your feelings?

Today reflect on whether you are still in denial about your addiction. Is there any way in which you are holding back from a full admission that you can't drink and use anymore?

# January 17

*"A Moment of Clarity"*

When people come out of denial and suddenly realize that the cause of their problems is their addiction, it's called "a moment of clarity." This is the Twelve Step version of Right View. At that point we see the truth clearly, and now we can move forward into recovery.

This is a precious moment. In fact, it is a "spiritual awakening," something we're told we will acquire through working the Steps. At first this moment might seem like a moment of failure—"Oh, no! I'm an addict!" However, it's a great gift. We can't solve a problem if we don't know what it is. And, while this clarity might come at a terrible time, at our bottom, it opens the potential for the wondrous experience called recovery.

Clarity is what the Buddha's path is all about. To see the truth of our situation, whether it's an addiction to a substance or simply the ordinary fascination with ego, the practice of mindfulness points towards clarity in every moment. And for the addict, the initial moment of clarity is only the first of many along the winding path of recovery.

When we practice meditation, we try to awaken and reinforce this clarity. This is why a daily practice is so important. We can't live on yesterday's clarity. The habits of self-seeking are persistent and deeply conditioned, so it requires vigilance to keep them at bay.

Today reflect on whether you are taking the actions that support and maintain your clarity.

# January 18

### *"Identity"*

The Buddha taught that the sense of self is a construction, formed by the confluence of thoughts, memories, sense experiences, and consciousness. We only know life through these elements and assume that there is something unifying behind them. This assumption, he said, was wrong.

The implications of this insight are enormous, and its full realization is one of the expressions of enlightenment.

However, the intellectual understanding of this teaching is far different from the insight itself, an insight that transforms our very experience of life. Some people use the *idea* of identity being a construction as a way to avoid or excuse behavior or responsibility. This is one of the negative intersections of Buddhism and recovery.

Some Buddhists resist identifying as an alcoholic or addict because they believe identity is a construction. They feel that saying, "My name is Joe, and I'm an alcoholic" is somehow "un-Buddhist," that they shouldn't be taking on another identity.

While this has the ring of truth, when closely examined, it's a hollow argument. The purpose of saying, "I'm an alcoholic," is to reinforce the fact that you can't drink anymore. It's not about fencing you in to a limiting role in life. As for adding an identity, if one has truly abandoned all attachments to all identities, then certainly, they could drop the identity as an alcoholic, but how many people have actually done this?

In fact, going into an AA meeting and saying you are an alcoholic can be seen as *stripping* identity rather than adding it. You are letting go of your last name, your status, any title or other role in the world. You are simply one of a group, nothing special. Ultimately this is closer to "not-self" than our ordinary identity. And AA's Twelfth Tradition makes this explicit when it says, "Anonymity is the spiritual foundation of all our traditions," anonymity being a synonym for non-identification.

Today reflect on how you relate to your identities. Which ones are useful and which ones are not so useful? Try to let go of unhelpful identities today.

# January 19

*"Counting breaths"*

When our mind is more agitated than usual during meditation, it can be helpful to have some simple tools for calming the thoughts. A useful one is counting breaths. There are a few ways to approach this.

The typical way is to count on each in-breath, up to ten breaths. On the out-breath say "out" to give the mind something to do. So, you would be saying "1, out, 2, out, 3, out," and so on up to 10. (Both the numbers and words are spoken silently in the mind, not aloud.)

You can also reverse this by saying "in" on the in-breath, and the number on the out-breath.

While this may sound like a simple task, you will probably find that many times you don't make it to 10. You wind up lost in some thought or nodding off. When you notice this happening, at that point just come back to 1. Don't try to figure out where you got lost; just start at 1 again.

Some` people will tend to make this a competition and find themselves getting frustrated when they can't get to 10. This is not a competition, and getting frustrated is just another ego manifestation. Try to keep it simple. Recognize that your mind is unruly, that you don't control it, and that acceptance of that will elicit more calm than judging brings to the situation.

Some teachers suggest that since 10 is such a familiar number, people can go on automatic pilot when doing this practice. They suggest counting to another number like 8. This is worth exploring.

Finally, another, perhaps riskier practice, is just counting up and up, not returning to 1. In this practice, when the mind wanders, you try to pick up wherever you got lost. There's a tendency to get somewhat hypnotized in this approach, but it can be effective. Again, experiment and see if any of these approaches help your concentration.

Counting is mostly for times when you are especially agitated or restless. It's not recommended as a core or ongoing practice because its main function is simply calming body and mind. It doesn't tend to arouse mindfulness or insight.

# January 20

## *"Right Intention"*

"Right Intention gives clarity, direction, and resolve on the path. With Right Intention, we are never entirely lost, no matter how much we stray. Right intention guides us back to ourselves and the values of kindness and wisdom." *Burning Desire*, p.78.

Once we have developed some degree of Right View, we begin to see what we need to do to live more skillfully. We see how we create suffering and how we can end it. Now we need to put into practice what we see. That means we need to set an intention.

All action is preceded by intention, even if we aren't aware of the intention. This is a fundamental Buddhist concept. In fact, the Buddha is quoted as saying, "Karma is intention." What this means is that the results of our actions depend not just on the actions themselves, but on the impulse behind them, the intention. For instance, we can give someone a gift out of kindness, or we can give them a gift hoping to get something back. The karmic results of these differing intentions will be very different, maybe not externally, but certainly internally because generosity always feels better than greed.

Sustained recovery depends upon sustained intention. No matter how bad a day we are having, we need to maintain our commitment to recovery. Life is hard, even without drugs and alcohol, and we're going to have ups and downs. It's only our trust and commitment to the path that sustains us through the tough times.

The Buddha says there are three things that qualify as Right Intention: the intention to let go, the intention to be loving, and the intention to be compassionate. While most of us won't be able to have a pure intention all the time, we can use these guidelines in making choices and taking actions.

Today reflect on the intentions that are guiding you.

# January 21

*"Lovingkindness"*

The practice of lovingkindness, or "metta," in the Pali language, is one of the primary practices found in Buddhist teachings. It is based in the understanding that everyone wants to be happy, and yet, we all struggle with challenges and pain in life. Knowing how difficult life is, Buddhists are encouraged to wish happiness for all beings.

For addicts, love is a central issue. Many of us carried resentments that we've had to address in recovery, and lovingkindness practice can give us a way to start that process. Further, many of us struggle with negative feelings about ourselves, the so-called "inner critic," and lovingkindness helps us overcome those struggles as well.

The traditional practice begins by sending love to ourselves, then to: dear ones, a neutral person, a difficult person, and finally outward to all beings. In the coming months we'll cover all these categories. Today, though, just take some time to reflect on whether you treat yourself in a loving way or not. Have you been kind to yourself? Consider how you treat yourself physically: do you eat in a healthy way? Get enough rest? Exercise?

How do you talk about yourself? Do you denigrate yourself to others? Brag?

How do you think about yourself? Do you put yourself down in your mind? Do you abuse yourself for simple mistakes? Or do you have an inflated idea of your own specialness or uniqueness?

Treating ourselves kindly and honestly are essential elements of recovery. If we are ever going to find happiness and serenity, it will begin with loving ourselves.

Today pay attention to whether you treat yourself with loving kindness or not.

# January 22

*"Cost–Benefit"*

How important to your happiness was your addictive behavior? Did you fear that all the fun would go out of your life if you stopped using or acting out compulsively? Many people only realize when they get clean how little fun they'd actually been having in the later stages of addiction, and that even before that, the state of intoxication they'd so often achieved left them with a feeling of emptiness and lots of regrets. Finally, many discovered that in recovery they were *more able* to enjoy life, that the clarity, health, and energy that came with being clean, along with the newfound sense of connection with others in Twelve Step programs, enriched life much further than the supposedly mood-lifting effects of drugs and alcohol that they'd used to have "fun." In fact, for most of us, it stopped being fun a long time before, if it ever really was.

Today, consider the benefits you get from your addictive behaviors, whether, emotional, social, or anything else. Then consider the costs: social, emotional, professional, physical, economic, etc. Here you need to be what AA calls "rigorously honest." Maybe you don't have cirrhosis of the liver, but what about a cough from smoking cigarettes or pot? Hangovers? Fights with your partner? What could you have done with all the money you spent? Then consider the benefits from dropping your addiction; again, think: social, physical, financial, etc.

For most of us, the benefits of recovery far outweigh those of addiction. Seeing this truth is one of the strongest motivations for maintaining our recovery.

- Adapted from *Buddhism & The Twelve Steps Workbook,* p. 53.

# January 23

*"Sila"*

*Sila* is the Pali term for morality or ethical integrity. It is considered the foundation upon which the practice of meditation and the development of wisdom and compassion are built. Without basic moral boundaries, our behavior can undermine any spiritual efforts. The same is true for recovery.

*Sila* is grounded in the Five Precepts of Non-Harming, essentially not to kill, not to steal, not to commit sexual misconduct, not to lie, and not to use intoxicants. While recovery might seem to be grounded in just the Fifth Precept, it depends, in fact on all five. This is a truth often overlooked by people outside the recovery community.

Recovery is not just abstaining from intoxicants or one particular behavior. It encompasses a lifestyle of morality, kindness, and service. Just as a Buddhist meditator will not get far if they are breaking the Precepts, a person in recovery will often relapse if they continue to lie, cheat, and steal, not to mention act out sexually or violently.

Following the Precepts, practicing *sila*, isn't about rules. It's about recognizing the suffering we cause ourselves and others when we act out in these ways. Violence, stealing, sexual misconduct, and lying both cause and require, a closing of the heart, a numbing of our conscience, and a cynical, hardened view of the world. This numbing and hardening open us to drug and alcohol use. For one thing, if we've become that nihilistic, there seems to be no reason to restrain our behavior around intoxicants. And the pain of guilt and shame calls for further numbing.

The Buddha called following the Precepts "the Bliss of Blamelessness." In recovery we discover this joy in the pleasure of doing the right thing, making simple acts of kindness, and knowing we aren't bringing more harm to the world.

Today take some time to enjoy this bliss. Take joy in your *sila*.

# January 24

### *"Triggers: HALT"*

If we are going to sustain our recovery, we will have to learn to live with and not react to triggers for relapse. One of the classic acronyms, HALT points to the tendency to relapse when hungry, angry, lonely, or tired.

Hunger affects us emotionally and physically. The emotion makes us irritable and feeling empty. We want something to soothe us and fill us up. For alcoholics, this ties into alcohol's "nutritional" quality. Its sugar base helps us cope with hunger. That's kind of the reason for "cocktail hour" and "Happy Hour." Instead of having dinner, you have a drink. Of course, for people with eating disorders, hunger presents a whole other challenge that must be dealt with multiple times each day. It generally requires a disciplined and organized approach to food.

Anger can trigger craving for something to cool the heat and agitation. But anger can also turn back on us. Self-hatred drives a lot of addiction. And we can even harm ourselves in a perverse attempt to harm someone else. "Drinking at" someone is the classic version of this.

Loneliness is a real challenge for addicts. Oftentimes we actually wanted to be alone so we could indulge our addiction with no one to judge us or get in the way. But the empty feeling of loneliness also wants filling and soothing. Self-pity can creep in and the feeling that we "deserve" the pleasant experience of being high, even if we know the consequences will ultimately be harmful.

Tiredness is an odd trigger. With alcohol and many drugs, we can cover our fatigue, so instead of getting rest, we go to the bar or pop a pill. For food and sex addicts, fatigue can be a trigger for binging. For all addicts, being tired lowers our resistance and capacity for self-care. We seek the comfort of food, sex, or intoxicants. Finally, many addicts simply associate using with late nights, so we fall back into that habit when tired.

Today, reflect on how any or all of the elements of HALT are relapse risks for you. Try to take care of yourself so that these triggers won't arise. If they do come up, determine that you will take wise action in response rather than reacting with dangerous activities.

# January 25

*"Triggers: Family"*

Addiction is a family disease. Few of us escaped childhood unscathed or have perfectly happy relationships with our whole family. The wounds we absorbed when young stay with us and are often part of the story of our addiction. In recovery we must find a way of reconciling with these scars.

If we find that spending time with our nuclear or extended family is triggering our addiction, we may have to decide to distance ourselves from them. This can be very painful and probably a last resort.

Barring that extreme, we might still find that there is a lot of work to be done around these relationships. We might have to make amends to a variety of family members, even ones who harmed us. The Twelve Step view is that we don't benefit from blaming others, but solely by taking care of our side of the street.

If people in the family have harmed us, there is also the work of forgiveness. This is where we face the greatest challenge. Here we'll want to discuss how to handle these issues with a sponsor or trusted friend or mentor. If the person has changed and is taking responsibility for their past actions, or if they at least aren't continuing those behaviors, we'll be more likely to want to forgive them. If, on the other hand, they continue to be abusive or in denial about their part, we might consider separating ourselves from them.

Dysfunctional families are systems that depend on everyone going along with the implicit denial, codependence, and role-playing. When someone steps out of this construct or points to its rotten core, it disrupts the entire system. Families can be torn apart by the truth; the person in recovery can be scapegoated and ostracized from the family. That's the risk we take when we go against the history of a family's dysfunction. However, if we are going to prioritize recovery, it's a risk we must make.

Today, reflect on how your family relationships are helping or hindering your recovery. Is there work you need to do in healing or separating from these relationships?

# January 26

*"Triggers: Intimate Relationships"*

Some say that the number one cause of relapse is intimate relationships. A painful breakup or a turbulent affair can send us spinning off into our addiction. In long-term recovery, the work and healing we do around intimacy is some of the most important we can achieve in creating a happy, productive life.

After overcoming a substance addiction, many of us realize that we have an underlying love, sex, or relationship "addiction." Whether this can really be categorized as addiction might be questionable, but the dysfunctional patterns that play out, whether around sex, power, or conflict can be deeply problematic and will have to be addressed in some way if we are going to establish healthy, happy, and sustained recovery. Programs like Al-Anon, Co-Dependents Anonymous, Sex and Love Addicts Anonymous, and Adult Children of Alcoholics can be great tools in dealing with these problems, as can therapy.

As addicts we may have been used to protecting ourselves from the vulnerability that intimacy demands. We stayed loaded so we didn't have to really feel, or we avoided commitment altogether. In recovery we have to learn how to be truly honest, to drop defensiveness, and not to run when we feel threatened by that very vulnerability.

If your partner is an addict, too, it's going to be challenging to stay together and not relapse if they don't also get into recovery. On the other hand, trying to convince your partner to get clean can cause fractures in a relationship. Many people find that they can't sustain the relationship they are in when they come into recovery.

Today reflect on how relationships trigger you. Is there work you need to do in this realm?

# January 27

*"Triggers: Work"*

At the end of a long day or week of work we can feel as if we "deserve" to have a drink or to overeat or act on some other addiction. This ties in with HALT, but has special issues. We can't just stop working. We all need a job and income. But sometimes we get caught in situations that are particularly stressful or even ethically challenging. Such pressures can easily become triggers for relapse.

Although we can't necessarily change jobs, we may at times face a decision, whether it's worth it to stay in a particular position. Sometimes we have to step back and ask what's most important, our job or our sanity. The momentum of ambition and professional progress can seem inevitable, but when we look at the broader picture in recovery, we realize that we always have options.

Creating boundaries around what you are willing to do at work is healthy. In fact, if you are a valued employee, you'll often be respected for taking such a position. And if you aren't treated respectfully, maybe you aren't in the right place.

When we do get into stressful work positions which can't immediately be fixed, we have to make sure that we have other supports in place. Going to a meeting or to meditate on your lunch break; stepping outside to call a friend; making sure you get enough rest; and even planning for a vacation or retreat that you can look forward to. All of these can help us to handle the immediate pressure. The bottom line is, we are committed to not drink or use no matter what, and at times that's the final protection we lean on.

Today reflect on your work situation. If it's a good one, take some time to appreciate that. If it's not so good, consider how you could move forward to improve or change the situation.

# January 28

*"Hindrances"*

The Five Hindrances are the mental and bodily states that get in the way of peaceful meditation, and indeed, a peaceful life. They're not personal flaws like the "character defects" the Steps talk about. Rather they are natural states that arise for everyone. That means we don't have to feel bad about them if they come up—either in meditation or in life. Our mindfulness meditation practice can be a kind of inventory of these hindrances. They are so common and persistent that we have to learn how to work with them if we are going to benefit from meditating.

The hindrances are desire, aversion, sloth and torpor, restlessness and worry, and doubt. These five qualities are the most common obstructions both to a peaceful meditation and an insightful one. Working with them takes practice and determination. You can't simply push them away, nor would you want to. To work with them, we must begin by applying mindfulness. In order to see them clearly, we need to allow ourselves to feel these energies fully. While this can be unpleasant, it's often very revealing. Because our natural habit is to react to the hindrances, in our ordinary lives we rarely really examine them or have a clear experience of them.

Once we are able to be with the experience of a hindrance, we see its unsatisfactory nature clearly, which motivates us to let go of the hindrance instead of acting on it.

In the coming months, we'll look at each individual hindrance. Today, begin to notice when one of these experiences appears in your body or mind and allow it to arise without fighting the experience or blaming yourself for its arising.

# January 29

## *"Antidote to Desire: Disenchantment"*

One of the things that brings Buddhism and the Twelve Steps together is their emphasis on desire or craving. The Buddha identified desire as the cause of suffering, while addicts know that it is their craving that keeps them stuck in a self-destructive cycle.

Since desire is such a challenge for addicts to manage, it is worthwhile to see how Buddhism suggests dealing with this hindrance. The first strategy for dealing with desire is to see the unappealing and ultimately unsatisfactory quality of the object of desire. With drugs and alcohol, this relates to what the Big Book refers to as "recoiling as if from a hot flame." If we have done a thorough First Step and seen both our inability to control our using and the awful results of our addictive behavior, we become disgusted with drugs and alcohol (and other addictive substances).

Disgust means literally, "losing the taste for" something. The appeal of intoxication is gone. A Buddhist term for this is "disenchantment." This means we are no longer under the spell of the substance or the addiction, not enchanted. With either disgust or disenchantment, the craving itself has been uprooted. It simply doesn't appear anymore.

The unsatisfactory quality of addiction is embodied in our clarity about how our addictive behavior inevitably worked out. It rarely ended well. A night of drinking or drugging might have been fun at the time, but it didn't lead to lasting happiness or satisfaction. Rather it usually led to regret, guilt, depression, and physical pain—and often more craving. Again, this clarity depends upon a thorough First Step, one in which the complete and true nature of our addiction was revealed and fully accepted.

Today reflect on whether you have become disgusted and disenchanted with your addiction. Is there more work to do on Step One to complete this break with your desire?

# January 30

*"Body Scan"*

One helpful form of mindfulness meditation is the Body Scan. Here, instead of focusing on a single thing, like the breath, the attention moves very slowly through the body, examining the sensations in each area.

Begin by closing your eyes or just lowering your gaze and taking several mindful breaths. Have a sense of softening the body, letting the attention come to a general sense of awareness of sitting.

Now put the attention on the top of the head. Focus on a relatively small area a few inches around. Move the attention from the front to the back of the head, feeling any sensations. Be aware of temperature, solidity, pulsing, tingling or any other feelings.

Move the attention down the left side of the head, the temple and the ears. Then down the right side.

Scan across the face: the forehead; the eyes; the nose; the cheeks, lips, and inside the mouth. Make sure your jaw is relaxed.

Move the attention down the neck and across the shoulders. Take the attention down the left arm little by little, the left hand; then the right arm and hand.

Now bring the attention to the chest, scanning across the chest, the armpits, and down to the belly. Go to the back and slowly scan from top to bottom.

Feel the sensations in the groin, the hips, and buttocks.

Now scan down the left leg, thigh, knee, calf, shin, and ankle; then the right leg, thigh, knee, calf, shin, and ankle. Move the attention over the left foot; and then over the right foot.

Now take a moment to see if you can feel the whole body at once, as a single object. Feel the energetic life of the body and its myriad sensations. Rest in that awareness.

# January 31

*"Spiritual Awakening"*

It's only Step Twelve that makes the claim of spiritual awakening, but in fact, each Step holds its own element of transformation.

The spiritual awakening of Step One is the realization that our behavior was not only destructive, but unnecessary. When we realize that we don't really need the drugs or booze, the binging or gambling, the sexual acting out or the co-dependent behavior, it frees us for the first time from that trap. Buddhist practice and teachings reinforce this realization by showing how craving itself causes suffering. It was not only the behavior of addiction that caused us pain, but the very impulse behind the actions.

With that realization may come the further freedom of no longer even craving our drug or behavior of choice. But even if we still have a lingering desire, our new insight makes it possible to restrain ourselves from acting out. As we watch the mind in meditation, we start to dis-identify with the desires and cravings that appear, seeing them as impermanent energies that are simply passing through the mind.

Spiritual awakening doesn't have to be a mystical experience or magical moment of oneness with the universe. Rather it is an understanding paired with a change of attitude. We no longer live in the illusion that our addiction is serving us in some way. And we begin to turn our life in a new direction.

Step One sets us on a path of recovery. It shows us the fruitlessness of a life spent chasing a fix, of hiding from life, from pain, and from challenges. It opens us to new possibilities and new dimensions of ourselves. We even begin to question our very identity. Who we thought we were was part of the prison of our addiction. Now we set out to discover who we really want to be; what brings us real happiness; what is truly important for us. This is all part of the journey of awakening that starts with Step One.

Today, reflect on how you have been transformed by your work with Step One. How has spiritual awakening manifested in your life?

# February: Step Two

*"Came to believe that a Power greater than ourselves
could restore us to sanity."*

# February 1

*"Came to believe"*

Belief is a problem for many people who come to the Steps. Perhaps you are a cynic, hardened by the losses and wounds of life; or perhaps you've been alienated by a faith-based religion or teacher; maybe your scientific mind views any talk of spirituality as naïve or simplistic. Whatever blocks your ability to connect with Step Two will have to be addressed.

Step Two says that there is help for us. "A Power greater than ourselves," doesn't have to be religious or mystical. If you go to rehab you have some belief that the "power" of the rehab will help you recover. The same is true if you go to a Twelve Step meeting.

What Step Two requires is the belief that we have the potential to grow and change. We need to see that we aren't destined to be addicts for the rest of our lives.

Of course, this doesn't mean that it's easy to adopt this belief. Many of us felt completely controlled by our addiction—that's its nature, after all. If we thought we could live without it, we might have quit a long time ago. So, "coming to believe" is not something we will likely achieve overnight. It's a process. This process involves all the elements of recovery: community, individual support, Step work, and more. New friends, a new attitude, new goals, and of course, new behaviors are all part of this process. As we change these things externally, we start to change internally. And this is how our trust in the process, in the Steps, and in ourselves, begins to grow.

The process of learning to meditate can be much the same. As we begin a practice, we might have the same doubts we have in recovery. We think we can't do it or that it's not working. As with recovery, we have to have a little trust in the process, to stick with it for a while and let the power of mindfulness take hold.

Today, reflect on where you stand in relation to "coming to believe" both in recovery and meditation. Have you wholeheartedly embraced this Step, or are you still holding something back in your program or your practice?

# February 2

*"The Third Noble Truth: Suffering Can End"*

The Buddha's Third Noble Truth, that freedom is possible, parallels Step Two in that it gives us hope. As the Buddha offers his teachings, we see that there is suffering (First Truth) and that it is caused by craving and clinging (Second Truth). These revelations can be challenging and even overwhelming without the Third Truth. But the statement that suffering can end points to the way out.

The essence of this statement is that if suffering, or addiction, can be created, then it can be *un*created. This idea, like the whole pattern of the Noble Truths, is based on the idea of karma, of cause and effect. Suffering has a cause; likewise, the end of suffering has a cause. The Fourth Noble Truth, then, is the cause that ends suffering: namely the Noble Eightfold Path.

Like Step Two, the Third Noble Truth is fundamentally about belief or faith. Even though Buddhism doesn't seem to be a "faith-based" religion, it requires some faith or trust to engage fully. Deciding to spend time meditating implies faith that the process works. If we don't have some faith in this process, then we won't engage in it.

Our level of commitment tends to grow over time, as our belief in the efficacy of this works grows. That growth manifests as more time meditating, more time studying the dharma, and more involvement with a sangha and teacher. At each stage, this increased involvement reinforces our faith, and a positive feedback loop is established.

Today, reflect on your commitment to dharma practice. How much effort and energy are you willing to put into meditation, to study, and to community? Are you clear that the benefits that arise through practice are directly correlated with the amount of time and effort you put in?

# February 3

*"Sitting"*

The way you hold your body is a key part of meditation. It's easy to overlook this aspect of practice and go right to focusing on the breath. But it's helpful to start a period of meditation by getting a more general feeling of how your body feels, setting the body in balance and alignment.

Unless you have some physical limitations, it's most helpful to sit upright, not slumping or slouching, and preferably on a firm cushion or chair. If you are sitting on a cushion, you should look at some pictures or videos for guidance on how to arrange the legs. When sitting cross-legged, it's important that the knees are touching the ground, so your posture is very stable. If the knees are unsupported, you'll quickly grow uncomfortable and have trouble being still. If you are sitting in a chair, both feet should be firmly on the ground to create a stable posture.

Beyond the specifics of physical alignment, what's even more important is to sit still. Any kind of movement, even subtly shifting or scratching disturbs the concentration and mindfulness. In fact, when there is an impulse to move, that should be taken as an opportunity to explore the sensations behind the impulse as well as the emotional desire, the wish for change or comfort.

For some addicts, restlessness and impulse control might make sitting still particularly difficult. Here we might face the same energy that drove our addiction. This makes the benefit of working with this energy especially useful. Getting in touch with the underlying forces that drove our self-destructive behavior gives us insight into our addiction and can help us to learn how to hold such feelings with kindness and balance.

Today, try to practice perfect stillness in your meditation. Notice how powerful the impulse to move is. See if you can relax and let that feeling pass without fighting it or indulging it.

# February 4

*"Restored to Sanity"*

Newcomers often rebel at the suggestion in Step Two that they were insane. While recognizing that their behavior had certainly been destructive, even irrational, they might argue that it fell short of out-and-out insanity. Fair enough. Step Two isn't a clinical or medical diagnosis.

Rather than quibble about language (one of the ways people avoid addressing the actual issue of recovery), it's more helpful to reflect on what is being restored.

First, many of us suffered from physical deterioration through years of addiction. Simply stopping ingesting intoxicants (aka, poisons) into our body will begin a return to health. Further, for many people, as they come out of the haze and delusion of addiction, other behaviors improve, including diet, exercise, and sleep, thus restoring the body.

Delusion is the word the Buddha uses to describe our foolish thinking and the choices and behaviors it leads to. And delusion is a synonym for insanity. So, from a Buddhist viewpoint, our addictive behavior itself was a form of madness. When we reflect back on how we lived, this will make sense.

It is this delusive thinking that is most in need of healing. Our belief that we needed to be high to be happy; that we couldn't live a healthy normal life; that we were, perhaps, unworthy of happiness; and all the rest of the patterns of negative belief are what supported our addictive behavior. They were the rationale that allowed us to persist for years in acting in a way that some would call "crazy."

So, maybe we were never put in a straight-jacket or had schizophrenic hallucinations (though plenty of us did get institutionalized at some point), but can we really claim that we were living in a rational way?

Today, take some time to reflect on the insanity of your life as an addict. Then think about how you are living today. Have you been restored to sanity? What else do you need to do to further this process of recovery?

# February 5

*"The Hindrances: Skeptical Doubt"*

Skeptical Doubt is the fifth of the Five Hindrances, and it is said to be the most dangerous because it will knock us completely off the path.

Doubt takes two major forms: doubt of the teachings and doubt of ourselves. If we doubt the teachings, then we won't study or do the practices. "What's the point of meditating?" you might say if you doubt the efficacy of the practice. If we doubt ourselves, then we don't have the confidence to engage in the work because it seems pointless. "I'm no good at this anyway," you might say.

In Twelve Step work we see the same two forms of doubt at work. People look at the Steps and are skeptical of their value. Especially if they have trouble with the idea of God or a Higher Power, they might be turned off before even getting started. This, of course, means nothing will change for them. If we don't try the Steps, how are we ever going to know if they work or not? This attitude is called "contempt prior to investigation," a particularly pernicious form of doubt. Recovery requires that we change our thinking and our behavior, that we try something new because the old ways only led to trouble. We have to put aside some of our habitual skepticism and try another way.

Doubt of ourselves is another impediment to recovery. "I may be an alcoholic," someone says, "But there's nothing I can do about it. I can't stop." Again, this becomes a self-fulfilling prophecy. And doubt for the person already in recovery is a major reason for relapse. The thought, "Maybe I'm not an alcoholic," is ironically often followed by going out and getting a drink.

Today reflect on how skeptical doubt impacts your life. Be aware especially of doubt that you really are an alcoholic or addict. Notice, too, doubt of your own capacity to meditate or grow and change in your life.

# February 6

*"Persistence"*

For addicts, hiding, bailing out, and giving up are habits that we have to break. Addiction is all about avoiding life, avoiding responsibilities and avoiding anything we find uncomfortable. That's why persistence is so important in recovery. First we learn to show up for meetings. We discover the importance of consistency and being part of a group. We see that, even when we don't feel like it, we benefit from following through on our commitments.

We persist at our work, in our friendships friends, with our family, and all manner of things, like it or not. We may have thought that success depended on some kind of lucky break or extraordinary effort. But we start to learn that what really makes for change and improvement in our lives is just being a reliable worker, friend, and partner in recovery. We see that what pays off is long-term commitment, not short bursts of inspiration.

Meditation, too, depends upon persistence. Many times we might not feel like sitting down and following the breath. It's not always exciting, and it can often seem as if we are spinning our wheels on our meditation cushion. But, like recovery, meditation benefits from a willingness to keep pushing, to learn to work with the difficult as well as the pleasant. In fact, with both recovery and meditation, we probably learn more in the difficult times than in the periods of smooth sailing.

One meditation teacher suggests we make a commitment to sit in meditation every day, even if it's only for one minute. He says that if he can't find time to sit on a given day, before bed he'll pull out his cushion and sit down at least for a few breaths. It's easy to tell ourselves we don't have time or we don't feel like meditating, but nothing good comes from skipping practice, anymore than it comes from skipping recovery meetings.

Today, make a commitment to sit every day and to stay close to your recovery program. Reflect on the importance of persistence, no matter what.

# February 7

*"Attitudes of Mindfulness: Non-Judging"*

(From the *Buddhism & The 12 Steps Workbook*)
"The tendency of the mind is to be constantly assessing our experience, ourselves, and others. In meditation this often appears either as a judgment of our own practice or of what is happening as we practice. We'll automatically put a label of 'good' or 'bad' on ourselves and everything that happens.

"So, if we find that we have a hard time quieting the mind, that it seems as if the whole meditation period is spent thinking and not being aware of the breath, we might fall into thinking, 'I'm no good at this,' or 'I'm not doing this right.' It's important that we catch this kind of thinking and remember to categorize it as thinking. We try to take the stance of an impartial observer. That means that a mindful response to the thought, 'This is boring,' is noticing that we are making a judgment. Sooner or later, as you start to notice judging, you may find yourself thinking, 'I shouldn't be judging so much,' and that is just more judging— judging the judgments. These are very powerful habits of mind. They aren't going to stop just because we decide they should or because we try to be aware of the breath. However, just learning to notice judgments objectively will have the natural effect of reducing our attachment and belief in our judging thoughts. This lets us begin to take a more objective view of our experience." *Workbook,* p. 42-43

Today begin to notice the habit of judging both in your meditation and in your daily life. See what happens if you question the immediate judgment and explore other ways of understanding the thing you are judging.

# February 8

*"Karma and Change"*

The belief that we can never change is one of the things that holds addicts back from entering into recovery. We've been stuck in the cycle of craving and self-harm for so long that we can't imagine another way of life. We come to believe that we are, in fact, fated to be addicts. This is potentially a fatal trap.

The word "karma" has often been misunderstood to mean "fate." Its actual meaning, though, is "action," and the Law of Karma says, "Actions have results." Those results are usually what someone means when they say, "It's my karma." But it's not your karma because of some mysterious force that is guiding the world. It's your karma because you have taken certain actions that created the conditions and causes for things to be the way they are. It's important in this regard to understand that in Buddhism, actions include thoughts, words, and deeds. So, our belief—the thought—that we can't get clean is an element of our karma. It's easy to see how this works: We believe we can't get clean, so we don't change our behavior. Therefore, we never get clean. We are proved right in our thinking. But actually, it was the thinking that created the result in the first place.

What's most important for us to know about karma is that the only time we can change it is *in this moment*. We can't go back and change the past, so the present moment is the time for change. We can change our lives, we can recover, and we can grow if we only work moment by moment to think, speak, and act differently. This is how we change our karma, how we change our lives.

The Twelve Steps are called "a program of action," and this is what it's all about.

Today notice what thoughts, words, or deeds you could take to change your karma for the better.

# February 9

*"Impermanence"*

The Buddha puts a special focus on the insight that everything is always changing. In the teachings on mindfulness, he suggests noticing the "arising and passing away" of every aspect of experience, whether physical, mental, or emotional. Why is impermanence such a persistent element of his teaching, and what does it have to do with recovery?

His logic probably goes something like this: we try to hold on to things that keep changing. Therefore, we're bound to be frustrated—in Buddhist terms, experience "dukkha." If instead we remember impermanence, we won't make the mistake of trying to hold on.

For the addict, we could say that one of the reasons we became addicted is that we were trying to maintain a steady state of being high. We were trying to make a pleasant mind/body state permanent. Or we were trying to recapture the perfect high we once experienced, something that is long gone. Our delusion drives us to keep chasing something that can't be attained or held on to.

It's often said that addicts don't like change. Perhaps that's true of everyone. Change disrupts our lives. Consistency lulls us into complacency. It's easy to follow a routine that never challenges us to question our lives. But one day we'll wake up and realize that change was happening even when we didn't see it.

Today notice the things that are changing in you and around you. Notice changes in your body, mind, and emotions; notice changes in your environment, in the weather, and in the world; notice changes in the people you encounter. Remember that you can't hold on to anything.

# February 10

## *"Mindful Self-Compassion"*

One of the great diseases of our culture is self-loathing. Many of us internalize an "inner critic" who is never satisfied with our behavior, our accomplishments, or even our thoughts and feelings. This negative self-belief is behind the crippling depression and anxiety that permeate Western society. Mindful self-compassion is an antidote to this disease.

Mindful self-compassion starts with the premise that someone who is in pain deserves care and compassion, not harsh judgment. It suggests that we look upon ourselves as someone else might, someone who cares about us. The Buddhist teaching on not-self can help here, because it shows us that no individual is unique, that we all share the same human traits. So, with mindful self-compassion we step away from "selfing," and take an objective stance toward this person who is suffering. And how do we respond to someone who is suffering? Hopefully, we offer them compassion.

We see how our thoughts are unkind and judgmental, and we try to take a different view. Is there another way to think about yourself? What would a kind thought be? A non-judgmental one?

We see how our behavior can cause us harm, whether through addictive actions, or things like overwork that result from our negative self-view. Even things like diet, rest, and exercise can be expressions of either kindness or harmfulness toward ourselves.

Today, ask yourself, how would a friend treat you? What might they say to you? What might they do to help you? Can you start to treat yourself more like a friend and less like an enemy?

# February 11

*"The Phenomenon of Craving"*

"The Doctor's Opinion" in the AA Big Book includes a term that has become part of the lexicon of recovery: "the phenomenon of craving." In that book it refers specifically to the overwhelming desire that is triggered by the first drink (or in the case of addicts, drug, taste of sugar, hand of cards, etc.). Every addict has experience with this phenomenon. While some may have stronger and more persistent cravings than others, we all know the feeling of "I've got to have it!"

This craving is the extreme version of the Buddha's Second Noble Truth, that suffering is caused by our desires. As addicts, this is not a theoretical or philosophical idea. It is a real, lived experience. Even for those who have been abstinent for some time, such cravings can arise. Learning to live with them is a vital part of recovery.

One of the main ways that Buddhist practice supports recovery is in the training of non-reactivity that mindfulness gives us. When we regularly sit in meditation, we are committing to not act or react (at least physically) for a certain period of time. During our sittings we might have many impulses, thoughts, feelings, and sensations. By resisting acting on them, we are learning not to act on craving. Each of those impulses is a craving, however small. In our daily lives, we typically give in to these impulses, whether they are the impulse to move or to check our phone or to open the refrigerator. That's normal. But for an addict, some of those impulses can be dangerous. So, learning to be mindful of the arising of craving and impulse, and seeing that we can let them go, is a valuable, and in fact, critical skill that meditation can help us develop.

Today notice the cravings that arise and how you respond to them. See if you can apply mindfulness to craving both in meditation and in ordinary life.

# February 12

### *"Two Benefits of Mindfulness"*

Mindfulness has two distinct and immediate benefits (among many others which are more long-term): calm and clarity.

Calm is the obvious benefit of any meditation practice, the relaxation and stress-release that come with taking quiet time and focusing the mind. One term for the kind of concentration one achieves in meditation is "calm abiding," which points to this settled state.

For addicts, this calm is a vital support for our recovery. Addiction is an agitated state, one of restless dissatisfaction that sends us searching for some kind of fix. The calm of meditation helps to break that cycle.

Clarity is the ability to see clearly what is arising in our mind and body. This means we start to be aware of our thoughts and how they lead us astray. Our negativity, obsessiveness, self-judgments, fantasies, and more are revealed when we bring mindfulness to our thoughts. This awareness then gives us the capacity to interrupt and let go of those thoughts.

Clarity also helps us be with the emotional and physical discomfort of anxiety and stress. Opening to these difficult feelings allows us to be more accepting and less reactive.

Much of addiction is a mental disease. Seeing into the thoughts that drive our craving helps us to break those mental habits.

Today, notice the calm that comes with meditation and bring awareness to the thoughts that arise while sitting. Let go of the thoughts and rest in the comfort of tranquility.

# February 13

*"Breaking Down the Breath"*

Often we begin working with the breath in just two parts, inhalation and exhalation. This establishes a basic connection with the sensations. The breath, though, turns out to be more complicated than that as our practice deepens.

Today, try breaking the breath into more granular parts. As you begin to work with more detail in the breath, explore each of these elements in turn before combining them all into a full mindful breath.

Start by feeling the beginning of the inhalation at the nostrils. Notice the initial impact of air touching skin. Watch this sensation for several breaths before trying to feel the next part.

Now, feel the inflow of breath, like a stream moving into the body. This inflow itself, when examined closely, can be experienced as a string of continually changing sensations.

After establishing awareness of the inflow, notice the end of the inhalation. This is another distinct moment that contains a variety of sensations. It's very quick, so you have to pay close attention to detect it.

Then, notice the beginning of the exhalation. Like the beginning of the inhalation, here we observe the impact of air touching skin.

Feel the outflow of the breath, a distinctly different experience from the inflow.

Then be with the end of the outflow, the completion of a single breath.

There is a moment between the end of one breath and the beginning of the next breath. Keep the attention on the tip of the nose for this moment to reveal itself and witness what that feels like.

By paying attention to all these details, there is a natural effect of deepening concentration. The mind becomes more unified.

Use this more detailed attention to breath whenever you are having trouble concentrating. It can be a good way to start a period of meditation, as well, since it tends to establish mindfulness quickly.

# February 14

*"Love"*

Addiction is an expression of hatred—hating ourselves, our feelings, the world, and those around us. It's a rejection of life. The healing of recovery is, in the words of Buddhist author William Alexander, an "awakening to love." We discover the richness, beauty, and fulfillment available in life. We discover our own inner goodness.

Love, though, is a word that has lost a lot of its meaning in our culture. It can mean lust, obsession, or simply liking something a lot. When the Buddha describes lovingkindness, he says, "Even as a mother protects with her life, her child, her only child, so with a boundless heart should one cherish every living being." He equates a mother's love more with care and protection than affection. While a loving mother might at times get quite annoyed and frustrated with her children, she will always care for them. To be clear, this is an archetype; we know that some mothers fail to care for their children.

What happens if we change our idea of love from affection to protection and care? Affection and passion tend to fade, and in romantic relationships are often driven by sexual craving, which also tends to fade. But if what guides our love is caring for someone, it's not subject to the same dissolution.

In the same way, if we think of our love for ourselves as caring rather than approving, we can avoid the pitfalls of self-judgment and disparagement. None of us is perfect, so there is always something to judge or disparage. If we view ourselves through this lens, we walk around despising ourselves. If, on the other hand, we think of loving ourselves as taking care of ourselves, then we eat when hungry, rest when tired, and seek comfort when troubled. In this way, we aren't loving ourselves because we've earned love or done something special, but just because we are human and need care.

Today reflect on ways you can care for yourself better. What if you thought of yourself as a vulnerable young child who needs protection? How would you treat yourself then? How would you treat others if you saw them as children as well?

# February 15

*"Disaster Thinking"*

We spend a lot of time worrying about the future. What if I get sick? Lose my job? My partner leaves me? The economy crashes? Our fear of all the things that might go wrong can create a background of anxiety that undermines our happiness. This fear in founded in a lack of faith, in ourselves and in the world.

Our lack of faith in the world isn't unfounded. It's true that many things go wrong, and that some of these might directly affect us. The company we work for might go out of business. A tree might fall on our house. A natural disaster might strike our town. But what do we gain by worrying about these things? As the Serenity Prayer reminds us, there is no point in fighting with things we can't control. Acceptance is the way to peace.

Our lack of faith in our own capacity to handle things or to manage our lives can result from the years of addictive behavior when we actually *couldn't* trust ourselves. But in recovery, hopefully we are different. As time passes in recovery, we face all sorts of obstacles, whether personal or professional. We learn that we can deal with problems and find our way through challenges. As we overcome one difficulty after another, we start to develop faith in ourselves—the faith that we won't be overwhelmed, that we can take whatever life throws at us.

This is the same kind of faith that Buddhism fosters if we live in accordance with the dharma. It's not that difficulties won't come, but that with mindfulness, wisdom, and compassion as our guides and supports we can face any challenge.

It's important for us to recognize the old disaster thinking that is left over from our days of using. We need to remember that things have changed, *we* have changed.

Today, notice your disaster thinking, and remind yourself that you now have tools for handling life's challenges. Remember that you will be okay.

# February 16

*"Control"*

Addiction is essentially a strategy to control how we feel. We want to be happy or high or just not in pain all the time, so we keep drinking, smoking, popping, eating, gambling, or otherwise finding ways to alter our consciousness to feel the way we want.

This habit of control carries over into other areas of our lives, including our relationships, our work, how we treat our bodies, and how we treat our own thoughts and feelings. But these efforts are bound to fail. As Step One reminds us, we are powerless over much of life. We can't control other people, the economy, or even our own bodies, much less our minds. So, this struggle becomes a painful battle against the world, and against reality.

The beginning of recovery is when we learn to let go of control.

We discover the same truth in meditation. When we first start to practice, we might have the idea that we should be able to control our minds, that we should be able to stop our thoughts and just focus on the breath. Soon enough we discover the futility of this kind of effort. We wind up in a battle with our own thoughts. We might go to our teacher and ask, "How do I stop thinking?" We're told that this isn't the point of practice, that we need to accept our thoughts and let them go.

At this point we are brought face to face with our wish to control everything, and the failure of this strategy. Now begins a process of letting go. We start to examine all the things we are trying to control, and we begin to dismantle that system. The practice of mindfulness meditation gives us a direct doorway into this work. It teaches us how to let go of thoughts and impulses in the present moment, giving us a tool that we can then apply more broadly in our life.

Today, reflect on the ways you can bring the attitude of mindfulness from your meditation into your daily living. See how the understanding that everything is impermanent affects how you address control; see the freedom that comes from letting go.

# February 17

*"Faithless"*

"When we've rejected our traditional faith without replacing it with anything, the world, and life, can be pretty dark. And this is a typical place for an addict/alcoholic to be. Such folks often live in bitter cynicism about religion—and a lot of other things. Their addiction has dulled their hearts. The density of their thoughts won't allow in the subtlety of the spiritual experience." *Burning Desire*, page 15

Recovery isn't just about drugs and alcohol or other addictive behaviors. It's also about recovering our hearts. Life is difficult and often painful. We become addicts to quell that pain. Unfortunately, we numb our hearts as well. When we shut down, we lose the capacity to connect with our better nature as well as broader spiritual ideas. When we carry these feelings into Step work, we can get stuck trying to work the explicitly spiritual elements of that process.

This is where open-mindedness and willingness are so important. We come to recovery in a state of surrender, having hit bottom and seen that our own ways of dealing with life and with the world no longer worked. Now we have to try new ways, new ideas and new behaviors. We have to open to the idea of a Higher Power.

That doesn't mean taking on some fundamentalist religion or going back to beliefs that we had abandoned years before. What it really means is opening to different ways of understanding spirituality. When we delve into these questions, we discover that spiritual principles are woven into the world. Love, service, and letting go are real parts of life, not esoteric principles. Generosity, compassion, and sacrifice are normal human behaviors that strengthen us, rather than weaken us.

Today, look for the spiritual in the ordinary. See where love and caring, service and generosity and many other positives qualities are playing out in your life and all around you. See if you can find the spark of faith within yourself.

# February 18

### *"The Power of Faith"*

What we believe largely determines what we do. If we believe recovery is possible, we'll be willing to embark on this journey. If we don't believe we can recover, we'll never try, a self-fulfilling prophecy.

In Buddhism, faith, or *sadha*, doesn't mean taking on some belief system, but rather trusting in a process. Rather than adhering to some text or teaching, we adhere to a practice—the practice of mindfulness. By working with this practice, we develop faith because we see that it works. The practice then reveals the teachings, that is, everything the Buddha taught is confirmed for us through direct experience.

The confidence that develops in this way is unshakeable. It's not dependent on an argument or on a tradition. It doesn't ask us to leave our intellect at the door of the temple. No one has to show us the scientific proof that meditation works or that the dharma is true. It's apparent when we sit down to meditate or apply mindfulness to an experience.

As our practice deepens over time, so does our faith. Each step on the path gives us more confidence. That leads us to take more steps, to fully embrace the teachings and practices of the Buddha.

Faith gives us the strength to go forward, to go deeper, and to broaden our practice to encompass our whole life. This is the power of faith.

Today reflect on the faith or confidence you have in Buddhism, in mindfulness, and in all the practices. Are you holding back in some way? Are you willing to take the next step in your practice?

# February 19

## *"Dharma"*

Dharma means truth or natural law, and also refers specifically to the teachings of the Buddha. These teachings provide guidelines for living, for meditation, and for the development of wisdom and compassion. The goal of a Buddhist is to live in accordance with the dharma. This is the great task of the path.

To live in accordance with the dharma means to live ethically, wisely, and compassionately. We follow the Five Precepts so that we don't hurt other people (or ourselves) and so that our actions are morally based. We practice mindfulness to be more awake in the world, in our bodies and in our relationships. With mindfulness, we develop wisdom as we strip away illusion and see reality more clearly. All of this tends to open the heart to kindness and caring for others and for the world. Finally, we study the words of the Buddha to understand more clearly his guidance.

Ajahn Chah, the great Thai Forest monk, defined dharma as "the truth of the way things are." To see the dharma is to see the truth, to come to understand how suffering arises and how to end suffering. As we walk a spiritual path, this is the task before us, to understand and live in harmony with the truth.

To fully understand the dharma we must practice, study, and commit to an ethical lifestyle. Each day we set out to cultivate all these qualities, to grow, and to serve. This growth happens little by little.

Today reflect on how you are living in accordance with the dharma. What aspects of this work do you need to emphasize more: practice, study, or ethics?

# February 20

## *"Spacious Mind: Hearing"*

Paying attention to the breath focuses the mind on a small point of sensation, either the tip of the nose or the belly. Spacious mind turns this practice upside down. To begin working with spacious mind, sit in your usual meditation posture, relaxing and settling in. Take a few mindful breaths.

The first element of this practice is working with sound. Shift the attention from the breath to sound. Notice what sounds you can hear. If you are indoors, notice sounds in the building such as other people, ventilation systems, voices, footsteps, radio, TV, or anything else nearby. Then notice sounds from outside like traffic passing by, construction going on, voices, or any other sounds. Finally, notice what you hear in your own body, like your breath, heartbeat, or the sound in your ears, sometimes called the "sound of silence" (more about this later).

Now you have scanned your environment for sounds. There are two ways to work with sound. One is to zero in on a particular sound. So, if a plane flies overhead, for example, you can follow the sound as it approaches and passes by. Listen not just to the general sound, but to hear the different frequencies. Most steady sounds have at least two frequencies or tones, a higher tone and a lower tone. If you listen closely, you'll be able to pick these out. Listening like this concentrates the mind.

The other way to listen to sounds is listening with an open attention, almost like listening to music. You aren't focusing on a particular sound, but rather trying to hear everything at once. This is the spacious mind of hearing.

In your meditation today, experiment with the two different ways of listening. Notice the effects on your concentration as you work with these different methods. If you find this helpful, make listening a regular part of your mindfulness practice.

# February 21

*"Don't Know"*

While faith is an integral part of Buddhism and recovery, some Zen traditions suggest that doubt actually has an important role to play on the spiritual path. So-called "Great Doubt" isn't so much an intellectual or emotional resistance to faith as it is an insight into the limits of our capacity to know the truth.

This is embodied in a practice called "don't know." How long am I going to live? Don't know. How will my life unfold? Don't know. What's going to happen next? Don't know.

We live our lives under the illusion that we know the answers to such questions. We think that our plans will play out as we imagine, and that we can control the unfolding of events. But that's not true. We may go along for a time with our life following a routine that we've laid out, but then one day there's a car accident, a health crisis, a job loss, or a phone call from a stranger that changes everything. Even nature can radically change our life if our house is destroyed in a hurricane, fire, or earthquake.

So, the truth is, we don't know. We don't know what's going to happen next. The wisdom of Great Doubt is that we don't live in this illusion. And when we don't live in this illusion, we are much more awake to life.

When we think we know what's going to happen next, how each day is going to play out, and what direction our life is going, we can fall into automatic pilot, not really paying attention to life. As John Lennon sang, "Life is what happens when you're busy making other plans." Buddhism encourages us to pay attention to life, so we don't miss it.

Today, make an effort to be present for it all, the known and the unknown, the expected and the unexpected. Every moment is unique, every moment precious. Keep practicing "don't know."

# February 22

## *"Restored"*

Recovery restores not only sanity, but many other things as well. Essentially what it restores is life. Just waking up in the morning with a clear memory of falling asleep, something often blurred in an addict/alcoholic's mind, can bring joy. Discovering the simple beauty of a walk in the woods, a cup of tea after dinner, or meeting a friend for coffee.

In our addiction, we forget that life is really made up of these small moments. In our search for thrills or transcendence, or our desire to escape from life's challenges, we lose touch with what really makes life worth living.

Relationships and connections with people come back. Although some connections might be permanently broken because of our past actions, many others will heal with time as people come to trust us and trust that we really mean it this time, that we are all-in with recovery.

A love of work comes back as we rediscover the joy of a job well done. Intoxication makes work a big hassle, an intrusion into the "party." Being clean and sober often fills us with energy and even inspiration that we channel into our job, service, or creative work.

The heart is healed, as well. The ability to feel, to care, to give love, and to accept love are reawakened as the fog lifts. Our capacity to sense a spiritual connection, be present, and develop wisdom grows.

As our body heals, the pleasure of exercise and physical activity returns. We join a gym or start running or biking. We're alive and remembering what it means to have a healthy, active body.

All of this and more may be restored as we begin to recover.

Today, notice the small moments of joy and connection, and remember it's all because of recovery. Stay with the gratitude and appreciation of what this path gives you.

# February 23

*"Daily Recollections: Aging"*

The Buddha recommends that each day we recollect five things: the inevitability of aging, sickness, death, and change, and our responsibility in the unfolding of our karma. Today we can talk about the first Daily Recollection.

Most people, once they become adults, are unhappy about aging. We gain weight or get wrinkles; we lose our hair, or it goes gray. Then, as we pass through middle age and into old age, we lose different capacities, whether our sight or hearing, our flexibility and strength, our energy and motivation. Aging starts to seem like one long decline, loss piled on loss.

How are we to hold these changes? How can we avoid letting aging seem like a depressing descent into darkness? And finally, why does the Buddha want us to contemplate aging every day?

One key thing to understand about the Buddha is that he was first and foremost interested in reality. He didn't sugarcoat the truth about life. But he didn't teach this way in order to cause us pain—quite the opposite. He realized that if we didn't squarely face the truth of our existence, when reality hit us, we would be caught unprepared. By reflecting daily on these basic truths, they become integrated into our understanding of life. And when we understand the truth, it is no longer frightening or overwhelming. We make peace with it and learn to accept reality.

Today reflect on your relationship with aging. Do you fight with aging or avoid thinking about it? How would it feel to be completely accepting of the aging of your body and mind? See if, at least for a few moments, you can feel the truth of your aging without any story or resistance. Aging is a natural, undeniable aspect of life. Breathe and take that in.

# February 24

*"Good Enough"*

At one dharma center they sell t-shirts with a stick figure in lotus posture and the words, "Good enough, dear." The image and the child-like printing all project a sense of innocence. The message is, "You don't have to try so hard." This applies to being a good meditator or simply a good person.

Many of us carry this sense of "not good enough."

When we judge ourselves as not good enough, we are comparing ourselves to an ideal that doesn't exist. What human being is perfect? We are all flawed; that's the nature of humanness.

What, then, qualifies as "good enough"? The truth is, if you are reading a book like this, you are already trying to be a good person and probably avoiding most of the egregious harm that humans do.

As for being a meditator, if you meditate regularly, you are good enough. That's it, the sole criterion.

In recovery we can also get caught in this cycle of self-judgment. After wasting so much of our lives in addiction, it's easy to feel the need to compensate—and over-compensate. But, as with meditation, if we don't act on our addiction today, we are already good enough.

Sure, we can always be better, and it's part of our spiritual path to strive to improve. But that doesn't mean we should feel bad about who we are today.

Today reflect on the idea that you are already good enough. What would it feel like to stop trying to improve yourself and just accept who you are?

# February 25

*"Training the Body"*

Meditation is sometimes referred to as a training. This process is multifaceted. The first facet is training the body.

We begin training the body by establishing posture. This is a foundational part of practice. How we hold the body has a surprising effect on the mind, on thoughts, and on feelings. Think about the high school student slumped at his desk in the back of the classroom. Such a posture causes sluggishness and dullness of mind. This is why we want our meditation posture to be upright and stable. At the same time, consider the Marine standing at attention, the whole body rigid and tight. This posture promotes stress and tension. For this reason, we want our body to be soft and supple.

Not everyone can bend their body into lotus posture. But if you can, this is a good way to sit. In such a posture, there should be three points of contact, the two knees and the buttocks. Sitting on the traditional meditation cushion, a firm pillow called a *zafu*, one positions oneself on the front of the cushion so that the hips tip forward, allowing the knees to touch the ground.

Then you establish an upright position that feels balanced, neither leaning forward or back or to the side.

On a chair, the difference is that the feet are on the floor, but otherwise, we want the same feeling of balance and stability.

Establishing posture, however, is only the beginning of training the body. What's even more important is sustaining stillness. Stillness of body supports the arising of stillness of mind. At times this can be difficult. Some kind of discomfort will often arise if we try to meditate for a sustained period or, as we do on retreat, meditate repeatedly throughout the day. Working with discomfort in the body, then, becomes a central element of meditation, one that often comes as a surprise to people who are just learning how to do this practice.

Tomorrow we'll discuss working with difficult sensations. Today, just work with establishing a stable, upright, and supple posture.

# February 26

## *"Working with Difficult Sensations"*

The reason this section isn't entitled "Working with Pain" is that even that language creates a bias in the mind. From a meditative standpoint, sensations may be pleasant or unpleasant, but it is the mind that defines them as pain or pleasure. This realization is one of the key insights we develop through meditation. As our practice deepens, we see that it is aversion to discomfort that makes certain sensations unmanageable.

So, the starting point of working with difficult sensations is relaxing and trying to find a way to release aversion. Because aversion manifests as tension, relaxing gets us started. Even relaxing in the face of discomfort can be difficult. There can be resistance to releasing the tension because there is an underlying fear of being overrun by pain. The next layer of this fear is the sense that once we let pain in, it will never go away.

This is where another vital insight comes in: the realization that all pain is impermanent. When we remind ourselves that whatever we are experiencing will certainly pass, it gives us more confidence and strength in letting the pain come to us.

The next step is to explore the components of sensations, to deconstruct the experience. Tomorrow we can look at this part of the process.

For today, begin to notice the tension and resistance that arise around difficult physical sensations. See if you can let go of that aversion and just be present for the sensations themselves without labeling them as pain.

# February 27

*"Exploring Sensations"*

Exploring the life of the body is a gateway into deepening concentration, wisdom, and acceptance.

As a concentration object, the body provides us with a compelling set of experiences. We can explore these in a methodical way, as with the body scan or sweeping practices, or simply as they arise. The idea is to probe beneath the surface of sensations and look with more focus and detail. Because of the complexity of sensations, their constant change and subtlety, the mind can become quite still in examining them. We have to focus strongly to pick up the myriad experiences. And the closer we look, the more we see.

Nothing is stable in the body, and that ever-changing nature reveals the truth of impermanence. The clarity we have developed makes this reality even more apparent. Along with that insight, comes the understanding that nothing can be held onto: we can't possess something that is constantly changing. This realization can be one of the most powerful breakthroughs in our spiritual development.

As we overcome resistance to difficult sensations, another door can open in our practice. Fear of pain and the sense that we need to exert control over our experience can fade. Now we are living with openness and acceptance. Instead of fighting with sensations, we develop interest and curiosity. The line between pleasant and unpleasant blurs. Instead of reacting with aversion, we respond skillfully. If real pain or harm is happening to the body, we take care of it, not with a sense of panic, but rather with sensible kindness towards ourselves.

Today, start to examine your relationship to sensations. Work toward an open, curious, and accepting relationship to the pleasant, unpleasant, and neutral experiences that arise.

# February 28

## *"Spiritual Awakening"*

Step Two awakens us to faith. Our addiction was an expression of our lack of faith—in life, in ourselves, in whatever powers there are in the universe. We lacked faith that a life lived without substances or our overweaning control would be tolerable. We felt that we had to manipulate everything, especially our consciousness and our feelings.

We lacked faith in our own capacity to survive life's challenges without being loaded. And we didn't think we could overcome our addiction.

Finally, we felt that, in some way, the universe couldn't be trusted, that just doing "the next right thing" wasn't going to be enough.

Step Two turns these beliefs around. It challenges us to trust in ourselves and in a natural unfolding. While its wording suggests that a Higher Power will take over, its more essential implication is that there is a process by which recovery, healing, and, yes, sanity can be developed. That process is grounded in the Law of Karma, the simple truth that thinking, speaking, and acting skillfully brings positive results.

The Buddhist view is that humans have the potential for enlightenment if we let go of our lower impulses, the ego drive. Before we can start that process, though, we must believe that it is possible. This Step puts us on the path toward transformation by challenging us to believe that we can change.

Today reflect on your relationship to faith and the process of transformation. Do you believe that change is possible for you?

# February 29

*"Leap Year"*

Whether you read this page once every four years or decide to "cheat" and read it at another time, this can be a day to reflect on time. We build our lives around schedules, deadlines, and plans that are all based on time. In that process we create pressure for ourselves to get things done in that relative framework. The dharma implies something else, something timeless.

When we meditate and try to be present, we are trying to let go of the concept of time. In the present moment there is no past and no future, it is always just now. When we connect in this way, much of the stress and pressure of our lives melts away. A great sense of freedom can arise when we let go of accomplishing things, getting places, and fitting things into a schedule. On retreats this becomes especially clear, but we can tap into this feeling in our daily practice simply by reminding ourselves there is only ever this moment.

This doesn't mean that we stop showing up for work on time, throw away our clocks, or shed all relationship to schedules. It means that, within these constraints, we try to maintain a connection to the timeless, to the now, to what isn't moving on a clock face.

Take a breath and feel the reality of just this moment. Feel it in your body and in your mind. This moment and this breath can only exist now. It comes and then it's gone. To be caught in thoughts about the past or in plans for the future is to miss the only reality we really have: this present moment. Don't miss it.

# March: Step Three

*"Made a decision to turn our will and our lives over to the care of God, as we understood him.*

# March 1

*"Turning it over"*

Step Three brings us into the heart of the program and gives us a new set of challenges. To begin, there is a question of what it means to "turn our lives over," whether to God or anything else.

What many people find when confronting this Step for the first time is their own resistance to letting go, a desire to control the results of their actions, and their ongoing conflict with life and reality as it is. This is a good place to start in the process of turning it over.

Here the words of the Serenity Prayer are a guide: "To accept the things I cannot change." Many addicts have fought with life, unwilling to accept the failures, challenges, and even opportunities that arrived in their lives. Acceptance is the starting point of turning it over. "Things are as they are," as some Buddhists say. In other words, it is foolish to fight reality.

How do we do this, to begin to accept things as they are?

The first thing is to see how it feels when you fight with reality, when you willfully refuse to accept things. This is where mindfulness comes in. When you find yourself at odds with a difficult or challenging situation, bring your attention into your body and feel the tension and stress you are holding. This reveals the painful element of non-acceptance and can inspire you to let go, to turn it over.

Today, begin to make it a habit that when you are stressed, angry, or resistant, that you pay attention to how that feels. Then practice breathing and letting go. See how pleasant it is to cease fighting. Use that pleasant feeling as an inspiration to continue to let go.

# March 2

*"Acceptance"*

Acceptance is a theme that runs through Twelve Step recovery, starting with the oft-quoted line from the Big Book, "Acceptance is the answer to all my problems today." This suggests that *non*-acceptance is the *cause* of all my problems. Indeed, we could say that this is the cause behind our addiction: not accepting how we feel and believing that we have to control those feelings with a substance or behavior.

But the idea of acceptance is often misunderstood to mean that we should become passive or apathetic. In fact, acceptance is just one stage—the first—in a process that includes responding to how things are or to a situation.

Our ordinary way of being is to react impulsively and habitually to things without understanding or being aware of what is driving those reactions. That kind of impulsivity is what underlies addiction, the constant grasping after pleasure and pushing away of discomfort.

With mindfulness, we learn to observe and accept these reactions without judgment, resistance, or struggling to change—and without acting on them. The calm that comes with non-resistance brings more clarity so we can make wiser choices in response. Those responses can then be grounded in wisdom and compassion. They represent a truer and more reliable aspect of ourselves.

Today, begin to notice your reactivity, and try to let it go. See if you can accept the thing you are reacting to, then breathe, relax, and ask, "How could I respond to this situation wisely?"

# March 3

### *"Our will"*

When Step Three says we turned "our will" over to the care of God, in Buddhist terms it means aligning our intention with the dharma. If we are going to change our lives and our behavior, we are going to have to change our intentions. As addicts we've been driven by self-centered greed, craving for pleasure, resentments, and self-pity. In recovery, we need to find positive intentions to guide us, and that's what the Buddha's teachings provide for us.

In order to align our intentions with the dharma, we must understand the dharma. That's one reason we need to study. Fortunately, the principles of dharma aren't complicated. We are encouraged to be mindful, act morally, live compassionately, and look at the world wisely: to spiritually awaken.

To accomplish this, we start each day with mindfulness meditation. We take on moral guidelines of non-harming: we don't lie, cheat, or steal; we don't harm others sexually; we act for the common good, not just personal gain. We try to be generous, loving, and forgiving. And finally, we look at the world through the deeper truths of dharma, the impermanence, suffering, and corelessness of all things. With these ideas at the heart of our intentions, we can live a life free from guilt and shame. We discover the peace and joy of wisdom and non-harming.

As recovering addicts, the beginning point of all our intentions is to not act on our addictive cravings today. We set the intention to avoid substance abuse or acting on process addictions. We plan our day so that we aren't put in risky positions that might trigger craving or relapse.

Today reflect on your deepest intentions. What do you want to bring to the world and how can you act on those intentions today? Consider making such intention-setting part of your daily practice and program.

# March 4

*"…and our lives"*

When we turn our lives over to the dharma, we start to take actions in accordance with the Buddhist teachings. It's important to understand that in Buddhism actions include thoughts and speech because those, too, have karmic consequences.

The first way that we try to live in harmony with the teachings is by following the Five Precepts: not to kill; not to steal; not to harm others sexually; not to lie, gossip, or use harsh speech; and not to use intoxicants. Of course, for a person in recovery, the last of these, the Fifth Precept, is our starting point.

The Twelve Step program is not simply a program of abstinence. If it were, there would only be one Step: stop the behavior and you're done. But the program is much more than that. It's a guide for healing and living a life of integrity, service, and wisdom. These same principles are embodied in the Buddha's Noble Eightfold Path. As we embark on this path, we need to explore and come to understand each of the eight facets of the path so that we can practice them.

Here is the Eightfold Path with some of the places you will find them in this book:

Right View – Step One
Right Intention – Step One
Right Speech – Step Five
Right Action - the Precepts, throughout
Right Livelihood – Step Ten
Right Effort – Step Eight
Right Mindfulness - throughout
Right Concentration - throughout

Today, pick out one of these elements, and begin to study and reflect on it. Make this exploration a regular part of your spiritual work as you go deeper into an understanding of the path.

# March 5

## *"The Practice of Letting Go"*

What does it mean to "let go" while meditating? As we sit and watch the breath, it's common for the mind to wander. Oftentimes, just noticing the thoughts is enough to make them disappear. That's one version of letting go. Notice the thought, let it go, and come back to the breath.

Sometimes, though, the thoughts are more persistent, and keep coming back over and over. This usually means that there is some underlying emotion driving them, perhaps anxiety or grief or resentment. The emotions are feeding the thoughts, so that even when you are mindful, they continue to repeat. They seem to have their hooks in you. In this case, letting go means shifting the attention to the feeling and away from the verbal content of the thoughts.

The feeling is located in the body. This is an important thing to understand and become familiar with—the visceral, physical, energetic quality of emotions. Pay attention to the chest and belly where these feelings often reside. Then relax, open, and explore the feelings.

There may be some resistance to feeling the emotion because we resist paying attention to that which is unpleasant. But if you can relax and feel, you'll find that the thoughts tend to quiet down or soften. They aren't being fed by the emotions any longer.

A third way to let go is when there is a stream of thoughts flowing through the mind. In this case, you might find that neither do they stop by just being observed, nor is there any strong emotion behind them. These tend to be trivial thoughts, more like annoying background noise than real intrusions on the mind. In this case, we allow the thoughts to continue, to just come and go, without trying to push them away or quiet them. Instead, we put a little more effort into following the breath, letting the thoughts recede into the background. If we aren't bothered by them, they won't take hold or become more intrusive.

In your practice today, notice how thoughts are responding to your awareness and see if one of these approaches helps you deal with them.

# March 6

### *"Making a Decision"*

In many ways, addicts don't make decisions. We are driven by craving, impulse, and obsession. Little consideration of ultimate consequences or results comes into our thinking. Only what we want right now and how to get it. This is how we wind up broken and desperate, crawling into a Twelve Step meeting admitting we are beaten.

When Step Three says we "made a decision," it means that now we are actually weighing various options thoughtfully before taking action. This alone is an improvement over the impulsivity and self-centeredness of addiction. When we are driven by addictive craving, we have only one choice—to follow that craving. When we are guided by mindfulness, we see a variety of options. Then we can sort through them to make the wisest decision.

Decision-making is not just a solitary process. We learn to ask for help from sponsors, teachers, friends, partners, and other trusted people before making a change or taking any significant action. This reflects humility in recognizing the limits of our own knowledge and experience. It also acknowledges that we, like everyone else, have built-in, unseen biases we are often blind to. Sometimes people who know us well can help us to avoid those.

Today, consider how you make decisions. Do you take advantage of all the resources available to you? Or are you still making impulsive, desire-based decisions? Getting clean and sober doesn't automatically make us wise. We need to develop new ways of dealing with the world and the choices we make.

# March 7

*"The Higher Power of Dharma"*

The Steps' suggestion that we need a "Higher Power" to recover can seem daunting to someone who doesn't believe in God or has been wounded by religion. Many Buddhists in recovery consider the Dharma to be their Higher Power, allowing them to engage in the Steps without taking on a religious belief system. The Dharma is reality. Fighting with reality is what addicts spend their lives doing. That battle only creates more suffering. The Higher Power of Dharma gives us practical guidelines for how to understand and engage the world.

The first guidelines, the Four Noble Truths, help us understand suffering, its cause, and how to end it. The Noble Eightfold Path (which is the Fourth Noble Truth), provides a roadmap for living a life of integrity, kindness, wisdom, and happiness. Within the map, mindfulness offers a powerful tool for transformation. The whole map is built around the understanding of the power of karma to transform our lives.

The Dharma also points to the power of loving-kindness and compassion. Treating people with kindness and dropping contention lifts a weight from our hearts and minds and replaces it with joyful harmony. Letting go of self-judgment frees us from the persistent inner critic.

Seeing the world through the lens of wisdom inherent to the Dharma transforms our experience. No longer confused by or fighting with reality, we come into harmony with the ups and downs, the persistent changes that life presents.

Today take one element of the Dharma as your Higher Power. As you move through your day, keep remembering this truth and see how its power is influencing your life moment by moment.

# March 8

*"Not Unhappy"*

Oddly enough, how we define happiness actually affects how happy we are. If happiness means a constant state of joy or euphoria, we are going to be disappointed a lot of the time. And this wish to always feel great is one of the driving forces behind addiction. Conversely, learning to live with the challenges of life allows us to maintain more balance and find serenity.

One of the ways we do this is by learning to accept that difficult or painful emotions are a natural part of life, not a mistake. Mindfulness and Right View support this. Mindfulness helps us to be present with our feelings in a non-reactive way. Right View reminds us not to take feelings personally, not to build a story around them. And Right View helps us remember that feelings are always changing, so we don't have to fear some permanent state of despair or anxiety. These two elements are what help us to hold difficult feelings in the moment.

When we realize that happiness isn't about always being in a good mood, we can start to see that true happiness is about how we live our lives. How do we engage with others? With work? With our own inner lives? What is the direction of our lives? Are we focusing on the things that really matter to us, or are we trying to succeed on society's or our family's terms? These are the questions that guide us to finding true happiness,.

Today, ask yourself if you are fundamentally happy. Are you living the life you want to be living or the one that somebody else laid out for you? How can you find authentic happiness?

# March 9

### *"Training the Mind"*

Sometimes training the mind in meditation is compared to training a dog to "stay." While there's some appeal to this image, I'm not sure that it holds up when examined closely. Yes, there is the quality of coming back to the breath that is similar to a dog coming back to its master. But does the mind really respond like a pet?

Meditation training has several layers. The first is simply to stay in our seat—probably the closest parallel to animal training. Even that behavior is more complicated than simply getting a treat for doing the right thing. We stay in our seat because we understand and trust in the value of meditating.

Mind training develops the habit to come back to the breath, or whatever meditation object we are using. This too, with its repetitive form, has a similarity to training a pet, but to think that it will result in a mind that obeys us like a dog is to set ourselves up for disappointment. Sometimes the mind will become calm and concentrated, but it's just as likely to run off chasing a squirrel.

The training deepens when we learn to observe our thinking, the movement of mind, the squirrel chasing. This isn't so much a discipline as a shift in viewpoint. Through instruction and practice, we learn to separate ourselves from the thoughts. We learn to shift from identifying with and reacting to each thought, to seeing how they are moving, what they are telling us, and what is creating them.

This brings us to a third element of training, our response to the pet that refuses to be trained. It does no good to beat the dog that runs away. You only wind up with a frightened, broken animal. So it goes with our minds as well. Forgiveness and kindness must be our constant response to the squirrel-chasing mind. Only then will it relax and stop pulling on the leash.

Today, notice how you are responding to thoughts that arise in meditation. Can you let them go and come back to the breath without creating conflict in the mind? Are you still judging yourself, or pulling too hard on the leash?

# March 10

*"Understanding God"*

The end of Step Three tries to make the concept of God as open and personal as possible with the phrase, *"as we understood Him."* And yet, even the implication that we should understand God can be a trap. Too many people approach this question intellectually, and many times people reject the idea of God as *anti*-intellectual.

Certainly, having some conception of God facilitates working the Steps, but this conception isn't as important as understanding the process of the Steps. The process of Step Three isn't embodied in the word "God," but in "turning it over." This is the idea that we have "ceased fighting anyone or anything." God, in this sense, just represents reality, how things are, the things we can't change. Addicts spend a lot of time trying to control things: how they feel, how others behave, how they think they should be treated. We end up in conflict with the world and with others, but perhaps most importantly, in conflict with ourselves, with our feelings and impulses.

The simplest understanding of God, then, is as "reality," or "the truth of the way things are." This brings us back to the Dharma as a Higher Power, which at its essence is karma, the law of cause and effect. Living in harmony with God, turning it over, is living in harmony with karma. To do this, we need to understand how karma works and how to work with it. That is what the Buddha taught. It is what his Noble Eightfold Path describes.

There's nothing magical or even particularly complicated about this idea. The fact that actions have results, the process of cause and effect, is one of the most basic ideas we face as living beings. When we drink, we get drunk; when we don't drink, we don't get drunk. When we are kind, we feel good about ourselves; when we are cruel, a bitter seed grows in us. Our biggest problem isn't understanding the truth of karma, but turning our lives over to it, living in harmony with the Law of Karma.

Today reflect on how actions bring results in your life. And remember that in terms of the Law of Karma, actions include thoughts, words, as well as deeds.

# March 11

### *"Beginner's Mind"*

The founder of the San Francisco Zen Center, Shunryu Suzuki Roshi, is best known for his seminal book, *Zen Mind, Beginner's Mind*. His premise was that often when we become "experts," we stop learning, we stop being open. But if we retain the attitude of someone who doesn't know so much, like a beginner, we are likely to learn much more. This attitude is vital for people in recovery, especially as they approach the Twelve Steps.

Getting sober, breaking out of an addiction, is a new beginning. We thought we were experts, that we were managing our drinking or other addiction. When we hit bottom and realized that we had a problem, we became beginners. We realized that our entire understanding of our relationship to alcohol, drugs, food, sex, gambling, or whatever our addiction was, had been wrong, distorted by denial and delusion. As painful as this realization can be, it also means we have a tremendous opportunity to start our lives again. How we do that can determine the success or failure of our recovery.

What attitude do we bring to the Twelve Steps, that of an open-minded beginner or a closed-minded expert? Do we read them through and think, "This won't work," or "I don't need to do all this"? Or do we have an attitude of humility and curiosity?

If we carry the jaded and cynical mindset of the addict into our attempt at recovery, it's not likely to go well. With beginner's mind we put aside our know-it-all attitude, our pride, and our resistance. We admit that our former way of living didn't work, so it's time to try something new. We embrace the role of the beginner.

Today take each moment as a fresh start. Drop the sense of having it all figured out, and engage your life with curiosity and openness.

# March 12

### *"Refuge in Buddha"*

"Buddha represents the enlightenment principle, the germ of awareness inside us all. In simpler terms, it means being mindful, so taking Refuge in the Buddha can simply mean that we are committing ourselves to living as mindfully as we can today." *Workbook*, p. 91

Perhaps the closest Buddhist corollary to the idea of turning your will and life over to the care of God is taking refuge. The idea is that if you live in accordance with the Buddha, Dharma, and Sangha (the "Three Refuges" we'll look at over the next three days), your life will unfold in beneficial ways, and thus you will be "cared for," as Step Three suggests.

The word Buddha means "awake," so taking refuge in the Buddha can mean taking refuge in being awake, mindful and aware. This takes us out of the realm of faith and into the realm of action. You are committing yourself to being mindful in every moment to the best of your ability, taking Refuge in your innate capacity to be awake.

This commitment is not to be taken lightly. Being awake means that, not only are we present for the joys of life, but also the suffering. We don't turn away from other people's pain, or indeed, our own. This is the quality of compassion that the Buddha embodies.

So, taking refuge in the Buddha is an expression of our wish to fulfill our human potential. We want to live like the Buddha, with kindness, wisdom, and clarity.

Today reflect on how you can take refuge in the Buddha. Commit yourself to being awake in all activities and bringing loving-kindness into all your interactions.

# March 13

*"Refuge in Dharma"*

Taking refuge in Dharma is trying to live in harmony with the Buddha's teachings. We seek to understand our experience through the lens of wisdom. We see impermanence, suffering, and corelessness; we act with compassion, generosity, and forgiveness. We apply the Eightfold Path, living with Sila, moral integrity; practicing Samadhi, meditation and mindfulness; and acting with Panna, clarity of intention and view.

Refuge in Dharma is the essence of living as a Buddhist, whether you formally take that identity or not. It requires studying the teachings so that we can understand how to follow the Buddha's path. It requires self-examination to see the ways that our mind diverges from the truth of the way things are, from the Dharma. It requires a commitment to integrity in all aspects of our lives.

When we take refuge in Dharma we begin to look at the world differently. Instead of viewing things through the lens of self, through our own preferences and biases, we ask how the Buddha would see things. When faced with a decision or challenging situation, we bring to mind any applicable Buddhist teachings and see how they might apply.

The Dharma is founded on the principle of letting go: letting go of ego, of craving, and of attachment. When we take refuge in Dharma, we persistently ask ourselves the question, what am I holding on to and how can I let it go? This will naturally lead us toward happiness, since suffering is caused by clinging.

Today, reflect on your commitment to the Dharma. Could you deepen your understanding with reading or study? Could you deepen your practice with retreats or more daily sitting?

# March 14

## *"Refuge in Sangha"*

Sangha means the spiritual community. For people in Twelve Step programs, refuge in Sangha is perhaps the most familiar of the Three Refuges. Meetings, sponsors, and community are at the heart of the program and of Sangha. We understand that recovery doesn't happen alone. We need the support of not just one person, but a whole collective to gain and sustain sobriety.

Taking refuge in Sangha means being part of something larger than ourselves. It means offering yourself in service and support. And it means accepting support from others. One of the failings of many addicts is their tendency, instead, to isolate and go it alone.

This tendency sometimes come out of arrogance, but mostly it results from the fear of being known, of shame, or a sense of lacking something. When we are compelled to join a recovery and/or Buddhist community, many of these concerns can be alleviated. We discover that we aren't unique in our shortcomings or our idiosyncrasies. We find that there is real joy in participating, in being part of something. We feel a freedom as we engage in acts that serve others, not just ourselves. And we discover the safety—the refuge—in a loving spiritual community.

In traditional Buddhism, Sangha meant the community of enlightened followers of the Buddha, the monks and nuns. Over time the term came to mean more generally, any followers, including lay people. In Western Buddhism, though, the path is often depicted as a solitary journey, and so Sangha receded in importance to the other two refuges. This is one of the shortcomings of Western Buddhism and why connecting Buddhism with the Steps actually helps the Buddhist world as well as the recovery world.

Today reflect on how you are participating in spiritual community and how you might be holding back from participating fully. How could you contribute more and be more engaged with other Buddhist addicts in recovery?

# March 15

### *"Loving-kindness: Dear Ones"*

After practicing loving-kindness for self, we turn our mind to dear ones, our family and friends. This can be one of the most pleasant stages of this practice.

As with any period of meditation, begin by establishing a comfortable, upright posture that allows you to stay alert, but is comfortable enough to sit still (20 minutes is a good baseline). Let the body relax and settle. Close the eyes or lower the gaze.

For loving-kindness practice, the breath is felt at the heart center in the middle of the chest. Feel the chest rising and falling and have a sense of softening and opening, as though you were breathing right into the heart.

Now bring to mind people who are dear to you. Visualize them or imagine their presence. Begin to repeat phrases of loving-kindness in your mind. You can make up your own phrases or use traditional ones like "May you be happy; may you be peaceful; may you be safe from inner and outer harm." The particular words aren't as important as the feelings of connection that they evoke when you think of your dear ones.

Let the breath move with the words. One breath per phrase is a nice pace. If your mind wanders, just bring it back gently to the words, the breath, and the images of your dear ones.

If a negative feeling comes up about someone, let that person go and move on. For this exercise, just stay with the positive feelings.

Keep expanding the circle of dear ones, letting anyone come to mind who you care for.

When you feel that you've finished, come back to the simple feeling of breath in the heart center.

When you're ready, open your eyes. Notice your heart center. Do you feel more connected now?

# March 16

## *"Clinging"*

Addiction is clinging. It can be clinging to a drug, a drink, a person, a feeling, a thought, or a behavior. Any of these can be addictions if they become harmful to ourselves or others. And yet, clinging seems to be inherent to our humanity; otherwise the Buddha wouldn't have pointed to it as the universal cause of suffering.

Even if we are clean and sober, and relatively emotionally balanced, when we sit down to meditate, we will see how the mind clings. It is the pain in this experience that Buddhist meditation aims to free us from. But before we can release this clinging, we must know it clearly.

Mindfulness meditation doesn't start with letting go of clinging. Rather, that's where it ends. But to get there, we must explore the entire process of clinging and all its qualities.

As you meditate, first see if you can detect triggers for clinging. What thought, feeling, sound, or sensation sets off clinging? What mind states are most susceptible to the arising of clinging? What physical states? What memories trigger clinging? What emotions? This is discovering the landscape of clinging.

Now start to explore the feeling of clinging through the body. Notice tension, anxiety, sadness and how they feel in the body. Take the attention into the belly, the chest, and anywhere else feelings or sensations arise around clinging. Breathe with these feelings. Hold them gently, kindly.

When you see the pain of clinging, you are seeing the First and Second Noble Truths, suffering and its cause.

Our simple practice says, if we return to the breath and turn away from the triggers for clinging, we will let go, and then clinging will dissolve. See if this is true.

Today explore the whole process of clinging and letting go.

# March 17

### *"Relapse"*

Many addiction professionals say that relapse is a normal part of the process of recovery. Most people don't make it on their first try. On the other hand, people sometimes die when they relapse or simply never get clean and sober again, so it can't be taken lightly.

Relapse can happen at any stage of recovery, after a week or after a decade or more. This is why maintaining our spiritual condition is so important. Relapse doesn't happen out of the blue, but usually results from a buildup of conditions. For the newcomer who relapses, it's often that they simply haven't fully committed to their recovery and haven't developed the tools to sustain that recovery. This is why traditional advice like going to 90 meetings in your first 90 days, avoiding your old hangouts and friends, getting a sponsor, and starting to work the Steps right away are important guidelines. The early days and weeks of recovery are the most dangerous ones for relapse.

For people further into recovery, the buildup is typically more subtle. This often involves: cutting back on meetings and engagement in the program; overwork; a turbulent emotional relationship; and doubts about one's actual alcoholism or addiction. Each of these implies that recovery has become less of a priority. This is why Twelve Step programs say that recovery must come first, and if anything else supersedes its importance in our lives, we put ourselves at risk.

Relapse is often accompanied by significant emotional pain like depression or anxiety. Many of us are afflicted by these conditions. Getting clean doesn't necessarily alleviate them. In fact, for many addicts, our behavior was actually trying to self-medicate for these types of conditions. When we take away the drugs and alcohol, the underlying psychological pain can become more acute. This is why the tools of recovery, including the Steps, Buddhist practices, and other healing modalities are so important.

Today reflect on what risks of relapse are present in your life. Are you fully engaged in your recovery? Are you putting other things before your recovery? How could you protect yourself further from relapse?

# March 18

*"Recovery from Relapse"*

Recovery from relapse can be more difficult than initial recovery for a variety of reasons. These include self-doubt, shame, despair, and spiritual emptiness.

With relapse there can be a sense of failure, and this failure feeds into self-doubt. "Maybe I can't do it," is an insidious thought that undermines efforts to recover from relapse. This thought needs to be countered with the Step Two understanding that there is a way, that recovery is always possible. No one is uniquely incapable of recovery. That belief is simply a form of negative egotism.

Many people feel shame about relapse. Facing your friends in the program can feel humiliating. It's important to remember that most of those people have relapsed themselves. There is no shame in relapse because it's a perfectly normal element of the process of recovery.

Relapse often comes out of a period of depression or other emotional turbulence in our lives, so facing its consequences can actually feel like piling on more pain that leads to despair. Not only are you depressed, but now your life has taken a further turn for the worse with your relapse.

We must remember that our life has been better in the past and it can be that way again. All it takes is time. We have to walk through the pain, one day and one breath at a time. Showing up is the key. Showing up for meetings, for work, for relationships, and most of all for ourselves.

Finally, relapse can be triggered by a spiritual emptiness when our program has hit a wall, or at least a plateau. When coming back from a relapse, we need to re-engage in our spiritual life. This is a time when we must be open-minded and willing to try new things. The cynical attitude of the addict will kill us if we let it.

If you have recently returned from a relapse, see if any of these examples apply. If you know someone who is having trouble returning from one or more relapses, help them find the way through from these obstacles.

# March 19

### *"Emotional Karma"*

When people talk about karma, they often focus on the big externals, like money, health, relationships, and jobs. However, if we are looking closely at cause and effect in our lives, moment by moment, the greatest immediate karmic impact might be emotional.

When we have a thought, there is an emotional impact on our mood. You can see this moment-to-moment in your meditation practice. When we act, there is an emotional impact as well.

The typical way of talking about karma says something like, "If you are generous, you will be rewarded." So, we think that if we give money to a homeless person, we're going to get some financial benefit in the future. Whether this is true or not, what's certainly true is that we will feel an emotional impact whether we give or not—there will be emotional karmic results.

With this understanding karma stops being about some future point in time, whether in this life or another, or even about being good or accumulating points. Instead, its effects are felt here and now, motivating us to be more generous, more kind, and more present. We see the immediate impact of anger—it hurts; of generosity—it feels good; of compassion—it makes us feel connected. And for an addict, there can be powerfully negative emotional karma to our using.

To fully understand emotional karma, begin paying attention to the connection between thoughts and emotions while you are meditating. Notice the moods and feelings that arise in relation to different thoughts. And notice how just meditating itself has an impact on your mood.

Once you've gotten familiar with this connection, begin to notice emotional karma in your daily life. Use what you see as inspiration to be more mindful, compassionate, and wise day-by-day.

# March 20

### *"The Power of Non-Doing"*

The Twelve Steps are a "program of action," as they say, and it certainly helps most people in recovery, especially in the beginning, to stay busy. Being occupied helps keep our mind off using, and it gets us on a productive path after the wasted time and energy of addiction. However, there is also a value in doing nothing—intentionally. This is one description of meditation.

We practice meditation in silence and stillness. Although from the outside it looks as if we are just sitting there, meditation is internally active. What distinguishes it from ordinary behavior is that whatever thoughts, feelings, or impulses arise during a period of meditation, we don't act on them. This restraint is a vital teaching for addicts.

In Buddhism, this is called "renunciation," a turning away from the world and its allurements. You might think of renunciation as a vow of poverty or celibacy. In fact, meditation is a temporary form of the same thing. When we understand this, it allows us to see that letting go—another definition of renunciation—doesn't have to be a distant goal or unattainable spiritual principle. It is available to us right here and now.

The practice of meditation helps us see that we don't have to be driven by our impulses. Whatever is going on internally, we can let it go and act more wisely. Non-doing gives us the space to respond rather than react, to wisely reflect before speech or action. This is the power that meditation gives us.

Today in your meditation, notice the impulses, no matter how small, that you are not acting on. Notice how non-doing gives you a capacity to see clearly and act wisely.

# March 21

*"Deepening Our Practice"*

Meditation has great potential benefits on many levels: spiritual, emotional, and physical. For people in recovery it can bring more peace and clarity, and it can act as a buffer against relapse. But all of this only happens with our persistent effort and participation. At first when you sit down to meditate, it might not seem as if anything is happening. Even with sustained practice you might wonder how to find more quiet and insight.

The first thing that helps us deepen our meditation is time. Meditation doesn't act like a pill that you can just swallow and expect results. Time is the pill, and the length of time determines the dosage. The science shows that one minute of meditation has very different effects than one hour. This is one of the reasons that people go on meditation retreats, sometimes for months at a time.

Another way to deepen practice is to experiment with different techniques. Different people respond to different practices. For one person, mindfulness of the breath is most effective, while others might find that loving-kindness or mindfulness of sound work best. It's helpful to explore a variety of approaches and see how they work for you. Furthermore, you might discover that different practices are more effective at different times. So, perhaps you do one practice in the morning and a different one at night. You might find you need more effort when you're emotionally agitated or excited. You could call this, "broadening practice" rather than deepening it, because it's expanding your toolbox.

A third element of deepening practice is study, whether with a teacher or from books or recordings. Teachers help us to understand our experience and guide us through rough patches. Their wisdom can inspire us and open us to practices and insights we might not find on our own.

Today reflect on how to deepen your own practice. Try spending more time in daily meditation. Consider attending a residential retreat. Experiment with some new ways to meditate. And keep reading and studying with inspiring teachers.

# March 22

## *"Deepening Our Recovery"*

Recovery goes through stages. From the first days up to a year or two, most people need to adhere closely to the guidelines of the program and the suggestions of a sponsor and recovering friends. These early days are characterized by revelations and huge challenges. We may relapse or struggle with maintaining sobriety and being clean. It can be stressful, and we can fall into depression and anxiety. We can also find ourselves elated with a newfound clarity and purpose.

At some point, though, many people find that the reins are loosened, and recovery starts to feel more natural. The Steps have become internalized. We feel steady on our feet. We may still be working a rigorous program, but now it feels that it's integrated into a life of recovery.

Yet everything changes, including our recovery, and at some point, it's common that people sense a need for something more. The Steps might become rote, meetings predictable, and sponsors superfluous. This is a moment of risk, a time when we must dig deeper into the spiritual dimensions of recovery.

For many people, deepening recovery means deepening meditation. The study of Buddhism gives us a rich way to explore these realms. Our meditation opens us up to new insights into our hearts and minds; we gain greater clarity regarding our emotional life; compassion, generosity, and many other qualities expand and deepen. The Steps themselves take on new dimensions.

If we don't take on the challenge of deepening our recovery, we run the risk of relapse. Unless we continue to move forward in our spiritual life, we may start backsliding.

Today ask yourself if you are deepening the spiritual dimensions of your recovery. Is there more you can do to enhance your spiritual growth moving forward?

# March 23

## *"Attitudes of Mindfulness: Patience"*

"The ability to be mindful develops over time. How much time, there's no saying. It's different for each person. When we first sit down to meditate, we might have some hope that something is going to happen, and if it doesn't, we might get impatient. If we can just relax and trust in the process, it will unfold and develop. If we are trying to rush the process or get impatient, we actually undermine the natural quieting that the mind inclines to.

"Again, the attitude of observing our experience, rather than trying to control it, allows us to just sit with whatever is appearing, whether it's pleasant, unpleasant, or neutral. As we develop this quality of patience, we become less reactive and more balanced in our response to experiences. We don't feel the same urgency to fix or change things that we don't like. This in turn increases our inner peace and leads to more patience, more willingness to be with things just as they are." *Workbook*, p. 43

As addicts, patience tends to be very low on our list of qualities—addiction itself is an expression of impatience. We want to get loaded *now.* If we're going to stay in recovery, we're going to have to face this quality and find some way of dealing with it.

Patience and impatience are tied to both our meditation practice and our recovery. Mindfulness, rather than saying you should get rid of these feelings, suggests that you turn your attention to the discomfort. As you do so, you breathe and try to let the energies pass through you. You feel the discomfort of your own impatience and you don't fight it or try to fix it. This is patience. It's not about gritting your teeth until the unpleasant experience passes. Rather, it's about letting go of your resistance, your fear, your frustration, and surrendering to the reality of what is happening in this moment.

Today notice your impatience in practice and daily activities. Feel the tension in the body, the discomfort. Breathe with that and see if you can let it pass on its own, without resistance.

# March 24

## *"Tracking"*

Typically, people try to pay attention to their breath or some other object (mantra, sound, body sensations) when meditating. However, it can helpful to check in with several other things during a sitting session.

The first of these is your sitting posture. It's common while sitting for the posture to start to slump. As you meditate, from time to time check in with your posture. If you have slumped, don't just snap back to upright. Rather, gently, and with the breath, raise the body back up. If, on the other hand, your body has become tight or rigid, use the breath to relax and release tension, and then settle.

Another thing to track is energy, whether you are sleepy or restless, or your energy feels balanced. If you notice sleepiness, use the antidotes of straightening posture and opening the eyes to get energy back. For restlessness, again, use the breath to soften and settle the body. In addition, restlessness can be countered by broadening or opening awareness so that there is a sense of spaciousness for that energy to move.

A third thing to track is effort. Are you striving or struggling to be with the breath or push away thoughts? This common problem creates more agitation in the mind and body. Meditation isn't about getting it right or winning the race. It requires an attitude of openness, patience, and acceptance. If you stick with the process, everything will unfold naturally in its own time. If, on the other hand, you are not making enough effort, you might need to focus more intently on the breath.

A final aspect of experience to track is mood and emotion. Thoughts often trigger feelings, so even as you sit still with the eyes closed, you might find different emotions arising. Don't ignore these. Integrate them into your awareness.

Today, begin to apply these principles of tracking to your practice, noticing posture, energy, effort, and subtle emotional shifts. At the same time, don't lose track of your primary object of attention. With practice you will learn to move easily between your primary object and these secondary elements.

# March 25

*"Honesty"*

Dishonesty is to be a fundamental element of addiction. We are dishonest with others in an effort to get what we want or to get away with addictive behaviors. Perhaps more importantly, we are dishonest with ourselves. We deny our behavior and our condition. The opening paragraph to Chapter Five of the AA Big Book emphasizes this when it says that those who don't recover are usually people "who are constitutionally incapable of being honest with themselves."

We tell ourselves that we're controlling our using, that things aren't that bad. We say we'll figure things out soon, that we just need a break, or that the world is unfair to us. On and on the excuses stretch. The fact is we are addicts who are unwilling to face the truth.

Recovery begins with acknowledging this fact. And what freedom that simple admission brings! No longer trapped in our own web of lies, we step into the sunlight of truth and see ourselves and the world anew. Now we can begin to solve our problem—because now we know what it is.

The paradox of honesty is that shame is banished. Many of our lies were associated with shame and a sense of failure. Facing the truth of our addiction changes our entire point of view. Now we see our addiction as a human problem, shared by many. With the lies and deceit abandoned, we can walk through life with dignity and honor, not concealing our faults and not trumpeting our assets.

Honesty toward ourselves, then, allows us to be honest with others. Finally, it allows us to see the world more clearly. No longer living in illusion, we are able to face life's trials and triumphs fearlessly.

Today, consider how honesty about your addiction has transformed your life, and reflect on ways you can be more honest with yourself and others. This is the first step in "H.O.W:" Honesty, Open-mindedness, and Willingness.

# March 26

### *"Open-mindedness"*

The mind of an addict is closed. We know what we know, and that's all there is to it. We know what we need, and we don't want any advice. As a result, we stay locked up in our own painful reality. It's only when we finally open our minds to new possibilities that things begin to change.

First, we need to be open to the possibility that we have a problem, that we are addicts or alcoholics. Of course, this is often one of the hardest ideas to accept. It requires a complete realignment of our understanding of ourselves and our lives. Instead of viewing our using as something we are controlling, we have to realize that we've been controlled by our addiction. We look at our past and realize how much damage we've done (which we'll address in Step Four). We begin to glimpse the possibility of a new life, one not centered on using or escaping, but on growing and being more productive and useful in the world.

But open-mindedness doesn't stop there. We learn to bring this attitude into our lives in an ongoing way. We question our motives and actions. We question our beliefs, our thoughts, and our emotions. We ask for help, and we listen. We are always ready to learn. We question the very premise of our lives: what is my life's purpose?

We start to take advice, and we realize how much untapped potential we have. Instead of enveloping ourselves in a self-protective cocoon, we open to the wide world of spirituality and wisdom. We become like curious children, always on the lookout for new information and new insights.

Today, ask yourself what ways you are still closed-minded. Next, notice and take joy in the ways that you are now more open. This is the second step in "H.O.W."

# March 27

### *"Willingness"*

Following on open-mindedness is the willingness to act on our new understanding. Without engaging and making effort nothing changes. As a "program of action," this is a requirement of the Twelve Steps. Buddhism, too, points to the necessity of taking action if we want to achieve any growth or change.

As addicts we could be stubborn and extremely passive. Our closed-mindedness left us unwilling to try new things, to deal with change, or to take risks. We lived in what we perceived as a safe, comfortable world. But that world was really a prison of our own making. We could never step out of those four limiting walls.

Willingness comes from the understanding that we don't know everything, that if we want our lives to change, we're going to have to try some new things. Everything from our work lives, to our relationships, to our spiritual practice benefits from this new attitude. Once we make this shift in attitude, we develop new habits and new ways of responding to the challenges and opportunities that arise. Instead of shutting down or running away, we step up. Instead of a cynical detachment, we find the joy of trying new things, of learning and growing. We rejoin the human race.

The Buddha said that nothing happens without effort, and that intention creates karma. With willingness we express our intention. And with effort we create real change in our lives. Our recovery depends upon the ongoing attitude of Honesty, Open-mindedness, and Willingness. This is HOW we live the program and the Steps, how we grow, change, and find real fulfillment in our lives.

Today, ask yourself where you are expressing willingness and where you are still holding back. Are there ways in which your recovery could deepen with more willingness? This is the third and final step of H.O.W.

# March 28

*"Depression"*

For many addicts and alcoholics, depression is an underlying condition that exacerbates our addiction and makes our recovery even more difficult. Many people relapse when they fall into a period of depression. How to manage this without using alcohol and (recreational) drugs or indulging in compulsive or self-destructive behavior is one of the challenges many addicts face.

Although there have been debates in Twelve Step meetings over the years about whether anti-depressants are appropriate medications for people in recovery, generally speaking, it's accepted that these drugs aren't intoxicating, and thus create no danger of relapse. In the case of clinical depression or suicidal thinking, there can be no question that prescribed medication is appropriate.

However, there are many other variations of depression that respond to non-chemical intervention, and most addicts will want to at least try these before resorting to medical help. In fact, Twelve Step meetings themselves, not to mention Buddhist meditation groups, can be a source of solace from these painful states. Depression thrives on isolation (as does addiction), so simply getting out of the house and into the company of a supportive community can break the spell of a depressive mood.

Mindfulness itself also has a critical role to play. Depression thrives on negative, habitual thought patterns. Mindfulness deconstructs these sorts of beliefs and opens up a different understanding of our experience. It reminds us that all feelings are temporary. And by questioning thoughts, it helps us debunk the kind of self-loathing that drags down the mood.

Two things are for sure: depression is a dangerous condition and dealing with it takes real work and commitment. If you are seized with suicidal thoughts, contact a professional for help right away.

Today, bring mindfulness to your moods. Notice how intimately your thoughts are tied to the arising and passing of moods. When a painful emotion arises, breathe into the body, relax, and let it be. If you don't feed it with more negative thoughts, it will eventually pass.

# March 29

*"Smile"*

Meditation is meant to free us from painful mental states and help us see the truth more clearly, and yet, the very effort to do this can sometimes turn into a grind. If our practice becomes too serious, one antidote is to smile. This might sound like a simplistic solution; however, it can have remarkable effects.

Because mind and body are connected, the physical act of smiling has the mental effect of uplifting the mood. Of course, if the mood is one of despair, a smile might not cut through, but for many relatively neutral or dull states, the smile helps.

A meditative smile isn't a grin, but just an upturning of the corners of the mouth. Keeping the attention on the breath, you bring a smile to your lips and continue your mindfulness. Don't look for a special response, just stay with your practice. Notice what happens, if the mood, the energy in the body, or the focus and concentration change at all.

The smile practice can be taken into daily life as well. Just walking down the street, try bringing a smile. At the same time, look at your environment, whether you are surrounded trees or buildings or people, and see how smiling changes your perception of them. Remarkably, smiling can create a huge shift in the way you experience the world.

Finally, offer a smile to people you pass or meet. A friendly smile can break down barriers between strangers. We don't have to aggressively grin, just glance at someone and smile. They'll often smile back, and both of you have improved your day.

Today, begin to practice the smile in meditation and daily life. See if smiling more changes how you feel through your day.

# March 30

*"Commitment"*

At this point in the Step process we have acknowledged our problem (Step One), accepted that it's possible to recover (Step Two), and now we've taken our first real action on the path: Step Three. Step Three is about commitment. The decision we've made with this Step is the decision to follow through on what we've learned in the first two Steps. It's not enough to recognize the problem and see that we can do something about it. We must act. Turning our will and our lives over is the first gesture in this process. We're facing our problem and embracing the solution head on. Buddhism expresses this commitment as Taking Refuge.

In recovery this means going to meetings, working with a sponsor or other mentor, doing service, and developing our spiritual life. Recovery and the Steps have become the central axis of our lives around which everything else turns. This is how the program becomes our Refuge. It is the safe place we all long for and we all need.

Once and for all, we've abandoned our go-it-alone attitude and embraced our role as members of a community. That community is there for us, understands us, and supports us no matter what. Whether celebrating our successes or lifting us up from our failures (even our relapses), our commitment has made us part of something powerful and healing.

Besides this external commitment, Step Three is an internal commitment to self-examination that becomes the thrust of the succeeding Steps. Turning our will and our lives over requires us to question motives and behaviors in an ongoing way. Embracing Buddhist principles and practices gives us a practical way to fulfill this demand.

Today, explore the levels of your commitment. Are you fully committed to your recovery both internally and externally? In the same way, look at your commitment to mindfulness and the principles of dharma.

# March 31

### *"Spiritual Awakening"*

The revelation of Step Three, its spiritual awakening, is the tremendous power of acceptance. The Step embodies the spiritual paradox of surrendering to succeed. Such a principle is hidden from the eye of the ordinary person. It contradicts society's push to conquer, to move forward, and to guide our own destinies. And it contradicts the addict's need to control everything.

For many people, this Step is the turning point in fully embracing the path of recovery. They've overcome the conflict with drugs, alcohol, food, sex, gambling, relationships, or control, and dealt with their resistance to spirituality and the idea of a Higher Power. With this third surrender, they've decided to go all in, to trust that the whole project of recovery and working the Steps is *the* way.

This shift in perspective, putting acceptance in the forefront of our, lives seems to smooth out the bumps, to defuse the conflicts, and to ease the changes that life throws at us. Instead of trying to get around problems or manipulate events, now our attitude is one of problem-solving: "Here is what life is presenting me. What might be a wise way to deal with it?" Not looking to blame or fix, we simply want to do the "next right thing."

This attitude neatly parallels the Buddhist path of mindfulness and compassion. In focusing on the present moment, we are engaging what is, not wishing for what isn't. In meeting each situation with love, we are leading with kindness, not meeting it with resistance, which creates conflict. We see that our ego-centered, pleasure-seeking attitude inevitably led to dissatisfaction, disputes, and alienation.

This transformation doesn't happen alone. In Twelve Step programs, a sponsor can be a vital guide in understanding what the "next right thing" is. A dharma teacher provides critical wisdom as we navigate this new, open attitude. As addicts, our decision-making skills were broken. Our spiritual awakening depends on the support of those who have trod this path before us.

Today, notice how much easier life is when you are guided by an attitude of acceptance. Take joy in this realization.

# APRIL: STEP FOUR

*"Made a searching and fearless moral inventory of ourselves."*

# April 1

## *"Buddhist Inventory"*

The Twelve Step program lays out very specific guidance for making a "searching and fearless" inventory. The Buddhist path doesn't have such a structured inventory format, but the teachings point to the importance of self-examination and give us a variety of ways to carry out this vital inner work. This month we'll break down some of these approaches.

First though, it's worth noting that in a sense mindfulness meditation itself is a kind of moment-to-moment inventory of what is appearing in our mind and body.

The Five Precepts give us a moral framework for looking at our behavior. This is also the closest parallel to a Twelve Step inventory model. Buddhist monastics have a regular ritual in which they confess to their teacher or the community any violations of the rules that they may have committed. The Western lay community hasn't yet adopted such a form, though it might be time to consider it.

The Five Hindrances, which we'll explore again this month, offer another way to approach an inventory. Here we can explore the different ways that our meditation becomes disrupted, and further, look at how those qualities arise in our daily lives.

Buddhism also gives us some ways to look for the positive. The Seven Awakening Factors and the Ten Paramitas (six in Mahayana Buddhism) are qualities that we try to cultivate as Buddhists. They provide excellent templates for developing a positive inventory, something which tends to be neglected in the Twelve Step world to the detriment of those in recovery.

Today make a commitment to bring an attitude of mindful inventory into your life. With kindness and compassion, carry this effort into each day.

# April 2

*"The First Precept"*

The Five Precepts are the foundation of Buddhist morality. The first four—not to kill, steal, harm sexually, or lie—are shared by most religions and ethical systems, while the fifth, to not use intoxicants, has a special role in recovery.

One distinct aspect of the Buddhist approach to ethics is to broaden, rather than narrow, our understanding of various strictures. So, the first Precept, "To refrain from taking the life of any living creature," addresses all life, not just humans. This sets up an almost impossible task since even boiling water can involve killing living microbes. This sort of paradox is typical of Buddhism in that it forces us to find our own way of understanding and living in accordance with the teachings.

Many people take this precept to mean we shouldn't eat meat, though strictly speaking, the precept doesn't say that. Others take it as a general call to serve living beings and try to lessen suffering. If we take a first Precept inventory, whether formally or informally, all of these questions can be part of our self-examination.

Further, we can take this precept as an opportunity to look at any violence we may have committed in our lives. Addicts often commit such acts when intoxicated or even in moments of desperate craving. Other people might have had to be violent as members of the military or in situations of self-defense.

The point of such an inventory is not to punish ourselves for past wrongs, but to see what we carry within ourselves today. If we have suppressed memories or avoided responsibility for our behavior, then we are closing off a part of ourselves. To shed light on these shadows allows them to be integrated into our consciousness. Without such a process, we will forever be victims of our own misdeeds.

Today, recognize and accept the ways that you might have been violent or harmed other beings. Use the following practices of forgiveness and compassion to begin to heal.

# April 3

*"Forgiveness Practice: Ourselves"*

Without forgiveness the inventory process can turn into one of self-flagellation or blaming others. These attitudes serve no purpose, but simply exacerbate the failings our inventory uncovers.

Forgiveness has several dimensions. First, it is founded in understanding that we can never change the past, so we must come to some peace with it. Forgiveness also arises from our realization of human imperfection. Everyone makes mistakes; everyone hurts people. No one is perfect.

Here is a guided meditation for the first step of forgiveness:

**"Forgiving ourselves**: begin by contemplating all the ways that you harmed yourself, internally and externally. This of course includes your addictive behavior, but also ways that you gave up on yourself, whether in school, in a relationship, or in a job. How have you talked to yourself or viewed yourself in negative terms? Self-hatred is a common disease in our culture, especially among addicts, and the truth is, as human beings, we don't deserve to be hated. Repeat these phrases to yourself: *For all the ways I have harmed myself through thought, word, and deed, I forgive myself. I forgive myself.* We may not feel anything right away, but it's important to stay with this process, and not just in a single sitting, but to keep coming back to this process over time until the tightness in the heart starts to break up and we begin to have a sense of self-forgiveness." *Workbook*, p. 192-193

Mindfulness encourages us to recognize and accept our failings, then move on. If we continue to ruminate over past actions, we are only creating more negative consequences.

Today, start a regular practice of forgiveness for yourself. Notice any resistance or judgment that arises and let that go. Return to the simple principle of bringing kindness to your own suffering.

# April 4

## *"The First Hindrance: Desire"*

While a Precept Inventory addresses the moral dimensions of recovery, a Hindrance Inventory specifically addresses the meditative dimension, and more generally, our mental and physical challenges.

Desire, as the first hindrance, reflects the Buddha's teaching that craving is the cause of suffering. For this reason, addressing desire in meditation is one of the first ways to explore the mind. If we can uncover our habitual thoughts of desire and learn to let them go, we can begin to fulfill the path.

In addressing desire, we first need to understand how it causes suffering so we will be motivated to let it go. The essence of this understanding is founded in the realization that there is no end to desire. No matter how much pleasure or how many material possessions we attain, there will always be the next desire. There is no one object, person, feeling, or experience that can provide lasting satisfaction. In seeing this truth, we become much more willing to let go of craving as it arises.

While there is no end to desire, each desire is impermanent. Knowing this truth gives us faith and courage to ride out troubling desires without acting on them when they arise.

Mindfulness reveals the existential pain of desire: it hurts. It hurts to be caught in craving, in feeling that things aren't okay the way they are. What mindfulness *also* shows us is that this pain is caused by the thought of desire, and that letting go of the thought lets go of the pain. And, while this formula may not play out instantly, its logic is irrefutable: if a thought of wanting is painful, that pain must cease when the wanting ceases.

Today make desire the focus of your meditation practice. Notice how many thoughts are related to desire. Notice how those thoughts manifest as feelings, and how letting go of those thoughts relieves those feelings.

# April 5

*"The Second Precept"*

"To refrain from taking that which is not given." Simply put, the second precept tells us not to steal. As addicts we often had a very "flexible" attitude towards other people's belongings. If our friend was better off than us, we could rationalize that they didn't need their money or drugs as badly as we did. We might think stealing from a store or corporation wouldn't really hurt them, or even that a certain amount of shoplifting was built into their accounting. None of these excuses justifies our behavior, which was fundamentally based in selfishness and amorality.

People outside the Twelve Step world usually don't realize that recovery involves more than abstinence from drinking and using. Twelve Steppers know that the program includes a broad-based change in our behavior. Recovery really means embracing basic moral principles.

In practical terms, we take on these principles because we understand that when we lie, cheat, or steal, we operate in a netherworld of self-justification and self-gratification that better fits the life and attitude of an addict than that of a sober person. The same rule-breaking, boundary-less behavior of a shoplifter easily morphs into the sleazy lifestyle of a drunk or drug addict.

Buddhist teachings on karma give a more philosophical, though ultimately realistic, understanding of what it means to steal. Karma says that every action has an effect, and those effects can be immediate or delayed; they can be material, mental, or emotional. They can also be legal. Stealing might get us arrested or alienate our friends and family; it might make people trust us less; or it might cause us sleepless, guilty nights. While it may appear that some people get away with crimes, in the words of the late dharma teacher Ruth Denison, "Karma means you don't get away with nothing, dear."

Today reflect on your own relationship to stealing. If you are doing an inventory, you can recall times when you have "taken that which is not given." How honest are you today in relationship to material things?

# April 6

*"Awakening Factors: Mindfulness"*

While inventory often focuses on the negative, it's equally important to acknowledge the positive qualities and actions in our lives. Without this reflection, our self-view becomes skewed. The Seven Factors of Awakening are a helpful starting point: Mindfulness, Investigation, Energy, Joy, Tranquility, Concentration, and Equanimity.

Today look at how you are integrating the Awakening Factor of Mindfulness into your life. If you have adopted a mindfulness meditation practice, this is something to take joy in. You can also consider whether you would be willing to deepen your practice either by increasing the amount of time you sit each day or by going on a retreat. If you don't have a daily practice, are you ready to take that on? What would it take to make this commitment? What stands in the way of your daily practice? Time? Doubt? Fear? This then becomes part of your inventory, exploring the things that block your practice.

Besides formal meditation, mindfulness can be integrated into other activities. How much mindfulness are you bringing to your life? Are you mindful at work? In relationship? When driving? Exercising?

Eating is another place where we can bring mindfulness to bear. Many of us fall into unhealthy eating habits. When we actually pay attention to the food we are eating, we may be motivated to change those habits. Even grocery shopping mindfully can be helpful because we'll make more conscious, healthy food choices.

A mindfulness inventory is meant to be supportive, not destructive. We aren't doing this so we have another way to beat ourselves up for our shortcomings. Rather, we want to take some pleasure in recognizing how we are already mindful, and also look for ways we can fit more moments of mindfulness into our day naturally.

Today try to bring mindfulness into every activity. Notice where this is more difficult and look for strategies to improve. Notice where this is natural and enjoy those moments of being present.

# April 7

*"Meditative Inventory"*

Twelve Step literature mainly envisions inventory as a written activity followed by sharing. With meditation, inventory also becomes a mental activity.

Meditation doesn't turn off our brains. Thinking happens. Often meditation teachings encourage us to just let go of thoughts and return to the breath (or other meditation object). However, to simply dismiss thoughts as an intrusion into our practice is to lose out on an area of rich possibility. This isn't to say that we should spend our meditation period lost in thoughts, but when thoughts do appear, it can be helpful to do a certain kind of investigation.

This investigation needs to be distinguished from something like psychotherapy where we are exploring the personal psychological roots of our thoughts. In meditation, we are investigating in a less personal way. For instance, we might notice that we have a lot of thoughts of desire or anger or anxiety. We start to see patterns: in the morning you might have certain types of thoughts that are different from those you have in the evening. You might notice how certain situations, like work stress, trigger cravings or resentments. This process is done without judging what is arising. We don't place blame or even try to figure out why we are having these thoughts. We are simply bringing mindfulness to the patterns and forms of thinking.

This kind of inventory helps us to step back from our thoughts, to take them less personally, and ultimately become less attached to them. As we see these patterns play out over and over, we find that they have less pull on us; we just can't take them that seriously when we see how habitual, how conditioned, how automatic they are. They become more like static noise running through our minds, and less like commentary on our worth or on the quality of our lives.

Today begin to apply the idea of meditative inventory to your practice. As you become more familiar with these patterns in your meditation, notice how such thoughts appear in daily life as well. Keep letting go.

# April 8

### *"The Second Hindrance: Aversion"*

In the course of our inventories, aversion appears in many forms, such as anger, resentment, fear, judgment, and avoidance. Some or all of these qualities were integral to our addiction. Certainly, aversion to emotional pain is a central driver to addictive behavior.

The Buddha highlights these aversive qualities as some of the most destructive and counterproductive human feelings we can have. Even when confronted with rude and disrespectful people, he was determined not to fall into anger. Anger, he said, only gives your "enemy" what they want because it makes *you* unhappy, it causes *you* pain.

During mindfulness meditation we see the impact of aversion directly. As we sit and watch the mind and body, when an aversive thought arises, we see and feel the stress that comes with it. The body becomes tense or the stomach churns; the mood turns dark, and the mind is flooded with more negativity.

In our ordinary mind states, we might not notice these changes, and so we act on the feelings. We get angry or blame others; we criticize or avoid them. While this might bring some temporary satisfaction as we vent our feelings, the lasting effects are rarely positive. Whether directed towards ourselves or others, aversion just tends to create more aversion.

Letting go of aversion begins with mindfulness. This helps us to see its impermanent nature, so we don't identify with it. That allows the feeling to naturally dissipate. Furthermore, we see the painful results of our anger, internally and externally. That motivates us to let go because we realize we are only hurting ourselves. These are some of the benefits of working mindfully with destructive feelings.

Today, watch how aversion appears in the mind. Notice your reactivity and its painful consequences. Explore other, more productive, ways to respond to the triggers of aversion.

# April 9

*"Antidote to Aversion: Loving-kindness"*

As we shed the light of mindfulness on the painful feeling of aversion, we look for ways to let it go. Cultivating loving-kindness gives us an active way to respond to those feelings.

When we first notice that such a feeling has arisen, we bring attention into the body to sense it directly. We recollect the destructive and painful effects of aversion.

Now we turn our attention to arousing lovingkindness. We breathe into the heart, and then try to radiate the feeling of kindness and care throughout the body. Along with that breath, we recollect the object of our aversion, whether another person, situation, thought, or feeling.

We then bring phrases of lovingkindness to mind. Common ones are, "May you be happy; may you be peaceful; may you be safe." Depending on the object of aversion, these might not fit, so we can be creative in finding phrases that resonate.

Further reflection might also be called for. With aversion to others, we might think of their positive qualities or of the negative consequences that they will suffer from their behavior. With aversion to situations, we might find the Serenity Prayer helpful in guiding us toward acceptance. With aversion to our own thoughts and feelings, we might remember their impermanent nature and our deep intention for happiness.

It's best to do such formal practice in a limited time frame, not trying to push yourself for a long period. Take this practice easy. Try to make it into a habitual attitude and response to aversion. With persistence, these positive thoughts and attitudes gradually replace our habitual negativity.

Today commit to turning toward loving-kindness whenever aversion arises. Bring imagination and creativity to this process.

# April 10

*"Paramitas: Generosity"*

The Paramitas, or Perfections, are positive qualities that the Buddha is said to have developed to their ultimate degree. They provide us with a template for how to live and what to strive for in our spiritual life. Like the Awakening Factors, we can use them as a framework for the positive side of our inventory. Strictly speaking, such an inventory may show us qualities that we lack, but they are meant to give us something positive to strive toward and develop further.

Generosity was the first thing that the Buddha taught to lay people (as opposed to monastics). The idea was that, since clinging and craving are the cause of suffering, generosity is the most obvious, material way of letting go. The entire Buddhist tradition rests on the support the lay community gives to the monastic community. Giving is built into the tradition in a way that's obvious if you visit a Buddhist temple or monastery. There you will often see people excited and happy to give offerings to the monks and nuns.

Generosity is uplifting, filling the giver with lightness and joy. It shows, in a very real way, the truth of the Buddha's teachings. Practicing generosity also reveals to us where we are caught in clinging. What are we afraid to let go of? Where does our selfishness lie?

As a positive inventory, reflect on the ways that you are generous. This might involve material generosity, but there are many other ways to be generous: with time, with affection, with attention, and more. As you reflect on ways you are generous, notice the tendency to undercut or undervalue your positive qualities. So often when we try looking at our positive side, we downplay the good. While this is often couched as humility, it can also express a negative self-view. None of us are Buddhas, but that doesn't mean we don't have value and that we can't still embrace what is good about us.

Today, take some time to appreciate the ways you give to others and to the world. Notice how it feels to acknowledge this and really take it in.

# April 11

## *"Daily Recollections: Sickness"*

The second of the Five Daily Recollections is the reflection on the inevitability of sickness, of becoming ill. Like the others in this list, sickness isn't something we really want to think about, which is probably why the Buddha suggests we do it deliberately.

The recollection is more broadly on the frailty of the body. Even when we're not sick, we can experience various aches and pain. As we get older (the first of the Daily Recollections) these only increase. What is our relationship to the unpleasantness of illness and physical discomfort? As addicts, we often got into trouble when we tried to avoid pain. Many people become addicts simply by using pain medication. So, the way we relate to illness is not just a theoretical or spiritual question—it has real life consequences.

The Recollection is supposed to help us to accept illness. When we realize, "I am of the nature to be ill; I have not gone beyond illness," as the Buddha says, we see being sick as a natural result of having a body. This doesn't mean we don't try to get well or take medicine or any other medical intervention. It just means we don't see being sick as an aberration or a mistake. This shift in attitude can relieve a lot of the distress associated with illness.

One of the Buddha's teachings called "The Second Dart" gives a simile for this understanding. He says that ordinarily when we feel physical pain, we add to it with our mental pain, our resistance or agitation about the physical experience. He says this is like getting hit by a dart, the physical pain, but then adding a second dart, the mental. He says that if we can let go of the mental reactivity, which often comes as aversion to the pain, we reduce the actual suffering significantly.

Today, think about how often you have been sick or felt pain in your life. Although we don't like to think about it, for most of us these experiences come all too often. Consider how the experience of illness or discomfort would be different if you took an attitude of acceptance rather than adding a second dart.

# April 12

### *"Noting"*

The meditation practice of "noting" comes out of a particular Burmese Vipassana tradition. It is one of the practices often taught in Insight Meditation Centers (Vipassana means "insight" in Pali). Noting is a very structured form of practice that helps us to see our experience clearly and understand what is happening.

With noting, we use words in the mind to note what we are experiencing. We begin by noting the breath, either "In, out" or "Rising, falling," depending on whether we are following the breath at the nostrils or the belly.

When we notice the mind has wandered, we can note, "Thinking, thinking," before returning to the breath. (For some reason, noting is usually repeated. Perhaps to break through and away from thoughts.) If a sound intrudes on our awareness, we note, "Hearing, hearing." If a sensation draws our attention, we note "Feeling" or "Sensation."

As we practice, we can refine the specific notes on thinking. For instance, it can be helpful to notice desire and aversion in thoughts. Or we might become aware of a lot of planning or remembering, judging or analyzing. Any of these terms can be used as notes.

While it's helpful to be precise in the noting, since that requires us to pay close attention and it reveals patterns of thinking we may not have been aware of before, we don't want to spend a lot of time figuring out what the best note would be. This just leads to more thinking and wandering mind. If a note doesn't immediately come to mind, just use "Thinking."

Noting practice is a very specific way of doing meditative inventory.

Today, start trying out the noting practice in your meditation. Use it for a week or so to give it a chance. If you find it helpful, you can adopt it as your main practice. If you find it distracting or unhelpful, just go back to what has been working for you.

# April 13

### *"Awakening Factors: Investigation"*

We've already talked about "meditative inventory," so now it might be useful to look at the second Awakening Factor, Investigation. Sometimes this factor is overlooked or misunderstood in practice. It doesn't mean thinking about what's happening when we are meditating. Rather, it suggests an engaged awareness that makes intuitive connections as we practice mindfulness. So, when we notice that certain thoughts arise when we are in certain moods, that's the result of investigating cause and effect. When we become aware of the changing quality of sensations, that comes from investigation. What we are doing is seeing the underlying patterns behind our experience.

Investigation ups our mindfulness game because it's not just a passive stance, but an engagement in what is happening. We are bringing curiosity to the whole meditation project.

It's easy to fall into a passive mode in meditation, especially when we develop a certain ability to sit and relax. Although there is certainly value in this, it doesn't fulfill the greater purpose of spiritual growth and insight. These require an alert attention.

Certain approaches to practice are more conducive to investigation than others. For instance, the noting practice from yesterday highlights the specific patterns of thought. However, a concentration practice like counting the breaths (January 21) isn't going to bring this same kind of clarity to process (instead, such a practice is more useful for calming and quieting the mind).

Today, ask yourself if you are truly engaged in your meditation practice. To strengthen the Investigation factor, make sure you are alert when sitting, and remain connected to the meditation object, not just vaguely paying attention to it. This will naturally have the added benefit of increasing concentration.

# April 14

*"The Third Precept"*

"To refrain from sexual misconduct." The Third Precept opens a whole realm of inventory. Sexuality, as a primal instinct, has far-reaching effects in the world and in each of our lives. For addicts, our relationship to sexuality can be particularly troubling. In fact, for many people, that relationship is the basis of their primary addiction.

The first principle of the Buddhist precepts is to "do no harm." When applied to the Third Precept, this can give some clarity. The precept doesn't lay out rules around sexual preferences or behaviors, it simply says, don't harm anyone, including yourself.

In our Fourth Step inventory, we address our harmful behavior before getting into recovery. Intoxication unleashes suppressed sexual desires, and many of us have painful personal histories around our behaviors while under the influence. A high percentage of sexual assaults are carried out by people who are drunk or high. This is not surprising. What is more troubling is the sexual misconduct perpetrated by people ostensibly in recovery or on a spiritual path. Twelve Step and Buddhist communities have often been thrown into turmoil by such behaviors.

Practicing the Third Precept demands that we begin to investigate the ways we express our sexuality. This doesn't just mean sex acts. It includes how our mind becomes swept up in sexual thoughts or fantasies; how we talk about sex; and how we interact with people we are attracted to. If we are in a committed relationship, we look at how we might flirt or otherwise suggest an interest in someone outside our relationship. If we are dating or exploring alternative relationship forms, we make sure those we are involved with understand and agree with our boundaries and what we are mutually committed to. An incredible amount of harm happens when such issues aren't clarified.

Today, begin to explore your relationship to the Third Precept. Ultimately, it is up to you to determine how you understand this complicated area of life.

# April 15

### *"Living with Our Sexuality"*

While addressing the Third Precept is an important part of our recovery and spiritual work, it is only the beginning of dealing with our sexuality. When we hear celibate monastics talk about their own issues with lust, it becomes clear that simply abstaining from sex isn't a solution to the issues that living in a body can bring up. In fact, in some Twelve Step programs for sexual addiction, celibacy is referred to as "anorexia" when it is used to repress sexual desire, not express a healthy letting go.

Unlike with drugs and alcohol, we can't just walk away from our sexuality. It lives in our body. How can we hold that skillfully?

As with most things, Buddhism suggests we bring awareness to the matter. Watching how sexual feelings arise or don't arise, and how thoughts, sensations, and emotions move together, gives us an entryway into working with this energy. And then, seeing how deeply conditioned this energy is gives us some idea about how challenging it is to make any changes.

Finally, it's vital that we see how our thoughts and behaviors lead to suffering—starting with ourselves. Our conditioning can obscure the dukkha inherent to sexual craving because once that craving arises, we so quickly move toward thoughts and actions without feeling the actual craving itself. When we slow down enough to feel the powerful energy of wanting or desire, we discover its inherently uncomfortable qualities. The power of this drive is hard to resist without suppressing it, which only pushes it underground where it can work in the shadows.

It's an important aspect of our recovery to begin this work of bringing awareness to our sexuality. It's probably best to do so without a larger goal in mind other than to learn about ourselves. What we discover may motivate some further change, but this should always be done from a place of understanding, not from some preconceived idea of how we should be, or what is right or wrong.

Today, begin to explore how sexual thoughts and feelings arise, and notice how they affect your words and actions.

# April 16

### *"Feeling Feelings"*

Many of us come to meditation with the conscious or unconscious wish to deal with some painful emotions. Whether those are chronic or acute, whether they are old patterns or arise out of circumstances in the present like a breakup, a death in the family, a job loss, or a health scare, we might have the idea that there is something magical about meditation that will heal our pain. We get the idea that meditation is like taking a drug, but more spiritual. Unfortunately, this is not how meditation works.

Meditation only works to the degree that we put in a sustained effort to be aware. Few of us want to bring more awareness to painful emotions. In fact, what we want is *less* awareness, which is why many people living with depression and anxiety become addicts. However, meditation can only help us heal these emotions when we start to turn toward them and let them in.

The first step in this process is to discover what we are actually feeling. People who consider themselves to be emotionally sensitive are often surprised to discover that they've never actually explored their feelings. Rather, what they have done is react to them. This is a critical distinction. To explore your feelings means to bring mindfulness to the experience. This begins with bringing attention into the body and seeing where and how emotions manifest on the physical level. This alone is challenging because our minds resist feeling any pain, so we shy away from intentionally turning toward it.

To accomplish this, we use the breath as a gateway. Taking some deeper breaths, letting the chest and belly open, and bringing attention to the feelings in that part of the body, we start to connect on the visceral level. This must be done gently, easing our way into the pain, trying not to run, trying not to let the mind take over. Just feeling the feelings.

This is the beginning of a challenging and rewarding process. Today, just start with the work of feeling emotions in the body.

# April 17

*"Feeling Impermanence"*

As we begin the work of feeling feelings, it's natural to have resistance to this opening. The mind recoils, or it runs away with a story, a judgment, an analysis, or an escape. In order to soothe the mind, it's helpful to remind ourselves that feelings are impermanent.

One of the tricks of the human mind is that when we are having a feeling, we tend to think it will last indefinitely if we don't do something about it. But if we look closely enough, we will see that feelings are inherently unstable, always changing. When we stay with a feeling without running off into thoughts, we give the feeling space to play out its natural lifecycle.

However, what we often do is start thinking about the feeling, fighting or resisting it. This aversion actually feeds the feeling because, not only do we feel bad, but now we feel bad about having a bad feeling. This can start a vicious cycle of painful thoughts and feelings, so that eventually we feel trapped in a bubble of negativity and pain. This is how depression and anxiety take over our lives.

This brings us back once more to the simple practice of mindfulness. If we can just be aware of the pain without aversion, without trying to fix it, and without trying to escape it, in time it will naturally pass. This isn't to say we can't do other skillful things to encourage the pain to pass, such as forms of self-care, but we don't do them with aversion. Rather we engage the feelings with kindness and love towards ourselves.

Today, start to adopt this approach to working with emotions. The feelings don't even have to be painful to practice mindfulness. Just begin to open to what you are feeling both in meditation and in your daily life. Check in regularly, feel, breathe, and watch how everything passes.

# April 18

## *"Self-Care"*

Working on your inventory can bring up a lot of difficult feelings, as we've been discussing the last of couple days. It's especially important for people in recovery to have strategies for self-care.

From a recovery standpoint, self-care starts with refraining from harming ourselves with our addictive behavior. For drug addicts and alcoholics, that usually means abstinence, though harm-reduction strategies might be a starting point. For food or sex addicts, this is more subtle and usually takes wise guidance from a sponsor and caring support from a group.

From a Buddhist standpoint, self-care starts in the mind. Our meditation practice reveals the harmful ways we talk to ourselves and the destructive mental spirals we fall into. We must learn to interrupt such spirals so we aren't creating more suffering. Unfortunately, inventory work can trigger a lot of negative self-talk as we look honestly at our past behaviors. This is what makes both positive inventory and gentle forgiveness toward ourselves so important.

Self-care also includes things like diet, sleep, and exercise. These are all disrupted in an addict's lifestyle. When loaded, you don't tend to notice how unhealthy your food is; with drugs and alcohol that drain energy normal sleep patterns are disrupted; and consistent exercise habits are hard to maintain when so much time is devoted to binging and recovering from binges.

Today, reflect on the ways you are taking care of yourself on a daily basis. How could you improve on self-care?

# April 19

## *"Hang In"*

When people first learn to meditate, they're often intimidated by the idea of sitting still for even five or ten minutes. If we are restless, anxious, or have a hard time focusing, this can seem difficult. But most people find that they can manage such periods once they get some guidance and try it. However, if we are serious about deepening our meditation practice, we'll soon realize that more time is required. Most teachers consider twenty-minutes a baseline for practice, and encourage longer sits of 30, 45, or even 60 minutes at a time. This can become truly challenging.

Meditation isn't like an on/off switch. You don't just sit down and go into the deepest meditative state. The development of qualities like mindfulness, concentration, and insight only unfold over time. This means we need to learn to hang in when we hit a wall. Several strategies will help.

The first is, relaxing. If we meet the feeling of pressure and tension with gentle relaxation, we can begin to move through it.

The second thing is to increase focus. A restless body is often accompanied by a restless mind. If you refocus on the breath very closely as you relax, you will begin the process of moving past the resistance and toward a deeper experience of meditation.

Finally, it helps to make a resolution to sit no matter what. The urge to move is just an urge. There is no actual crisis or problem that feeling is pointing to. With determination, we can get through it.

Once we've broken through to a longer period of meditation, we'll discover our concentration building New challenges will arise, but having dealt with the resistance to sitting, we'll have more confidence and power to work through these as well.

Today, try stretching your regular meditation period by ten more minutes. Try this for a few days and see if you can make the longer session your new normal.

# April 20

*"Third Hindrance: Sloth and Torpor"*

The Third Hindrance has mental and physical elements. We get sleepy and our mind gets dull and spacey. As we start to stretch our meditation periods, this can become even more challenging. The deepening calm that comes with longer sits can tilt us toward sleep.

The starting point of working with sloth and torpor, as with all the hindrances, is mindfulness. This can seem paradoxical, since mindfulness is about increasing awareness, and sleepiness is about decreasing it. To bring mindfulness to the physical feeling of fatigue means feeling the sensations in the body. These can be quite subtle, like a heavy feeling in the limbs or around the eyes. Like many feelings, being tired is something we take for granted without examining the sensations themselves.

The mental state of fatigue can be dreamlike or murky. We might have visions or hear voices, or simply notice strange thoughts appearing. We're moving into the edge of sleep where the subconscious bubbles up.

With sloth and torpor, mindfulness alone isn't always sufficient for working with it. Some antidotes are called for. The most commonly recommended antidotes are straightening the posture, taking a few deep breaths, opening the eyes, and even standing up to meditate.

Our posture tends to slump when tired, so getting more upright will help. Breathing deeply brings more energizing oxygen into the body. Opening the eyes lets in light that naturally wakes you up. Standing up will keep us more alert.

Generally speaking, mindfulness has an energetically balancing quality. It tends to give us energy if we are tired and relax us if we are amped up. Once again, we find that the time we commit to practice has a big effect here. With sufficient time devoted to mindfulness practice, sloth and torpor will tend to subside.

Today, explore the effects of sleepiness on your meditation. If this is a persistent problem, see if one of the antidotes helps. If not, consider whether your fatigue needs to be addressed in another way like more sleep or less stress.

# April 21

*"Balancing Energy"*

As addicts, fatigue and dull mental states could feed into our addiction. Alcohol masks fatigue and many of us used powerful stimulants like cocaine and amphetamines to get us out of states of low energy. The resulting hangovers and crashes could plunge us into despair and depression. Our lives in addiction were often characterized by this yoyo effect of swinging from over-amped to exhausted and depleted.

In recovery we might find we have more energy. In an effort to make up for lost time, we wind up overworking. Exhausting ourselves in this way puts us at risk of relapse. Once again, we're faced with the addictive tendency to overdo things and get over-stimulated. Our meditation practice can help us to take the edge off this tendency.

Low energetic states also have an emotional component. Depression, as its name implies, is such a state. As we swing back from over-stimulation, we might find ourselves falling into dark and negative moods.

Our practice and our program will help us to manage these tendencies. With the program, fellowship at meetings will usually give us a lift. Connecting with others in recovery gives us a perspective on our feelings, letting us see that what we're going through is normal.

Besides bringing some calm, our meditation and dharma study will help us to see our experience as impermanent and impersonal. Energy is just that—not me or mine, but a natural phenomenon that comes and goes. The Buddha's teaching on the Middle Way gives us a model for what to work toward in our energetic states. Not too much, not too little. Attaining perfect balance isn't the goal. Rather with awareness of the tendency to swing one way or the other, we take steps to raise or lower our energy through self-care, the tools of recovery, mindfulness, and self-compassion.

Today, make an effort to track the waves of energy that pass through you. Make awareness of fatigue or restlessness a regular part of daily mindfulness.

# April 22

## *"Inventory as Trigger"*

In Twelve Step work, doing a "searching and fearless moral inventory" is considered a vital part of recovery. Some suggest that without this Step, sustained recovery is endangered. Whether or not that dire risk is true, there's no doubt that inventory offers tremendous opportunities for growth and self-awareness. But such a psychic upheaval doesn't come without risks.

Revisiting our past can be a trigger in a couple of ways. First of all, just thinking about drinking or using, acting out sexually, overeating, gambling, or any other addictive behavior we did can actually set off a craving. While we were certainly harmed deeply by that behavior, the addict's mind can still be drawn to the escape and temporary pleasure of intoxication. That's one reason why, when working on an inventory it's more important than ever to stay close to the program, to our sponsor, and to our friends. Lots of meetings are recommended, and lots of processing with others is a good plan.

Writing an inventory can also be deeply painful. To honestly admit the ways we hurt people can send us into a spiral of depression or anxiety. Many of us did real harm to the people we cared most about— our family members, lovers, and friends—and that truth can hit us pretty hard as we write about it and bring up all the details. Here it's vital that we practice forgiveness and compassion for ourselves. We have to remember that we are human, that many other people have done things just as bad, and that now we are on another path. It hurts to remember these things, but they are in the past now. We can't change them. The most important thing we can do is live kindly, generously, and wisely from now on. If we let our despair over the past infect our present, we are simply perpetuating the negative events, not moving away from them.

Today remind yourself that writing an inventory is an act of courage and love. The very fact that you are willing to take responsibility for your past actions shows growth and maturity. Appreciate your efforts to heal and recover today.

# April 23

*"Forgiveness: Others"*

The practice of forgiveness has several dimensions. In Step Nine we'll address "asking for forgiveness." Here we can look at the issue of the resentments we hold for others. In recovery, we are encouraged to stick to "our side of the street," not to blame other people for our problems. When people have hurt us, it can be hard to do that. But, ultimately it does us no good to hold on to resentments. They simply eat away at our own peace and happiness.

Here is a practice for forgiving others from the *Buddhism & The Twelve Steps Workbook* (page 193):

"Resentments are sometimes called 'the number one killer' for addicts, and certainly, many of us carry long-term anger, blaming, and trauma. Ultimately, this anger harms us as much as it does our enemy. We are the ones who are living with the nagging thoughts and obsessions. To forgive others does not mean we condone their behavior or that we will ever let them hurt us again. It just means that we don't want to carry this baggage with us. Bring to mind the people who have harmed you and the things they've done to you. Breathing into your heart, say to them, *For all the ways you have hurt me through thought, word, or deed, I offer my forgiveness. I forgive you.* Again, we can't expect instant results. But we need to stick with this process. Sometimes there will be a sudden shift or insight, and at others just a gradual melting of the icy heart. Stick with it."

You can use this practice in a formal way to work through longstanding resentments. You can also use it informally as a reminder when getting frustrated or angry with someone. The question we can ask ourselves is, "Who is my anger hurting?" The answer is, mostly ourselves. It certainly never solves a problem.

Today, explore whether you are holding any resentments or anger toward anyone. If so, try this forgiveness practice on them.

# April 24

*"Hindrances: Restlessness"*

From the *Buddhism & The Twelve Steps Workbook*, pp. 115-116:
"Restlessness and Worry are the flip side of Sloth and Torpor. In these states it's difficult to even sit still, and the mind spins out. The physical aspect is a sense of energy in the body, a need to move, change position, get up, walk, do anything but sit still. This, of course, makes sitting meditation very difficult. Nonetheless, sitting still is perhaps the best way to work through such energy.

"The mental aspect of this hindrance is the obsessive focus on a single worry. The mind keeps spinning with anxiety but never comes to any resolution. These thoughts intermingle with the physical anxiety of restlessness to create a pervasive sense of fear and loss of control. The extreme version of this is a panic attack. Mindful breathing, conscious relaxation, and deepening concentration are powerful ways to work with this challenging energy.

"Addicts often talk about wanting to 'get out of their own skin,' which is an expression of restlessness. When we feel this way it's important to recognize that we are being triggered. The tendency with Restlessness and Worry is to immediately act. Restlessness is a trigger for impulsive behavior, and so it's vital that we see its nature and catch it before acting unwisely."

In the beginning of their practice, many people find sitting still is the biggest challenge. We need a certain amount of faith in the process to get through this. It just takes time to settle down. Our culture of distraction makes this doubly difficult. With a smartphone as a constant companion, any moment of boredom or quiet gets filled up with whatever game, information, or social network we're drawn to. This tends to keep the mind on edge, never satisfied, always expecting to be entertained. In this way, when we sit down to meditate the mind can have that same forward thrust of energy which triggers restlessness.

Today, notice how much restlessness you are experiencing in your practice and in your daily life. Tomorrow we'll explore antidotes to restlessness.

# April 25

*"Antidotes to Restlessness"*

The classic antidote to restlessness is concentration. But one might ask, "When I'm so restless, how am I supposed to concentrate?" What this antidote really entails is doing a simple, repetitive practice that can gradually calm down the mind and body. Here are some suggestions:

*Counting breaths*: This practice was described on January 21. It simply involves numbering your in or out breaths (not both) from one to ten, then going back to one again. If you space out before reaching ten, go back to one and start again. This is harder than it sounds. Some teachers suggest using a different number, like eight, because counting to ten can become so rote that you are actually spacing out even as you count. Explore for yourself.

*Mantra*: In the Thai Forest Tradition monks are taught the mantra "Buddho," vocalized in the mind to fit a full inhalation and exhalation: "Bud" on the in breath, and "dho" on the outbreath. Simple and calming, this has us repeating the name of the great teacher. This practice is described more on October 23.

*Sweeping*: Also, called Body Scan (January 30) this practice, involves moving the attention through each sensation in the body. This can be done at any pace, and when you are restless it might be better to do it fairly quickly, in just a couple minutes.

*Spacious mind*: This practice was described on February 20, with an emphasis on hearing. Since restlessness can have a quality of claustrophobia, spacious mind imagines or senses the mind as a vast space so that there is plenty of room for the restlessness.

*Aim and sustain*: Sometimes we just need to be more intentional about the way we focus the mind. With aiming and sustaining we carefully place the attention on the object (aim), and make the effort to maintain the attention (sustain). In this way we are making sure the attention is locked on to the breath or other meditation object. We are really feeling it, not just vaguely paying attention.

Today, experiment with different ways of working with restlessness. See which practice works best for you.

# April 26

### *"Meditating in the Body not the Mind"*

The term mindfulness makes it sound as if meditation is all about the mind. That can lead to what you might call meditating from the neck up. If you are following the breath at the nostrils, and you have the sense that your thoughts pass through your head, you can leave the body entirely out of your practice. This is a mistake.

One way to work with the body is to develop a more open awareness of the whole body. This practice is somewhat more subtle than the body scan and takes some time to develop. But ultimately it can become a more natural, intuitive approach to practice than some of the more structured forms.

Begin by moving the attention through the body, just checking out the head, shoulders, torso, arms, hands, hips, pelvis, legs, and feet. Then see if you can open your awareness to feeling the whole body as a single object. You might have the feeling of being in a bubble or sense the body as a field of energy. There are many different ways to connect with this awareness. See if you can find one that works for you. The idea is that you are feeling the whole body at once.

This field of energy or single object contains all the different sensations of the body. As you hold your awareness on the whole body, there will be a sense of movement, or a feeling of flow as different subtle feelings catch your attention. See if you can just sit and take these things in, not trying to focus on any particular sensations, just letting them all come to you.

If you notice that your mind has drifted into thinking, first go to the breath to get refocused. Then let the attention open to the body again. Take a relaxed and easy approach to this practice. You can always zero in on the breath if you start to feel spaced out.

Today, begin to experiment with an open body awareness in practice and in daily life. The body is always with you. Allow its life to wake you up to the present moment.

# April 27

*"The Fifth Precept"*

The Fifth Precept, which addresses the use of intoxicants, is one that is often overlooked or downplayed by Western Buddhist teachers. Even the ways it is written can cause confusion. A typical version reads, "I take the training precept to refrain from the use of alcohol and drugs that cause heedlessness." The problem is that addicts and alcoholics will use anything as an excuse, so we can always claim that we aren't "heedless" when using. Unfortunately, that misses the point.

The precept is really about clarity. We are trying to develop mindfulness in all activities, to stay awake, wise, and compassionate. When we get loaded all these qualities are diminished. In fact, many activities can diminish our clarity, especially overuse of screens (TV, computer, smartphones), which might be the most pervasive addiction in our culture right now.

Rather than thinking of the precept as a prohibition on using drugs and alcohol, it is more useful to see it as a reminder to stay awake. Our minds are easily absorbed into daydreams, obsessions, resentments, and entertainment. To seek escape from daily life may be natural, and to some extent, needed. However, when such things take over our minds we can start to live in a kind of netherworld, disconnected from our bodies, our hearts, and the world around us.

The point is, we can become addicted to many things. As recovering addicts, we have to look out for that tendency in ourselves. Even meditation can be used as an escape to some degree. Addicts by nature tend to go to extremes; we tend to go overboard in our obsessions. With this precept we make the effort to be aware of that tendency and to try to live a more balanced life.

Today, ask yourself what you use to escape the world or cloud your mind. Is this behavior unhealthy or unhelpful? Would you be willing to moderate it? While strong habits are hard to break, the reward is more time awake and present for your life.

# April 28

### *"A Buddhist Glass of Wine"*

Many Buddhist teachers, apparently unclear on the risks of alcoholism, say about the Fifth Precept, "It doesn't mean you can't have a glass of wine with dinner." These are some of the most dangerous words you can say to an alcoholic, and they reflect an ignorance about alcoholism. An alcoholic *can't* have a glass of wine with dinner. That's never the last glass. But something else is missed in this statement, and that is the spiritual value of sobriety.

Sobriety is an intentional effort to experience life in an unvarnished way. It's saying, "I'm not going to run away from my feelings or the difficulties that life puts in my path." This is the heroic element of sobriety. Whether we are alcoholic or not, sobriety is a spiritual way of life. That's why monks include it along with celibacy in their way of living. They don't try to paper over life's rough edges with indulgence in sense pleasures.

The monastic life is more rigorous than simple sobriety or living clean, but it points to the same thing. The path of recovery demands that we question our attempts to escape from life and see whether what we're doing is actually causing more suffering. When we discovered how much pain our addiction was causing us, we made this question a central part of our philosophy of life. We learned that behaviors that seemingly brought pleasure could have hidden consequences, so we began to look for those consequences in all our pleasure-seeking behaviors.

This by no means meant we didn't enjoy life. Quite the opposite, what it meant was that we discovered the *true* joy of life, being awake and aware for all of it. This is the precious gift of living clean and sober. We embrace "the full catastrophe," as Zorba the Greek called it, not avoiding, suppressing, or glossing over any of this rich tapestry of experience.

Today, take joy in being awake and aware, no longer dulled by drugs, alcohol, or any addiction. This is the sacred state of recovery.

# April 29

*"The Gift We Give"*

Our recovery is a gift we give to ourselves and to the world. Many Buddhist gatherings end with a ritual called "Sharing the Merit," in which the participants dedicate any good karma from that gathering to the awakening of all beings. This springs from the Buddhist principle of service, one shared in the Twelfth Step's suggestion to "carry the message." This is the same thing the Buddha did after his own enlightenment, walking the dusty roads of Northern India to share his message of awakening and freedom.

As we grow in our recovery and get our life back, we receive many gifts. Some of us go back to school, find a partner, build a business or a family. Our selfishness and self-centeredness fall away as we gain a new perspective on life. We start to understand that true happiness doesn't come from satisfying personal desires, but from living a life of service and love.

When work moves from simple survival to service, we find true meaning and purpose in our lives. While making a living is always necessary, we often discover that focusing on how we can help others actually attracts support that takes care of our material needs.

When an intimate relationship stops being just about satisfying our own sexual and emotional needs, we find the joy of building a life and maybe a family with our partner. Love is no longer just a feeling, but an action, doing what we can to help another person find happiness and contentment.

Having children, sometimes seen as an obligation or an expectation, even a burden, becomes a way of contributing something to the world. When we overcome our own addiction, we can break a cycle that may have lasted for generations. Watching a child raised in a clean and sober home can be a revelation to someone whose family history was one of dysfunction and addiction. And the joy of such parenting is one of the greatest gifts of recovery.

Today, reflect on the gifts you have received from recovery and those you have given back through your service in recovery.

# April 30

### *"Spiritual Awakening"*

The spiritual awakening of Step Four is the awakening to our inventory. This starts with seeing the unvarnished truth about our past. No longer trying to justify or defend our behavior, we take in the harm we've done and use that history as a stepping-stone to deepening our recovery.

If we are going to move forward in this process, we must first look back. If we hope to become different people, we must see who we have been. As painful as this work can be, it is also one of the most valuable aspects of Step work. Rigorous honesty is at the heart of recovery, and the inventory is where that really begins.

As we've seen over this month, inventory can't be solely a negative examination. If it is going to be truly honest, it needs to include the good as well. At times looking at our good qualities can be as difficult as seeing the bad. Many of us have a hard time taking credit for our goodness. But this too is part of the spiritual awakening of inventory. This is the joyful part.

Once spiritually awake, we can never fall fully back to sleep. Even with relapse, a seed of knowing stays alive. What we learn in our inventories informs our lives in an ongoing way. Our patterns of behavior, our mental habits, and all the conditioning that drives both are revealed in the inventory process. We need to remember what we have learned here, for it will now be our guide.

With Step Ten, the inventory process becomes inscribed in our daily life. The work we did with Step Four trains us to look honestly at ourselves from now on. The old self-indulgence and self-deception can't take hold anymore with this newfound understanding. We've turned a corner and given our Step work a momentum that can carry it forward.

Today, reflect on what you've learned about yourself in your inventory work, and how that has changed your life. Remember to include the good things, as well as the so-called bad.

# May: Step Five

*"Admitted to God, to ourselves, and to another human being the exact nature of our wrongs."*

# May 1

### *"Self-revealing"*

When we share an inventory, whether the formal Step Four version or any other, we are opening ourselves up in a way that's not usually comfortable for addicts. Will we be judged? Will what this person learns be held against us? Will they think less of us? We all want to look good to others, so sharing our most painful secrets naturally feels threatening. Nonetheless, we've learned that holding back is even more dangerous.

To hide our failings, our mistakes, and our flaws only leaves us isolated, alone with our pain. With no external viewpoint to balance our self-judgment, we only go deeper into our own story. Step Five is the beginning of getting out of this self-destructive cycle.

When we reveal ourselves to others, a burden is lifted. We discover our shared humanity as the person who is listening to us reflects back what they are hearing and how they, too, have made mistakes. You may be amazed to discover that you weren't the worst person in the world, that, in fact, you are typically imperfect, like every other human being.

If you haven't already done formal Fourth and Fifth Steps, find a sponsor and begin the work. If you have, today consider if there is anything you are still concealing or something you are afraid of sharing. If so, find a trusted person or sponsor to whom you can unburden yourself.

As Step 10 reminds us, this is not a one-time process. We each need people with whom we can unburden ourselves. Besides a recovery sponsor, a dharma teacher or peer can sometimes fulfill this role. Make sure there are people in your life with whom you can share your secrets and struggles.

# May 2

*"Speaking the truth"*

"Speaking the truth is vital to recovery, as lies and secrets are so tied into our addiction." *Recovering Joy,* p. 26.

Right Speech holds a central place in Buddhist teachings. It is both an element of the Noble Eightfold Path and one of the Five Precepts. When the Buddha taught the dharma to his son, Rahula, the first thing he emphasized was the importance of having integrity in speech. The Buddha's definition of Right Speech comes down to three essential elements: to speak the truth, in a timely manner, and only if useful and kind.

To speak the truth isn't always a simple matter. Certainly there are facts that are indisputable. However, often when we speak, much of what we talk about can be conjecture or opinion. When you say, "You should do this," you don't know if that's true or not; it's just your opinion. So, if you are trying to speak more accurately, you could say, "*I think* you should do this," making it clear that you don't actually know.

The same can be said for statements like, "I never" do this or that. Instead you could say, "I rarely" do this, or "I feel like I never," or even "I can't remember ever doing that." This may seem like nitpicking, but in fact, these kinds of absolute statements have an effect. They communicate something to others and to ourselves. When we leave no room for exceptions, we build a kind of wall around our beliefs, and this can box us in. We develop beliefs about ourselves and others that are inflexible and lacking nuance.

These simple examples point to the complexity of speaking the truth, and in fact, of truth itself. As we commit ourselves to Right Speech, we face a whole new challenge on our spiritual path, one that goes to the heart of that path: seeking the truth.

Today begin to explore how you use language to say things that aren't 100% true or provable.

# May 3

*"In a Timely Manner"*

We've probably all had experiences of saying something and afterward realizing we'd picked the wrong moment to speak. The Buddha says that it's not enough to speak the truth; it also needs to be the right time.

The point of Right Speech isn't to prove a point or to win an argument. Right Speech is meant to be of benefit to the speaker and the listener—and maybe others who will be affected. Therefore, if we are going to say something, we need to consider the readiness of the listener to take in what we have to say. If someone is angry or upset, it may not be the best time to criticize or correct them, even if the criticism is accurate. If someone is sad, it might not be the best time to remind them of the inevitability of death; if they are anxious, it might not be the ideal moment to talk about the risks of climate change.

This orientation goes to the heart of communication: it's a two-way street. When we are caught up in our own thoughts and concerns, it's easy to forget the impact that our words might have on others. We're just excited about sharing or disturbed about some issue, so we want to blurt it out. This can wind up having the opposite effect we hoped for if our listener isn't interested or ready to hear what we have to say. Then we might walk away frustrated, disappointed, or angry that we weren't heard or appreciated.

For these reasons, bringing mindfulness and our intuition to bear on when to speak is vital. That attention will naturally cause us to take a moment before opening our mouth. That moment is one of getting out of ourselves and our own obsessions. It's a moment of letting go of self, of connecting and opening.

Speaking in a timely manner, then, isn't simply something that helps us to get our point across, but it deepens our spiritual practice in and of itself.

Today, before you speak consider whether this is the best time to say what's on your mind. Is the person you are talking to in the right frame of mind to hear what you have to say?

# May 4

*"Useful and Kind"*

There are different ways to characterize the third element of Right Speech, and we have to be careful we don't misunderstand what the Buddha is saying. It's not that we are supposed to always say nice things to everyone. Sometimes we must confront challenging situations forthrightly; sometimes people's feelings will be hurt; and sometimes strong words are needed.

If we speak the truth without considering the repercussions, we risk hurting people unnecessarily. This doesn't mean we have to lie, but perhaps it would be better not to say anything. We need to ask ourselves why we are speaking. Are we naively making speaking the truth an absolute good?

In other situations, we may find that we can use more skillful words to express what we want to say. In intimate relationships this is a vital skill. Blurting out even a legitimate criticism without considering how the words will be received can turn into an unnecessary conflict. Rather, taking a few moments (or longer) to consider if there are useful and kind ways of saying what we want to say can make the difference between a well-received comment and the trigger for a nasty fight.

A key reflection in this process is to consider what our purpose or intention is in speaking. If there is something we want or need, what is the best way to ask for that? Perhaps we'll realize that we want the person to change. Is that a realistic goal? If we want to deliver a criticism, will that be received well if spoken out of anger or judgment?

This work requires careful reflection and effort. Right Speech is one of the most difficult skills to attain. We need to bring patience, care, and close attention to this process as we learn to speak the truth, in a timely manner, in a way that is useful and kind.

Today, notice the intention behind your speech. Try to orient your words toward love and service. Notice the results both when you speak skillfully and when (or if) you do not.

# May 5

### *"Mindful Speech"*

Above and beyond the guidelines for Right Speech is the issue of actually being mindful as you speak. This is one of the biggest challenges to our mindfulness practice. One way of explaining the challenge of mindful speech is to recognize that ego is made up of thoughts, and thoughts are what we speak. So, it's easy to see how speaking can just be an expression of ego.

To cut through this tendency takes a lot of commitment and attention. We need to start listening to our own words and hearing what we are actually saying. In this way we discover what we think about ourselves. When we denigrate ourselves—"I'm no good at xyz"—or characterize our emotions—"I'm always so angry (anxious, depressed, etc)"—these unconscious habits of speech perpetuate the very things they are addressing. And, most critically, we are not following the first guideline for Right Speech, to speak the truth. These statements are either untrue (you can't *always* feel one emotion) or unproven. Why is this important?

When we express negative ideas about ourselves, we are creating self-fulfilling prophecies. If I say that I can't do something, I may never try to do it. If I say that I'm always feeling something, it tends to trigger that very feeling. If we sincerely want to discover the truth, we need to examine and reject these simplistic formulations.

The same applies to how we speak about others and about the world. When we say things based either on our judgments and negativity, or our naivete and unsupported positivity, we reveal our bias and don't allow ourselves to see how things really are. Again, paying careful attention to our language uncovers our inner life. Over time, then, mindfulness of speech becomes mindfulness of thoughts as well.

Today, begin to pay closer attention to your words. Notice the habitual ways you talk about yourself, your feelings, your abilities, and also how you talk about the world. Making changes to your speech takes time and a strong mindfulness practice, so don't be too hard on yourself if you discover unhelpful elements in the ways you talk.

# May 6

### *"Meditating Together"*

The experience of meditating alone has a different flavor from meditating in a group. Sometimes people prefer one or the other. When meditating alone there is no one to determine how long you should sit. You can control your environment more easily and perhaps make sure everything is quiet. You might say there is less pressure in sitting alone, but that doesn't mean it's preferable for everyone. Alone, you might have trouble sticking with your practice, or you might have trouble getting yourself to sit down at all.

Many people, especially those new to meditation, find the experience of group practice to be a very helpful support. It forces them to sit for a certain period of time and reminds them to make more effort to sit still.

Other people might find themselves more self-conscious in a group or frustrated that they have to wait for someone else to ring the ending bell. There can be some anxiety associated with having your eyes closed in a group; in that case, it's better to meditate with the eyes open gazing softly at the floor a few feet in front of you. You might also find it irritating if other people are making noise, shifting in their seats or coughing and sneezing.

Rather than focusing on preferences between sitting alone or in groups, it's more helpful to simply notice the differences and work with them. It's easy to forget that mindfulness meditation isn't about creating the perfect circumstances so you can have the most pleasant experience. To bring an attitude of interest and investigation takes us out of the mode of preferences and into curiosity and openness. Whether we are getting restless from sitting alone or irritable in a group, we can work with that energy. Learning to sit through these challenges trains us to be more balanced in our daily lives as well.

Today, start to notice the differences you feel between sitting alone and sitting in a group. Notice your preferences; try to let them go and find an open acceptance and curiosity about your experience.

# May 7

## *"Sharing Inventory"*

The formal purpose of Step Five is to share the inventory you wrote in Step Four with a trusted person, traditionally a sponsor. This can be one of the most important moments in Step work, and a turning point in your recovery. Writing an inventory is usually pretty difficult emotionally. But thinking about sharing all of that information with another person takes this to another level.

Typically, you are going to read what you wrote, but it's important not to necessarily stick to the script if other things come up. Once you are talking with someone, a lot of things that didn't occur to you when writing might arise. If it feels safe to do so, share it in the moment.

As you are sharing, use mindful speech to track your experience. There may be fear, excitement, shame, or relief. Your feelings won't always make sense, but try not to judge them. You are going through something completely unfamiliar, an unmasking that few people will ever willingly do, so you never know how your psyche will respond. You might laugh or cry. Or you might feel nothing, at least for now. Trust the process and trust whatever feelings come up.

Usually the effect of sharing an inventory is a great sense of relief, at least at some point. To become unburdened of our secrets and shame, to be heard, understood, and not judged by another human being can be transformative. The whole narrative of our life can get a reset.

If you have already shared your Fourth Step inventory, today reflect on how transformative that experience was. Take some joy in the fact that you have had this opportunity.

If you haven't done this Step, imagine who you might choose to share your inventory with when you are ready. Know that you will gain immeasurably from the process.

# May 8

### *"Mindful Listening"*

Mindful listening presents us with a whole other challenge from mindful speech. When we're in conversation with someone it's easy to drift into thoughts about how we want to respond. There may be comparable experiences we would like share, corrections to what they are saying, or we may simply look forward to putting in our two cents. All of this takes us away from actual listening.

Mindful listening requires, first, that we drop our own agenda. To listen fully we need to let go of our own thoughts and give all our attention to the other person. When we do this, mindful listening becomes a kind of meditation itself, only instead of paying attention to the breath, we're paying attention to the speaker.

In the recovery world, it's common for people to jump in with advice when someone is sharing a difficulty. This is why crosstalk is disallowed in most Twelve Step meetings. But after the meetings, such a prohibition is dropped, and it's not uncommon for people to offer unsolicited advice such as, "You need to [go to more meetings, call your sponsor, find a Higher Power, etc]" without ever really hearing what's going on personally for this person.

While such advice may be useful in general terms, it might be just the *wrong* thing for this person to hear at this moment. Mindfully listening to what someone has to say might reveal that they previously relapsed over the Higher Power issue or that they just fired their sponsor. While it's true that many addicts have similar problems, and, in addition, we want to avoid thinking of ourselves as unique, we still need to recognize that a person's particular situation has an important bearing on what the best advice might be for them. Or, indeed, whether we really need to give them advice at all.

Today, begin to listen with your whole body and mind. When someone is speaking to you, try to drop your agenda and just be present for them. Let any response come out of your intuitive mindfulness, not out of an opinion or what you've heard before.

# May 9

### "Listening to Inventory"

One of the greatest gifts of recovery is to be the receiver of someone else's inventory, whether a formal Fifth Step or just someone taking us aside to share something painful, shameful, or confusing. This great responsibility needs to be met with presence, openness, compassion, and a non-judgmental attitude. This last aspect can be the most difficult to manage when someone confesses to harmful actions or words. Still, if we are to be of service, we must maintain balance in the face of such an inventory.

Clearly, this is a time when mindful listening becomes particularly important. We are being mindful not only of the person who is speaking, but of our own inner response. If we allow our judgments or even disgust to come out in any way, even in our facial expression, we can do great harm. At times this can be quite challenging. We are trying to help them to forgive themselves and move on. If they detect judgment from us, that process might be stymied

To be the receiver of inventory is a sacred role, like a priest, priestess, or confessor. It can be helpful to draw on such an image, to see yourself as the embodiment of forgiveness and compassion. Humans create so much harm in the world, lifetime by lifetime, generation by generation, that only such an archetypal figure can hold all the suffering.

The fact that someone is sharing their deepest secrets with you shows their willingness to change, which is what you need to remember. They are seeking redemption, and you are in a position to help them on their journey. The question to ask yourself is, "How can I help this person?"

Today, think about how you can listen to someone's inventory in the most skillful way. Can you let go of the judging mind and stay in your heart for the suffering addict who shares with you?

# May 10

### *"Noting Desire and Aversion"*

Besides learning to listen to others, mindfulness teaches us to listen to our own thoughts. One interesting way to approach this is to use the noting practice to focus on desire and aversion.

These two types of thought are the roots of most of our mental suffering or *dukkha*. The Second Noble Truth points to this fact: our craving is the source of dukkha. (Aversion is just another form of craving.) To see this clearly is the first step in letting go.

Settle in for a period of meditation and connect with the breath. When you find the mind wandering, notice if the thought that's arising is one of desire or aversion. These qualities might be subtle, but most thoughts have some taste of one or the other. Don't take a lot of time trying to figure it out, just take a quick look. Then make the mental note "desire" or "aversion" depending on which category fits best.

When you come back to the breath after noting the thought, notice how your body feels. Notice if there is any unpleasant feeling or emotion present. Often feelings of desire and aversion manifest as tension or some kind of distress in the body. Or, the mood shifts, and we feel an unpleasant mind state. Keep breathing. If you don't go back to thinking right away, that feeling will likely pass fairly quickly. However, if you aren't careful, you'll wind up having another thought of desire or aversion toward the previous thought. This is how the cycle of negative and agitated thinking is sustained.

The illusion that desire and aversion present is that by following them we will feel better. A close examination, through mindfulness, reveals that the opposite is true. When you see, over and over, how unsatisfying and subtly agitating thoughts of desire and aversion are, that can be your inspiration not to fall into those patterns.

Today, start to notice thoughts of desire and aversion in your meditation and in your daily life. Practice letting go of those thoughts.

# May 11

*"Habitual Thoughts of Desire and Aversion"*

When we adopt the practice of noting desire and aversion, we discover underlying patterns in our mind. It can be very disturbing to realize that we've spent much of our life walking around with these thoughts in our head. Psychotherapy is a place where we can explore the roots of these issues, but in the context of recovery and Buddhism, there are some helpful strategies for working with them.

One key principle of Buddhism is the interconnection of all things. Nothing happens in a vacuum; everything is part of a causal chain. When, for instance, a thought of desire arises, it's helpful to explore where it is coming from. Perhaps you have a fantasy of a vacation, then you realize that you are feeling overworked. Perhaps you are dreaming of getting in a relationship, and you realize you are lonely. These sorts of insights aren't exactly earth-shattering revelations, but they can give us guidance as to how to respond. You don't have to go to Hawaii to get a break from work; you don't have to have a new romance in order to be with people. This isn't to say that we should always be trying to cancel out our desire or aversion, however, putting them in context and taking wise action in response to them is part of our practice.

Fundamentally, though, the Buddhist approach to desire and aversion is to let them go. While this will be a major topic of Steps Six and Seven, here we can say that feeling the suffering associated with these mind states is the biggest motivator for letting go.

Today, notice the forms of dukkha that arise with desire and aversion. Use that awareness as a motivation to let go.

# May 12

*"Fourth Precept"*

The precept on Right Speech has multiple layers that we can address over the next few days: "I take the training precept to refrain from false or harmful speech." First of all, it's about speaking the truth. Lying is the most direct and obvious way we break the precept. As addicts, lying to others was a way of life; lying to ourselves was a means of survival. We didn't want to see or accept the truth.

The cost of lying to others is the loss of trust. Once people know that you don't reliably tell the truth, they no longer believe anything you say. Many people who get sober have found that it's a long road back to earn people's trust again.

The cost of lying to ourselves is that we never face our true situation or condition. This is how denial is sustained. We can never grow or overcome our problems if we don't face ourselves honestly.

As has been mentioned, the first paragraph of Chapter Five of the Big Book of Alcoholics Anonymous, which is perhaps the most commonly read piece of Twelve Step literature, includes the word honest or honesty three times. Clearly, the founders felt this point needed to be emphasized. The Buddha, too, saw honesty as critical to awakening. Reality was what he wanted us to experience. In fact, the practice of mindfulness he taught can be viewed as a kind of existential honesty—seeing the truth of the present moment.

The inventory process is how we unpeel the layers of self-deception and form new habits of honesty. We have to learn new ways of being, new ways of thinking, and new ways of speaking. Like the entire recovery process, this takes time. It's almost like learning a new language: the language of truth. We learn to question our thoughts, our beliefs, and finally, our words. This is the beginning of practicing the Fourth Precept.

Today, begin to notice how your thoughts try to deceive you, in both positive and negative ways. You might have positive thoughts that are really fantasies or delusions, or negative thoughts that are just expressions of self-hatred. Notice how these thoughts affect your speech and try to speak more truthfully.

# May 13

*"Harsh Speech"*

While speaking the truth gets the most attention, avoiding harsh speech is also one of the elements of the Fourth Precept. While intoxicated, harsh speech may have been natural, whether with swearing, angry outbursts, or insulting comments. These habits are hard to break. As we wake up and become more mindful, we realize how harmful these ways of speaking really are. Just paying attention to the body gives us insight into how speaking harshly hurts us. Paying attention to others makes it abundantly clear how painful it is for them.

While getting clear about what is true takes more thought and reflection, harsh speech is easily detected emotionally. When we're loaded, we might not feel these feelings, but when clean they stand out. This is an important part of bringing mindfulness into our daily lives. When we have a commitment to live wisely and compassionately, the harm done by offhanded cruel, rude, or angry words clashes with that intention. While we can feel the dissonance of such speech internally, we can also see it externally in the way it's received.

Harsh speech includes sexist, racist, homophobic, and other words expressing biased views. Again, our thoughts are revealed in our words, and these thoughts, while deeply conditioned, must be seen for what they are: hateful forms of prejudice with no basis in reality. Such words are not only harsh, they are untrue. Here we see how the precepts are not merely moral guidelines, but give us a path to truly transform ourselves. To heal as addicts, to realize our spiritual potential, and to find true happiness, we must be willing to uproot the tangled roots of hatred within us, to shed light on the shadows, and to embrace love, tolerance, and truth as sacred principles.

Today, start to pay attention to the quality of your speech. Notice whether you habitually use harsh or biased speech. Find new ways of expressing yourself that are less harmful to others and to yourself.

# May 14

*"Saccharine Speech"*

The guidelines on harsh speech are a valuable tool in our transformation as addicts, but they shouldn't be turned into a false way of speaking where everything is coated with sugar and smiles. Anger isn't a "bad" emotion, and suppressing it isn't helpful.

In certain spiritual circles people become passive and conflict-avoidant. They develop a fear of saying anything critical in case they get labeled as "negative" or hostile. This is by no means what the Buddha taught. When he felt it was necessary to speak strong words, he didn't hesitate. When his monks were behaving unskillfully, he let them know in no uncertain terms. Avoiding harsh speech doesn't mean avoiding the truth, or even avoiding criticism or expressing anger. What's important is that we don't express these feelings through emotional outbursts that harm people and are counterproductive.

The tendency toward false sweetness comes out of fear. In trying to establish new speech habits you might be wary of falling back on old behaviors and losing control. If anger or reactivity has been a problem, it's easy to adopt an idealized way of being: never angry, always nice. However, since such attitudes are unsustainable in any practical sense, all the unacknowledged feelings are suppressed and must come out some other way. For an addict, this puts us in danger of relapse or behaving as a so-called "dry drunk."

To maintain a healthy recovery, it's vital that we find ways to hold and express difficult feelings. Developing such skills takes time, effort, and patience.

Today, reflect on how you can skillfully express difficult feelings, like anger, sadness, and anxiety. Consider how you can communicate them without harsh or harmful speech.

# May 15

*"Relative and Universal Truth"*

Most people live entirely in relative truth, the personal view. Our culture supports this way of living by its emphasis on material things, on worldly success, on power, and on pleasure. Buddhist teachings point to the limits of these things. While this way of living can work for a while, even for years, at some point life will throw something at us that isn't manageable, that we can't control, and that doesn't fall into our way of handling things. Someone close to us will die; we'll get a life-threatening diagnosis; our partner will leave us; a professional setback will throw our finances into disarray. If we have no universal perspective on these types of events, we can fall into despair or profound confusion.

In the relative, personal experience of life we easily become attached; the universal view reminds us that attachment causes suffering. In the relative view, things are stable; the universal reminds us of the impermanent, fragile nature of everything. In relative thinking, we have control over our lives; the universal tells us that such control is limited and illusory.

The universal view helps us accept the limits of money, power, and pleasure. Not that we shouldn't have these things, but that we don't see them as the end goal of life. Learning to dance between absolute and relative, between universal and personal is the art of life. To be neither lost in emptiness nor enchanted with form is to live wisely. We need to understand the universal truths to truly understand life; and we need to live skillfully in the personal world to do no harm and to actually enjoy life.

Today, reflect on the ways you relate to these two truths and consider how you could more skillfully move between the two.

# May 16

### *"Easy to Admonish"*

In one famous sutta the Buddha tells his monks they should be "easy to admonish." This is recorded in the formal language of the suttas. Admonish isn't a word we use a lot these days, but it simply means, "criticize" or even "scold." So, he wants us to take criticism without resistance. It's very similar to what we learn from the Twelve Steps.

No one likes to be criticized. It's never easy to hear someone's negative thoughts about us. But there are two things that are particularly valuable about this experience.

First is the obvious opportunity to learn and grow from our mistakes. No one is perfect, so criticism gives us the opportunity to look at ourselves honestly and consider how we might behave or speak more skillfully. This is one of the primary ways that we can develop ourselves.

The second valuable opportunity of being criticized is that it helps us develop humility and non-attachment. When we are attached to being right or good, we set ourselves up for failure because no one can be right and good all the time. To be reminded of this helps to free us from such attachments. When we admit our failings, we no longer have to protect our ego or our image. What a relief!

Being easy to admonish, then, becomes a part of recovery. Our new way of living includes this surrender to our imperfection and frees us from the need to pretend to be something we are not. Nothing to protect, nothing to prove.

Today, reflect on your own capacity to take criticism or admonishment. How does it feel when this happens? Commit yourself to using criticism as a spur to growth and to deepening humility.

# May 17

### *"Compassion for All Beings"*

Stepping out of a focus on "I" opens up the world of "We." This is a key element of spiritual practice. It appears in Step Twelve in the suggestion to "carry the message," and it appears in Buddhism as awakening compassion for all beings.

In Buddhism, we see compassion arising naturally out of mindfulness practice. As we pay attention to our experience day by day, exploring the nature of suffering—how it arises and how it ends—the sense of separation between self and other starts to dissolve. We realize that our experience is universal, and an internal shift occurs.

Now we no longer see suffering as unique to us, but as inherent to the human condition, and further, in the condition of all living beings. Out of this insight arises compassion for all beings.

How we respond to this opening of the heart is highly personal. Each person finds their own expression of compassion. It might mean changing your diet or being more conscious of how you use resources; it might mean engaging in service; it might mean becoming socially or politically active. And it certainly means responding to the heart's longing for connection.

Buddhist compassion practices use the imagination to help develop this sense of connection. Breathing into the heart, we feel our own tender vulnerability; we recall our own experience of suffering and letting go of suffering. Then, we have a sense of radiating from the heart out to the world around us, to all those who are suffering.

We might visualize people who are sick, poor, or oppressed; people who are suffering emotionally, physically, or spiritually. We can think of animals who are struggling to survive in a deteriorating environment. We do all of this with a sense of equanimity and acceptance so that we aren't overwhelmed by these reflections.

Today, begin to focus less on "I" or "me" and more on a sense of "we" and "us," radiating kindness and compassion for all beings. Consider making such reflections part of your daily meditation.

# May 18

*"Working with Anger"*

Anger is one of the most difficult emotions to manage. It can come on so fast and be so consuming that it's difficult to respond to mindfully. Further, anger is often viewed as "un-spiritual," something we shouldn't be feeling, much less expressing. Thus, we can be thrown into a double-bind with anger: trapped in reactivity, yet ashamed of it at the same time.

Anger isn't inherently bad. It has its logic, its purpose, and its justification. We don't work to let go of or transform anger because it's bad, but because it's painful and harmful. To work with it, we first try to become aware of the feeling of anger as it arises. What we discover is heat, agitation, and hijacked emotions. Anger takes control of our mind and body, sweeping away logic and kindness, compassion and reflection. All we are left with is a roiling, violent energy. It's the unpleasant, painful nature of this energy that is one of the motivations to let go.

The other motivation is the recognition of the effects of anger on others. Here we see that we alienate and undermine others with angry outbursts. We trigger their own anger or their shame and despair. Unleashing anger on children can cause lasting trauma.

Once we understand the unproductive nature of unbridled anger, we begin to look for ways to hold it more skillfully. To suppress or push aside anger doesn't help, but rather subverts it in unhealthy ways. First we need to allow ourselves to feel anger without acting on it. Then we need to explore the triggers for anger. Anger is often rooted in some unmet need or memory of some harm done to us. When we understand those triggers, we can be more intentional and skillful in how we respond, using the tools of Right Speech to communicate our frustration without creating more conflict.

Today, start to work at developing wise and helpful ways to channel and express anger.

# May 19

*"Internally and Externally"*

Mindfulness is sometimes presented as solely about our internal experience: feeling the breath, noticing thoughts, sensations, and emotions. But this only covers one side of the practice. In fact, the Buddha in the Satipatthana Sutta tells us to practice mindfulness "internally and externally." What does it mean to practice mindfulness externally?

The simplest way to think of this is that you should be aware of your environment and the other beings in it. If we become too fascinated with our inner life, we may neglect the impact our words and actions have on those around us. Bringing awareness to these things makes mindfulness an authentic part of our whole life, not just a personal experience. Becoming more sensitive to others is one of the key components of compassion. And it helps us to be less self-centered.

The typical Twelve Step inventory tends to be more of an external reflection: how did my behavior harm others? On the other hand, many of the Buddhist or meditative inventories, like exploring the hindrances or the Awakening Factors, are more internal. Having said that, a thorough Buddhist inventory should also include our behavior, since that's what the Precepts and all the elements of sila are about.

To operate in this complicated world, reflecting on the experience of others is an important way that we grow and become more conscious. While there are universal aspects of being human, the experiences of different genders, races, sexual orientations, abilities, body types, and much more are quite particular. To understand these diverse viewpoints, it's not enough for us to imagine ourselves, with all our own conditioning and history, in someone else's place. We have to imagine their history and conditioning as well. Most of us will benefit from educating ourselves on these issues to come to a fuller understanding of the diverse experiences of others.

External mindfulness is an entire practice in and of itself. Today, begin to reflect on what this might mean for you.

# May 20

*"Looking Good"*

We all want to look good in the eyes of the world. Admitting we have a problem with drugs or alcohol is hard for this very reason. But if we want the freedom that recovery brings, this is the path. We have learned that trying to protect our image only backs us more into a corner. We spend all our energy keeping up pretenses, all the while inwardly knowing that we're living a lie. To open up and drop those strategies is a great relief.

Sharing an inventory is a humbling experience. Here you are exposing your worst behavior to another human being. There's no cover, nowhere to hide. And that turns out to be what's freeing about it.

People also try to look good in spiritual communities. This is one of the pitfalls of Buddhist groups where there is often a subtle pressure to act wise and peaceful, even if that's not how you really feel. When you come into a meditation hall everyone looks so serene, and the message can be, "This is what enlightenment looks like." If you could see into all those meditators' heads, though, all the thoughts and feelings bubbling up, you'd realize that their looks are deceiving.

Some Insight Meditation communities have started what are called "Kalyana Mitta" groups, or "spiritual friends." These small groups meet regularly to discuss their practice and the dharma. Here you are more likely to get an honest view of what people are really thinking and feeling inside.

Today explore the ways you try to look good. Are you hiding aspects of yourself that would be better exposed? Have you had the freeing experience of sharing your inventory yet?

# May 21

*"Back to Basics"*

From time to time it's helpful to go back to the basic instructions in our meditation practice. Today we'll work with some of these.

Start with posture. How are you sitting (or lying down) when you practice? Is your posture supporting you in being awake and relaxed? If your posture is too casual it can cause you to get drowsy and dull when meditating. If your alignment is off, you might feel pressure on the back or neck. Check whether you are tipping forward, back, or to one side or another. If you need to lie down to meditate, make sure you are alert. It's probably best to keep the eyes open in the lying posture.

Tension in the body is often a reflection of anxiety in the mind. Check through your body to see if you are carrying tension in meditation. Make sure the belly is relaxed as this is one point where tension often resides.

Are you really feeling the breath? It's easy to develop a vague connection to mindfulness of the breath. You might sort of know you are breathing, but not feel the actual sensations in any immediate way. As part of your practice, make sure that you spend some time focusing in closely on the breath, whether at the belly or the nostrils. Feel the actual sensations and sustain that attention. You don't have to maintain this tight of a focus through the whole sitting, but it helps to at least start your practice this way.

What is your relationship to thoughts in practice? If you get lazy, meditation can just wind up being a time to space out. And, while it's not helpful to push thoughts away or try to make the mind blank, if you just let thoughts carry you away, you're not getting much out of practice. Your relationship to thoughts is at the heart of your practice. Finding a balanced Middle Way takes a subtle and intuitive effort. Try to be aware of thoughts without struggling with them; just let them come and go without following them. This may be the biggest challenge in the art of meditation.

Make a check-in like this a regular part of your practice. Keep your practice fresh and engaged.

# May 22

*"Sinking Mind"*

At times when meditation gets quieter and more relaxed, random images, scenes, shapes, voices, or sounds can appear in the mind. There can be a pleasant, dreamy quality to these perceptions, and one can get the sense that the practice is going somewhere quite interesting. However, this is almost always just a sign of what's called "sinking mind," a drowsy state on the edge of sleep.

In sinking mind what appears to happen is that the lid is taken off the subconscious, as in sleep, thereby releasing random mental impressions. Because you are still awake and have a certain degree of consciousness, you might infer some meaning or importance to these impressions. Mindfulness teachers, however, don't endow them with such significance. In fact, the most common advice is to snap out of this state and clear the mind.

In this case, you can use the antidotes to sleepiness. First, open the eyes, which will tend to dispel any hallucinations. Then adjust the posture so that you are more upright and can regain some alertness. Take some deeper breaths and bring a strong focus to physical sensations.

While sinking mind itself isn't a helpful state, the fact that one has become that relaxed while remaining awake is generally a sign that calm and concentration are becoming stronger. However, that concentration needs to be balanced with energy.

Try focusing on just the in-breath as a way of bringing more energy to the body. And keep the attention broad, not focusing too closely on any particular sensation or perception.

Today, start to work with balancing concentration and energy. Notice when one or the other dominates, and try to find creative strategies to counterbalance those effects.

# May 23

### "Interrupting the Karmic Flow"

The Zen teacher Judith Ragir refers to the unfolding of Steps Four through Nine as "interrupting the karmic flow." This is the effort to change the direction of our lives for the better.

Our karmic flow is created by the conditioned and habitual thoughts, words, and actions we have taken in our life. They create tendencies that keep getting played out over and over—like our addiction. They result in the circumstances of our life. So, if we want those circumstances to change, we need to change the karma behind them. These Steps have the potential to bring about that change.

Beginning with the inventory, we are, in a sense, examining our past karma, our past actions. If we are going to bring about any change in our life, we first need to see clearly what needs to change. Step Five exposes this karma to another person, allowing us to get perspective as well as reaffirm the nature of that karma (spoiler alert: it's not good).

Steps Six and Seven are where we start to uproot and alter our habitual thoughts, words, and actions. And Steps Eight and Nine help us to heal the past harm with others.

All of this work tends to change the direction of our lives. We develop new ways of thinking, of speaking, and of behaving. These new behaviors bring new results, and our life circumstances begin to change in significant ways.

This is interrupting the karmic flow. Recovery depends upon it.

Today look at the ways you are trying to think, speak, and act differently. Are you moving your karma in positive new directions or are you stuck in the same negative patterns?

# May 24

### *"Stepping Outside"*

Nature is one of the great healers for the heart and mind. Humans spend a lot of time in artificial, indoor environments that can become stifling. The Buddha's journey to awakening happened largely in the forests and plains of Northeast India. Much of the time we find him sitting under a tree or speaking to monks outside. Many spiritual teachers recommend daily time in nature as a support for peace and contentment. This goes double for people in recovery.

Of course, not all of us have the time or the access to go to a forest every day. But it's easy to forget that simply stepping outside puts us under the great roof of the sky, and even in many urban environments there are trees, birds, and squirrels at hand. The clouds, the breeze, and the warmth of the sun or cool drops of rain are all mindfulness bells that wake us up to our essential aliveness.

Stepping outside can lift the oppressive weight of busyness and stress. Moving our body, even taking a short walk, brings us back to the present moment. We feel ourselves as living beings standing on the earth. We can bring attention to the world around us, just observing whatever is available in our natural environment.

The walls that surround us indoors also seem to create walls around our thinking and our emotions. We can feel trapped in limiting ideas and views. In our addiction we might have slumped on a bar stool or sunk into a couch, our bodies and minds stuck in a morass of negativity.

Somehow, the simple touch of air on skin in the outdoors frees something inside us. It's as though our spirit is returning to something essential, even primal.

Today make time to go outside. If there is a park nearby or trails, take advantage of them. If not, simply enjoy the freedom of being under the sky. Whatever the weather, see if you can appreciate the purity of nature.

# May 25

*"Advice"*

In the Twelve Step world, sharing our "experience, strength, and hope" with another member can often turn into giving advice. While this usually comes from a good intention, we need to be careful in telling other people what they should do with their lives.

There are standard forms of advice in the Twelve Step world: go to more meetings, write inventory, talk to (or get) a sponsor, and find a Higher Power. While such suggestions might be helpful for some, if they land at the wrong moment or on someone not ready to hear them, they can actually be harmful. When they are accompanied by the claim that you will drink if you don't follow this advice, they become predictions. That mean the dispenser of this wisdom thinks they know exactly how karma works and what the future will be.

Advice is usually based on personal experience, which means that it's been tested by exactly one person. The tendency to universalize our personal experience is a risky one.

This isn't to say that we can never give useful guidance to other people. However, it's vital that we listen first before telling someone what they need. What are you hearing from them? What are their particular issues? Try to let go of your habitual response, and allow something deeper, more intuitive, to arise.

Instead of giving direction as to exactly what someone should do, it can be helpful to suggest various alternatives, so the person starts thinking for themselves, weighing possibilities. It doesn't hurt to give anecdotes of your personal experience, but it can be wise to also offer other stories or situations you are aware of, perhaps quoting the Buddha or Twelve Step literature. Remember, if someone takes your unvarnished advice, you are essentially becoming responsible for the outcome. Is that something you want to live with?

Today notice how you approach helping other people work through their problems. Could you be more skillful in your advice giving? Are you able to listen first and trust your intuition?

# May 26

*"Meetings are Meditation"*

Recovery meetings provide a unique opportunity for practicing mindfulness in a community. While a group meditation is largely conducted in silence, meetings involve people speaking. And yet, except for the few minutes we might share, we are silent for most of the time. This means we can bring our mindfulness skills to bear in this group setting.

Although it's not necessary, some people choose to actually close their eyes while listening to others in a meeting. Others choose to look at whomever is speaking. Either way you can use the mindful listening instructions to be present. Notice your breath, your posture, and your body sensations. Notice how your mind reacts to each speaker's words: agreement, judgment, inspiration, boredom. Thoughts and feelings just come and go as you listen. Your mood might brighten, or a difficult memory might be awakened. Just keep noticing what comes up and keep listening.

As you listen, notice your own impulse to join in and share. Where is it coming from? Notice if there is an egotistical impulse, a healing impulse, a generous impulse—or something else. Sharing has various purposes, from helping the newcomer, to processing your own feelings, to exposing a dangerous craving. It can also come out of a wish for attention. Before you raise your hand, check your intention.

If you get called on, stay mindful. Notice any nervousness or excitement. Keep some attention grounded in your body. Notice the energy that comes from speaking in public. Breathe, stay present, and speak the truth.

Next time you go to a meeting, see if you can make that a time for mindfulness meditation.

# May 27

### *"Sharing Meditation with Others"*

As much as there is to learn about meditation, given the subtle and complex process it can be, in some ways it's quite simple: sit down, breathe, and when you notice your mind has wandered, bring it back to the breath. This is probably why even relatively inexperienced meditators sometimes want to share it with others.

Clearly, to be a meditation teacher you need a fair amount of experience and training. You need to be able to address the many challenges and mind states that can arise in meditation. In order to do that, you need to have experienced those challenges and mind states firsthand. Ideally you need to have navigated the hindrances, worked with the range of energetic states, studied with different teachers, and read a wide range of texts.

Barring this extensive training, you can nonetheless be of service by simply showing someone the basics. If this is done carefully and with full disclosure of your own limitations, you can certainly help someone get started. You should always encourage them to find a trained teacher and do some study on their own, as well.

One of the principles of teaching meditation is that you don't try to teach something you haven't done. Just because you've read about a practice, you shouldn't try to share it unless you've done your own work with it. In this way you can really address how the practice works, its particular challenges, and how to handle them.

If you do decide to share meditation with others, you will quickly learn your limitations, which can be a motivation to take your own practice deeper. This is perhaps the most valuable thing you get from sharing with others. You are forced to dig deep, explore, and verbalize your own experience, which means you understand your experiences better. Then you see what you still need to learn.

Today, even if you have no impulse to share the practice, consider how you might guide someone who is new to meditation. This reflection in itself might help you with your own practice.

# May 28

### *"Limits of Sharing"*

In recovery we're encouraged to share our secrets. We are often told, "You are only as sick as your secrets." When we do this in Step Five there can be a huge sense of relief as we unburden ourselves of painful memories and experiences. Keeping secrets is risky behavior for addicts who might be triggered to use if the shame and guilt over some past behavior builds up inside. Inventory can be a way to relieve this burden.

Even with these guidelines, we also need to be aware of times when sharing isn't wise or appropriate. One of these is sharing our sexual history in a mixed group, and sometimes in any group at all. Addicts often have troubled and messy sexual relationships. To share the details of those relationships in a group can cause a lot of discomfort. The same is true of a history of violence, incarceration, and institutionalization. While we'd all like to think that Twelve Step groups are full of open-minded, non-judgmental people, the truth is, we are all human. Certain stories can be shocking or cause pretty strong judgments to come down. This isn't to say that one can never address these or other sensitive subjects in a meeting, just that you should consider your audience before sharing.

Step Five is somewhat ambiguous when it says we shared the "exact nature of our wrongs." If we take the word "nature" in its typical meaning, this could mean that we just tell someone that we were, for instance, violent, without giving the details. But in this context nature can have a different meaning, one not as commonly used today, to mean, "exactly what happened." It's hard to say what the authors of the Steps meant. What is most important is that we are clear about why we are either holding something back or sharing it. If we feel that our spiritual growth demands that we give the details of some very troubling behavior, then we should find someone we trust who will be able to hear what we have to say in a compassionate way without judging us.

Today, ask yourself if there are any aspects of your inventory that you choose not to share. Be clear about why you made this decision.

# May 29

*"Breaking Anonymity"*

Although the Twelve Traditions suggest we shouldn't break our anonymity in the media, on a personal level there are no specific guidelines. For some people it feels important to keep their addiction and recovery private, shared only with others in recovery and maybe close family and friends. People might have a range of reasons for this decision, from the personal to the professional. However, there may also be situations where we find that breaking our anonymity with someone is an act of service.

It's clear that the public perception of addiction and recovery has changed significantly since AA was founded. In those days there was little or no understanding of the condition of addiction. It was largely viewed as a moral failing, so that to reveal your condition was to risk being ostracized in your community or your profession. Today there is much more understanding and compassion about addiction. While there are still debates over the causes and nature of addiction—whether it is a disease, or caused by genetics, trauma, or something else—few people still view it as a moral failing. This change in attitudes makes anonymity a less important issue in many circumstances.

Addiction is of a hidden or invisible condition. When we let others know what we've been through and how we are handling things better today, it allows people who are struggling with their own addictions to open up as well. And it also allows friends and families of addicts to get some guidance.

Much of the pain of addiction is due to the sense of isolation and hopelessness addicts often feel. When we share our story with others who are struggling, they don't feel so alone, and they realize there is hope. This can be a great gift we offer.

Today, consider where and when you want to break your anonymity. Only do so where it is safe, where you won't risk professional or personal problems, and where you believe that sharing might help others.

# May 30

*"Self-judgment"*

Sharing our inventory forces us to admit to the most harmful behaviors of our life. This is only helpful if we are sharing with someone who is compassionate and wise, someone who can help us to see our past behavior as simply human, the unskillful acts of someone caught in the vise of addiction. Still, as this story goes around in our mind, it's hard to avoid harshly judging ourselves, at least some of the time.

The judging mind views everything through the lens of good or bad, right or wrong. It is always pounding the gavel, convicting ourselves or someone else. When we start to watch the mind in meditation, we often find that judging is a major part of our thinking.

With the noting practice it can be helpful to just start naming destructive judgments as they arise. Soon we might feel overwhelmed with the flood of thoughts that want to determine the rightness or wrongness of practically everything.

Joseph Goldstein, the renowned Buddhist teacher, sometimes suggests that people beset with this problem on a retreat start to count their judgments. Sooner or later, as the judgments pile up—10, 11, 12...50, 51, 52...500, 501—we just start laughing. "Who do I think I am? What do I think I am doing? What is the *point* of all this?" We start to see that our mind is just an infinite judging machine, detached from any reality. We lose faith altogether in these judgments—and that's a good thing.

It isn't so easy to let go of these thoughts. A lifetime of judging creates a lot of forward momentum. We need to bring patience and self-compassion to this process.

Today, try counting your judgments in meditation. Then, start to notice when they arise in daily life. See if you can take your judgments a little less seriously.

# May 31

*"Spiritual Awakening"*

The spiritual awakening of Step Five is the realization that our inventory isn't unique, our story isn't special, and everything we've done deserves compassion and forgiveness. This awakening connects to the Buddhist principles of not clinging to identity and holding all beings with kindness and love.

As painful and difficult as writing a "searching and fearless moral inventory" can be, sharing it with a wise and caring sponsor can relieve much of that pain. As long as the inventory stays trapped in our mind or even written down, it is held in our ego's view. Strangely, the ego would rather suffer than die, so it's more willing to embrace the idea that we are uniquely flawed than the possibility that there's nothing special about our mistakes.

A good sponsor helps us to see the universality of our failings, and the absurdity of taking it all personally. They will point to the many similar and even worse stories they have heard in the rooms of recovery and in interactions with others. And they will reveal enough of their own inventory to see how much you both share.

The realization that we aren't unique in our behavior is part of the larger door of compassion opening for us. Stepping out of the realm of addiction, we can see that everyone, not just addicts, makes mistakes and hurts other people. We see that the world is full of this pain. Everyone wants love, yet everyone hurts those they love.

We've woken up, now, to the universality of suffering. Our recovery is starting to make a turn that will play out over the succeeding Steps, a turn away from the personal and towards service, connection, and interdependence.

Today, reflect on any sense of spiritual awakening you have experienced with Step Five. Are you now becoming less attached to the idea of a unique and separate self? Do you see how developing self-compassion helps you to bring the same caring to all beings?

# June: Step Six

*"Were entirely ready to have God remove all these defects of character."*

# June 1

### *"Who Removes What?"*

The question of how the Steps actually work starts to come to the forefront in Step Six. The idea that some outside force—"God"—is going to remove our shortcomings doesn't make sense from a Buddhist viewpoint, which says everything arises out of causes and conditions. This means we need to take a completely different tack when understanding this Step. Instead of thinking about God removing our defects of character, a Buddhist view is that we are finding a way to let them go.

In this view, Step Six is one of the "intention setting" Steps, along with Two and Eight. Each of these three Steps prepares us for the next by establishing Right Intention. As the Buddha says, all actions are preceded by intention, and those intentions then determine the nature of the results from those actions.

The intention of Step Six is to prepare us to let go, to become ready to abandon our unwholesome qualities. Why do we need to *prepare* for this? Why not just do it?

What we discover in working the Steps is that, even when we know what we should do, sometimes the depth of our conditioning holds us back. This is why it takes so long for most of us to let go of our addiction. Rarely does someone think that their drinking and using is doing them a lot of good, but it's hard to find the willingness to change. We could say that everything leading up to working Step One was our preparation to letting go of our primary addictive behavior. And then, through the Steps, we realize that many of our underlying thoughts and behaviors were also problematic. That's why the whole process of inventory work is so important.

When we come to Step Six, we are facing what we uncovered in Steps Four and Five and setting the intention to change.

Today, begin to reflect on your willingness to change your thoughts, words, and deeds to come more into alignment with the dharma.

# June 2

### *"Whose Defects?"*

"This tendency to view ourselves as inherently flawed, can make the phrase 'defects of character' a difficult one. It suggests something personal, something which is mine. Buddhism might take a different view.

"In Buddhist thinking, the self is a construction, a collection of processes and experiences which have no center, which are inherently empty of substance. In this sense, although we may have tendencies and habits of mind, we don't have a hard and fast 'character.' Who we are is much more fluid than that, more dynamic." *One Breath at a Time*, p. 150

This view that self isn't solid actually makes change more possible. If we had a fixed character, how would we ever let go? When we see that our habitual thoughts, words, and behaviors are conditioned, we realize they can, in a sense, be unconditioned, or altered through reversing that conditioning.

What makes it so hard to begin this process is the very sense of identification that we are trying to dislodge. It can be painful to look honestly at ourselves. Even though we may understand that everyone has acted unskillfully, it's still really difficult to dis-identify with our particular flaws. And, even having written and shared an inventory, we might not want to go right at these issues and try to change. With the inventory, it's easier to think of what was revealed as something past, not something we still have to deal with.

Today, notice how it feels to accept your own shortcomings. Can you see those qualities without taking them personally, without either judging yourself or trying to disavow them?

# June 3

*"What Defects?"*

It's possible to write and share an inventory without necessarily seeing particular defects or shortcomings. The inventory can just look like a list of bad things we did. That means there's another level of investigation that has to go into this process to understand what Steps Six and Seven are about. We need to look at what was behind the destructive actions we uncovered.

When we hurt others, what impulse were we acting on? What was behind our anger? Our craving? Can we see the fear, the selfishness, and the wounds? Are there patterns that emerge?

Like the inventory itself, this is delicate business. When we try to define the exact characteristics and impulses behind our worst behavior, it doesn't exactly cheer us up. We need to keep some perspective on this, to remember that these qualities don't define us, but rather are conditioned habits that we developed unknowingly, with no intention to harm others or ourselves. It's like learning to speak your native language: you're taught it directly and indirectly before you even attain real consciousness, so you aren't responsible for speaking those words. To carry that metaphor further, now is a time when you need to learn a new language of behavior.

Our Buddhist practice can help in this process. Because mindfulness meditation includes watching our thoughts and how they arise, we can get a direct view into our own mind in this process. Here we aren't doing an inventory of behavior, but something more intimate, an inventory of the mind. When we study these thought patterns in our meditation practice, they can help us to see how the patterns of behavior in our inventory arose out of the mind.

Today, begin to examine the patterns of thought and behavior you uncovered in your inventory and your meditation in order to understand what needs to change.

# June 4

### *"Ready or Not"*

We might think that someone who is engaged in recovery and developing a spiritual practice is by definition ready to change. And yet, one of the truisms of spiritual life is that obstructions can arise at any stage; resistance to change and letting go can appear whenever vigilance slips. So, "readiness" isn't a one-time or constant thing. This means that part of our inner work is to keep track of such resistance, to stay honest with ourselves about when we are blocking our own path.

Readiness impacts every step of this journey. We must be ready to let go of our addictive behavior to begin to recover. We must be ready and open to accepting different spiritual teachings and concepts. We must be ready to look honestly at ourselves. And we must be ready to let go all the time. With Step Six we confront this requirement in a direct way.

Here, having overcome so many challenges in our Step work, we might be surprised at the difficulty we now face. We certainly had to work hard to carry out our inventory work, but now we are being asked to really change. To change behavior and beliefs, yes, but even more vitally, to work at the underlying habits of mind, the so-called "character defects." In many ways, these defects are old friends. We might have thought of them as defining us in some essential way, even if in negative or painful ways. It turns out that being entirely ready to let go of such qualities is the challenge of a lifetime. And for many people, it is a challenge that will *take* a lifetime to resolve. However, it is possible to change if we stay ready and do the work.

Step Six is an ongoing process. It takes a persistence to keep digging, to keep letting go. Just as the inventory isn't completed with one fell swoop, the readiness to change is needed over and over.

Today, reflect on how ready or not ready you are to change. Where are you stuck meeting resistance, and where are you free?

# June 5

### *"Intention to Change"*

One way to inspire readiness is to examine intention. What do we want from our life? What are we willing to do to get it? Most people will say that they want happiness and fulfillment, or at least to end suffering, as the Buddha put it. We want love and connection; we want meaning in our work; we want purpose in our lives. And what stands in the way of these things? Our character defects. This means that on some level, these defects are blocking our highest intentions.

The Buddha's guidelines for intention give us a rigorous challenge: only act out of love, compassion, and letting go. This mean that selfish aims won't be rewarded. It suggests that the most satisfaction will come if we care for others without attachment.

If we look honestly at our inventory, we'll see that our destructive behaviors were driven by unskillful and selfish intentions.

Our intimate relationships suffer from our wish to control others, our defensiveness, our unreasonable expectations, our neediness, and other qualities. If we want to sustain such relationships, we have to look at our own side and be willing to change, be willing to let go. We have to examine our intention and be guided by the principles of love and non-clinging.

Our professional lives suffer when we aren't willing to cooperate, when we give up after facing setbacks, when we lie, cheat, and steal, and when we choose careers for the wrong reasons, like fear and greed. To find success and satisfaction, we need to make decisions based on wise principles. Again, getting clear about our highest intentions will be our guide.

Today, ask yourself what it is you want from your life, especially in relationship and work. Are you acting with the wisest intention in these areas?

# June 6

### *"Getting Ready: Feeling"*

The fundamental question we are faced with in Steps Six and Seven is "How do I let go?" The AA Big Book makes this almost sound like magic—just say a prayer, and you're good to go. Of course, that's not realistic, and from a Buddhist view, any change must involve actions: thoughts, words, or deeds.

The beginning of this process is being present with our difficult emotions. Feeling the pain of our behavior, feeling the pain of our words, feeling the pain of our thoughts. When we bring mindfulness to bear on these karmic causes, we are motivated to change them. The same thing that made us stop our addictive behavior, seeing the pain we were causing ourselves and others, becomes the motivation for changing other harmful behaviors. It's not enough to take an inventory and see what's not working. We have to feel it and be ready to change.

This is where mindfulness is so important. If we aren't really tuning in to our direct, moment-to-moment experience, we can wind up avoiding feeling our pain, and thus put off making any real changes. We might feel things are "good enough," allowing ourselves to skate through life without realizing our potential for greater happiness or fulfillment.

The Buddhist path, which takes us deep into the truth of our experience, forces us to fully face our own suffering, which paradoxically becomes the doorway to letting go. Until we learn to really feel, to be with our underlying agitation, anxiety, sadness, and anger, we won't be able to release any of it.

Begin to connect with your feelings throughout the day. Notice how your thoughts, words, and actions trigger different moods and emotions to arise. Let yourself fully feel those feelings.

# June 7

*"Breathing with Feeling"*

Integrating emotions, moods, and feelings into our practice broadens our mindfulness beyond the ordinary focus of breath and thoughts. However, as we open to feelings, there can be resistance or fear to really letting them in. We can use the breath to ease into those experiences and to stay grounded and present with them.

As you sit, first connect with the breath and the larger sense of your whole body. Next, take the attention to the chest and belly region, allowing whatever emotions are present to show themselves. Feel the breath rising and falling here. Particularly for difficult feelings, let the breath be expansive but easeful. You might breathe a little deeper and slower, not forcing that, but just sensing how bringing care to the feelings naturally makes the breath more gentle.

Notice any tension, resistance, or fear of the feelings that arises. With your inhalations, sense that you are opening, allowing the feelings to be fully felt. With your exhalations, sense that you are releasing the feelings and the resistance. Feel the energy, the weight, and the tone of the feelings.

Be watchful of the mind so that analysis or judgment doesn't take hold. No matter how difficult the feelings might be, remember that they will pass, that they are impermanent. If the experience gets too intense, open the eyes, move the body a little bit, and then, if it feels safe to continue, begin again.

As you move forward with your practice, apply this approach whenever strong emotions are sweeping you away or when sticky thoughts are persistent and agitated. When you let the emotions in and allow yourself to fully feel them, it often provides a release as you watch them naturally recede on their own.

Today, work with this breathing practice, whether there is a strong emotion present or not. Get used to checking in with your moods and feelings while meditating.

# June 8

*"Depressed about Depression"*

Depression is a common experience for addicts. Many were drawn to intoxicants because of painful feelings they wanted to suppress, while others experienced depressive states when hungover or in withdrawal. Drained of energy and resilience by a binge, the mood sinks along with the physical state.

Depression is different from sadness or the blues in that it is sustained over time and has a pervasive quality that seems to envelop one's life. Everything seems to go dark and negative. Of course, psychologists have debated causes and cures for ages, and the pharmaceutical industry is always coming up with a new pill to fix it. When the mood gets to the point of self-destruction or paralysis, no doubt medical intervention can be appropriate. But Buddhism offers insights that can be helpful, especially for milder cases.

The most direct way Buddhism can help is in seeing how we get depressed about feeling depressed. If you are susceptible to depression, when a feeling of sadness comes over you, there can be an immediate sense that a dark hole is opening. The thought, "Oh, no, I'm getting depressed" might arise. Interrupting this negative spiral is vital to avoiding falling into depression.

Instead of ruminating on the possibility of something bad happening, if we go back to the simple experience of feeling, bringing mindfulness to the emotion, we can avoid falling further. Then remind yourself that everything is impermanent, that a depressed feeling must surely pass. This realization alone can break the cycle of negative thought. Certainly sad, depressed feelings are unpleasant, but when felt without additional fears, they are just that, unpleasant, not overwhelming.

Today, notice the mind's reaction to difficult or unpleasant emotions. Do your best to interrupt them with mindfulness and the reflection on impermanence.

# June 9

## *"Right Livelihood"*

The Noble Eightfold Path includes the work we do in the world, Right Livelihood. This brings our spiritual work into the practical realm and points to the all-encompassing quality of Buddhist practice. This puts it in sync with recovery, which also challenges us to live by spiritual principles.

Although plenty of addicts are able to function effectively in a profession while using, few of us were at our best. Many of us looked on work as an annoyance that got in the way of our using. In recovery, as we learn the spirit of service, our attitude changes dramatically. Now we see our livelihood as another way to express our wish to bring something of value to the world.

It's not unusual to hear people share in meetings about going back to school or entering into a new profession. The joy of recovery often spreads far beyond the meeting rooms and finds us impacting people's lives through our work.

Buddhism encourages the same sense of service. It emphasizes compassionate activity.

When considering potential professions, you can get confused or frustrated if you feel that you have to attain some high spiritual standard in your work. Not everyone is suited to be Mother Teresa or to work for Doctors Without Borders. Instead of measuring yourself by such a standard, it is more helpful to consider intention. Ultimately the benefit that comes from your livelihood is tied more to the loving, mindful, and generous intention you bring to the work than to a specific job. The simplest task—customer service, office assistant, or landscaper—can be done with this spirit, and when it is, that work becomes Right Livelihood.

Today reflect on the intention you bring to your work. Are you acting out of kindness and a spirit of service?

# June 10

*"There Is a Body"*

The "Satipatthana Sutta," translated as "The Four Foundations of Mindfulness," is the Buddha's most specific and extensive instruction on mindfulness practice. Mindfulness is, he says, "the direct path...for the attainment of the true way." This is one of his strongest statements about his teachings, so we should take it seriously.

The First Foundation of Mindfulness is Contemplation of the Body. In the instructions for bringing mindfulness to the body, after many other suggestions, is found a phrase that points to a simple way to meditate: "Mindfulness that 'there is a body' is simply established in one to the extent necessary for bare knowledge and mindfulness."

Thus, "there is a body" becomes an instruction in itself, as the Buddhist scholar, Venerable Analayo points out. Sitting down, we simply feel our body as it is. We recognize that we are living in this organism, what the Buddha calls "this fathom-long body." We feel its weight and density; the flow of energy; the movement of breath and pulse of heart; emotions and moods. In short, we feel life. This is a wonderful way to connect to the present moment, and indeed, to our very own life right here and now, simply and directly.

"There is a body," boils the practice down to its simplest component. This is what is. Not my body; not an attractive or unattractive body. Not a good body or bad body. This reflection takes us out of thoughts, judgment, and analyses. It points us away from "I, me, mine." It puts us right here, right now,

Today, begin your practice with "there is a body." Notice if it makes you feel more connected and alive.

# June 11

*"Loving-kindness: The Neutral Person"*

The instruction in metta practice to send loving-kindness to a neutral person often seems to stump people. First, the idea that people are neutral to us might be a new one. However, since we don't know the vast majority of people in the world, upon further reflection, we realize that many people are neutral to us. We don't like or dislike them; we simply have no feelings about them at all.

In developing metta for the neutral person, we try to think of a specific individual, so we have someone in our minds to send those thoughts to. If we think about people we know, we're probably going to find that we have positive feelings, negative feelings, or a mixture of the two toward most everyone. So, we need to think of someone we don't exactly know, but whom we encounter in our lives and can visualize in our minds. Typically, this might be someone who serves us at a café, bank, or store; a neighbor in our building or our neighborhood; or someone we see at work or in some other public sphere. It's easy to get caught up in trying to figure out the perfect person, but that's not necessary. Better just to pick someone and try them out. The main thing is to be able to picture them clearly in your mind.

When we first begin to work with the neutral person, there likely won't be a lot of feelings of love. This is natural, and in fact, to be expected. If we find that we start out already loving them, then they aren't really neutral. To send phrases and feelings of love to a neutral person can feel awkward and forced, depending on your own tendencies and your mood at the time. The important thing is to stick with it. Don't judge your own ability to love the neutral person. Try to be patient with what can seem like a tedious process. Over time you'll see how this step in the metta process expands your capacity to love all beings.

Today, begin to include a neutral person in your loving-kindness practice: "May you be happy; may you be peaceful; may you be safe."

# June 12

*"Challenges to Loving-kindness"*

The practice of loving-kindness can sound romantic and spiritual, as though we are going to be uplifted, our hearts opening in joy and bliss. While these feelings can arise, there are plenty of times when it's not like that at all. In fact, metta practice can be more about seeing how closed we are or remembering that we need to make more effort to bring kindness into our lives.

As we work through the different elements of the practice, every stage can be challenging. Loving ourselves can seem selfish or undeserved; giving metta to loved ones might suddenly reveal the fissures in a relationship; the mind might drift when trying to send love to the neutral person; a wall of resistance might arise when turning toward the difficult person or the enemy; and radiating love to all beings may seem unrealistic or beyond our capacity. This is all part of the process. The most important thing is to let go of expectations or judgments regarding our own practice, and just carry on. Just as with recovery, the key is to show up, one day and one breath at a time.

All meditation practices, from mindfulness, to concentration, to metta, or any others, depend first and foremost on the time we put into them. Metta gives us a nice, simple structure with specific people to send love to and basic phrases to repeat. Combining these elements with an awareness of the breath gives us a process to stick with, allowing us to drop any ideas of what should happen. If we simply put in the time with this process, the results will unfold naturally.

Today, notice the obstructions to your metta practice. Try to let them go and continue to send love.

# June 13

### *"We Are Not saints"*

When we see a phrase like "entirely ready," in Step Six we can end up setting unachievable standards for our personal and spiritual growth. The AA Big Book addresses this when it says, "We are not saints...We claim spiritual progress, not spiritual perfection." What a relief those words are to many of us.

It's ironic that people who had spent years getting drunk or loaded on drugs can get into a program where they start measuring themselves against the holiest beings. Now, somehow, despite years of dissipation, we think we should be perfect meditators, top-flight employees, constantly loving spouses, Step geniuses, and service gurus. These attitudes just reflect the tendency of addicts to go to extremes. And it's not helpful to have such lofty expectations of ourselves.

Many of us have to work hard to discover an appropriate level of effort and set reasonable expectations for ourselves. In meditation, we learn that we can't simply control our minds, but that just showing up and putting in the time is in itself success. At work, we find that avoiding workaholism and being a worker among workers is the way to avoid burnout and frustration. In relationships, we learn to seek peace over drama, contentment over bliss. In our Step work, we grow increasingly humble the more honest we get. And in service, we accept that we can't save the world.

Recognizing all these limits is what brings real serenity to our recovery. No longer trying to be the best at everything allows us to settle back and enjoy life as it is. Intoxication was a way to make life seem more glamorous and exciting. In truth, it only created an illusion of happiness. With recovery we find something more lasting and valuable: peace of mind.

Today, reflect on the ways you strive too hard or have unrealistic expectations of yourself, your program, your practice, and the rest of your life. Appreciate the ways you have stopped striving and accepted the simple joys of life.

# June 14

*"Naming Feelings"*

The practice of feeling our feelings objectively is vital in learning how to let go or be less identified with them. Often there are subtle, underlying moods and emotions at work that we need to recognize and identify to get at the roots of our clinging. Interestingly, it turns out that how we name these feelings is of great importance.

When we name something "fear," "sadness," or "anger," we are reifying an essentially insubstantial experience. Without these labels, feelings are just sensations or energies in the body. When we name something, as with the earlier discussion of depression, we give it a reality, a solidity that takes on a life of its own. As we've seen, the thought, "I am depressed" can trigger more depression. With mindfulness, we can work at a more elemental level by just tuning into the felt experience.

This is one of the places where learning to let go of thoughts comes in handy. As you turn toward a feeling or as a feeling pushes itself into your consciousness, you might be able to catch the arising of the naming function, what Buddhism calls "perception." This naming or labeling is based on memory and conditioning. It's a valuable ability that allows us to understand our world, but it can also get us stuck.

When working with feelings, it's most helpful to avoid naming them right away, and try to stay as close as possible to the raw, visceral experience. You'll see the impermanent nature of the feeling in this way, because feelings are never static. You can feel them as dynamic energy, moving, vibrating, pulsing. They may be pleasant, unpleasant, or not particularly either one, but what they are not is an absolutely definable thing.

Today, begin to work with emotions on this pure, raw level. See how the mind wants to name feelings, and see what you learn when you don't name them.

# June 15

*"Embracing Joy"*

Working through the Steps can begin to feel like a never-ending process. Facing our addiction and powerlessness, writing and sharing inventory, making amends, and all the rest don't seem to promote actual happiness. And isn't that the ultimate reason we got clean and sober (besides wanting to end the misery)?

Perhaps we associated feeling good with being loaded. Now, as addicts in recovery, maybe we are afraid to have too much fun or be too happy. But at some point, we need to learn what happiness really is and embrace it. Happiness is much more than being in a good mood. It's about having a life that works, where our values are integrated with our behavior, where we have satisfying relationships and work, a sense of purpose, and a certain degree of security. For addicts, aligning all this starts with getting clean and sober, because none of it is possible without establishing that first. Then it grows and develops as we overcome the crippling effects and habits of our addiction. As recovery progresses, we come to a place where things are finally making sense.

What can hold us back is the sense that we have to constantly be working on ourselves, that any of our imperfections are unacceptable and must be eradicated. This attitude can be fostered in the Twelve Step world if inventory takes too prominent a place. While the inventories of Steps Four and Ten are vital, if they come to dominate our recovery, we'll have a hard time finding joy.

It seems apparent that if you sincerely work the Steps for several years and align your life with those values and principles, at some point you ought to be able to let up on intensive inventory work. This doesn't mean that you let up on your spiritual work. Meditation, service, and the development of wisdom and compassion are ongoing practices. But they are ultimately meant to bring joy, not be a dreary slog. Inventory itself can continue, but not as a search for perfection or constant demeaning of our worth, but rather as an investigation of the natural and inevitable failings of a normal human being.

Today, reflect on things that you can appreciate about yourself and your life in recovery. Is there joy to be found?

# June 16

*"Embracing Fun"*

As we begin to open to the idea of finding more joy in our lives, one good way to do that is to find playful or joyful activities. Since the activities we have learned to embrace as adults are mostly around our addiction, we might turn back to our childhood to rediscover things we enjoy. As addicts we needed dramatic, intoxicating entertainment, but children find joy in simple things.

We might try taking a mindful walk; watching a movie with a friend or child; riding a bike or going for a swim; sitting in a café with a good book. Such activities may not be exciting or thrilling, but for a sober person they can be deeply pleasing. We learn in recovery the joy of contentment. Just to be at ease is a gift.

You might want to go further and take up a sport or art form. In recovery we start to realize that many of the limitations on our life were self-imposed. Why not take piano lessons? Learn to ski? Take a creative writing class? Try improv? Addicts tend to live in a narrowly circumscribed world. Not only are certain activities a problem—a two-hour movie without a drink or a drug can be unmanageable—but our beliefs about our capacities and preferences also tend to be very limited. We either don't think we have the ability to do certain things, or we develop a strict set of things we "don't do," or don't like. These are simply based on aversion and judgment that's atrophied in our addictive soul.

This aversive attitude often overtakes the thinking of an addict. We become deeply cynical, closed to life and its myriad beauties. Our addiction has poisoned our hearts.

Recovery is all about breaking these barriers. The barrier of addiction was only the first of these. Our whole life can become one of discovering ourselves, our potentials, and our possibilities.

Today, consider what new (or old) activity you might bring into your life just for fun. Was there something you were passionate about in your youth that you might revive? What doors might you open to new opportunities for joy and engagement in life?

# June 17

*"Fear of Change"*

Our resistance to getting clean and the transformation that recovery promises come out of fear. "We are afraid that if we give up what we know we'll be left with nothing, or worse still, with what we don't want. Something has to happen—like hitting an alcoholic bottom—to make us willing to change." *A Burning Desire*, p. 178.

As active addicts we were confused about who we were and even what our life was about. We became so identified with ourselves as addicts and stultified in our limited life that we couldn't see the prison bars that surrounded us. We'd rather live with our known suffering than venture into something unknown, even if it might mean true freedom and happiness. It's only when we hit bottom that we were willing to try something new. But even then, our willingness might have been limited to changing our addictive behavior. Step Six is about having willingness to change the embedded thoughts, words, and behaviors that went along with our addiction.

Who will we be if we take up this task? Will we lose some essence of ourselves? Will we become mindless drones? These are the thoughts and fears that block our progress on the path. We need only look back at Step One and our initial resistance to see through these fears. The freedom that came from abandoning our addiction is just a sample of that which awaits us if we take on the full implications of Step Six, if we embrace the transformation that recovery promises.

Do you really believe that your potential is limited to who you were as an addict? Is it possible that your life has much more waiting for you if you are just willing to let go of the limitations you place on yourself? Step Six is the opportunity to open to change, to take the challenge of recovery to the next stage.

Today, reflect on your own resistance to change. Are you willing to let go of this resistance to find the freedom that awaits you?

# June 18

*"Who Am I?*

Our fear of change is based in something fundamental. "The root of this fear seems to be clinging to *I*, to a sense of self. We could probably say that all our 'defects of character' derive from this one point. This is actually what the Twelve Step literature already says: 'Selfishness—self-centeredness! That, we think, is the root of our troubles.'

"Buddhism takes the idea that self-centeredness is our problem to another level when it says that the very idea of a self, this *I*, is a delusion—so, we're clinging to something that doesn't even exist as a separate, solid entity. Now *that* is a problem.

"Who we are, our identity, our personality, is a conglomeration of memories, feelings, thoughts, conditioning, genetics, all of the stuff of the mind/body. It's a dynamic, living, constantly changing process more than an entity. Our survival instinct, that which makes us want to protect our bodies, also wants to protect this illusory identity. In the same way that we are afraid of our bodies dying, we are afraid of ego death, of the death of identity. And in the same way that we try to protect the body, we try to protect the ego." *A Burning Desire,* p. 178

Step One feels like a huge attack on this ego, which is why it takes so long to get there and is so difficult to complete. The rest of the Steps continue with this dismantling.

Buddhist practice helps us to hold this experience differently. As we deepen our meditation, we see the truth of what the Buddha taught: the dynamic, fluid, changing nature of mind and body. This insight has the potential to loosen our attachment to self, to ego.

Today in your meditation, notice change: changing thoughts, changing feelings, changing sensations. Recognize that these are what make up your sense of self and that they are never static or stable. Reflect on the implications of this insight.

# June 19

*"Probing Self"*

In recovery, everything gets upended, including, especially, our self-view, our sense of who we are. The Buddhist insight that identity isn't fixed can help us to manage this upheaval.

Wisdom shows us that we have many identities based on our relationships and positions: we might be a boss, a mother, a friend, and a recovering alcoholic. In different situations we have different roles. None of them define us. We need to learn to slip each of these on and off when appropriate, without becoming attached to any one identity or self-image.

Many people in recovery find that their old life and identity don't fit anymore. They need to change jobs, get out of a relationship, find a new group of friends, or go back to school. Someone who'd avoided responsibility all their life might suddenly be worrying about insurance and their bank account or paying their bills on time. We might begin to set our sight on things we never thought were possible for us.

If we are going to grow in recovery and truly transform our lives, we need to be open to change, to letting go of past identities. The freedom that recovery brings is that no identity has to truly define us.

Today, reflect on the various identities you have. Which ones do you cling to? Which ones limit you? Can you hold them all lightly?

# June 20

*"Radiating Energy"*

In mindfulness meditation we usually take a stance of observing what we are feeling, not trying to create some experience. However, at times we can take more active steps in our practice to cultivate particular states. This can be helpful for people in recovery when they are struggling with difficult emotions. Loving-kindness practice is an example of this. With simple mindfulness practice, we can also cultivate states. One way is to practice radiating energy through the body.

Start with some calming breaths and a focus on the whole body. Just feel yourself sitting still, sensing all the energy in the body. Then focusing on the chest, imagine that you are radiating outward from the chest through the torso and into the limbs. Bring the attention back to the chest: breathe and radiate again. After a few times of this wavelike practice, connect with how the whole body now is bright and filled with energy.

You may start to feel waves, jolts, or tingles—or you may not. Don't force it, and avoid judging or grading the results of this experiment. As addicts, we're often looking for the high, but in this case, such striving will only block the arising of positive experiences.

Work with this energy for five to ten minutes, and then begin to calm the energy. Again, using the calming breath, imagine all this energy settling, and picture behind it a serene, peaceful feeling. Sit with that calm, just enjoying a settled state for a few minutes.

You can begin to integrate this practice of radiating and settling into your daily practice whenever it feels appropriate. This tends to work best when you are already relatively settled, rather than when you are anxious or agitated. This can bring benefit to your concentration over time.

# June 21

*"Wounds"*

We all carry wounds. Some are so deep we don't even know they are there, or they only surface after years of inner work. Some are so painful that they alter the whole course of our lives—often violent traumas inflicted on us or by us or witnessed by us. Some of us have experienced more subtle wounds, unintentional emotional abuse or early losses from which we struggle to recover. Some traumas are passed down through generations and held in our bodies. Some of the wounds are just the "slings and arrows" of life, nothing special, but painful and difficult to hold, nonetheless.

How we relate to these experiences and how we learn to live with them determine to a great extent how happy and content we are in our lives. If we become embittered or resentful, we carry these scars around with us everywhere we go. If we become frightened or morose, we might withdraw from life, too afraid or passive to take risks or engage. If we don't learn to work with these scars, we are likely to relapse at some point.

The Buddha's First Noble Truth says that suffering is inherent to life. He points out how painful birth is, how difficult aging and sickness are, and that death itself is often miserable. His teaching shows us that we must accept the challenges of life as natural, not view them as aberrations to be fixed. When we understand that the wounds and scars we carry are the badges of a life fully lived, we start to relate to them differently. Did we learn from our pain? Did we grow? Did we come to understand life more fully? And were we able to use this understanding as a way to serve others? These are some of the questions we can ask.

As we grow older, these wounds are likely to accumulate as we lose friends, have health problems, and experience all the challenges life presents to us. If we are to live a fulfilling and purposeful life, we must learn to hold these wounds with care and compassion.

Today, reflect on your own wounds. How do you hold them today? What have you learned from them?

# June 22

*"Holding Our Wounds"*

Mindfulness gives us a tool for holding our pain in a new way. Instead of moving away, we open to pain and explore it. Instead of trying to fix it, we learn to accept it.

For trauma survivors, as many addicts are, this can be more challenging. Fortunately, resources to address such difficulties are available in such work as David Treleaven's *Trauma Sensitive Mindfulness.* With the help of these tools, even those with deep wounds can often develop an inner strength that allows them to be more fully with their pain while learning to move through it.

The first thing we see when we start to apply mindfulness to our pain and wounds is that there are two aspects to the experience: there is the pain itself and there is our reaction to it. The reaction is aversion, the wish to get away. This actually makes the experience harder to hold. When we are able to overcome this aversion, this fear of pain, we come to the raw wound that, while unpleasant, is often manageable in a way we may not have believed before.

This direct engagement gives us an inner power to engage life fearlessly. At the same time, our growing understanding of wounds as natural, not a problem to be solved but an experience to be felt, helps us as well. Seeing our experience in terms of the Four Noble Truths lets us accept that what is happening to us isn't unnatural.

This doesn't mean that we remain passive in the face of adversity. But mindfulness gives us the space—and the choice—to respond wisely. Is there something I can do that would be helpful or healing for this wound? When we ask this question, we do so from a place of acceptance, wisdom, and compassion. With humility, we ask for help when we sense that we need it.

Today, use your mindfulness practice to help you hold difficult experiences. Try to respond to your pain with kindness and wisdom.

# June 23

*"Repeatedly"*

Thoroughly working the Steps just once is a big job. You could be excused for thinking you deserve a break after enduring such a challenging process. But working the Steps is an ongoing process, one that must become an integral part of our lives.

Once you've thoroughly done the Steps in order, it's wise to set up a routine that includes regular work with Steps 10, 11, and 12, as well as referring back to earlier Steps as needed. Besides recognizing our powerlessness, our Step One work, Steps Six and Seven might be the ones that require the most consistent engagement.

Step Six is not a once and done Step. Over and over we are challenged to be ready, ready to let go, ready to change. We might think that a shortcoming has been removed, then find it sneaking back in. We might discover a "defect" or underlying tendency we never saw before. In fact, it might be *unwillingness* to continue to work this Step that is behind many relapses. The persistence of negative qualities must be met with an equal persistence in letting go.

It's hard to change. It's hard to let go. Our ego resists the self-inquiry and openness that this requires. As we grow in recovery through the Steps, we repeatedly return to the question of how ready we are to let go. Spiritual pride might tell us that we've already solved our problems, but such thinking only opens the back door to a gradual slipping away from the path. This is why "one day at a time" is our maxim, and why the daily practice of mindfulness is so vital. Honest appraisal of our current spiritual condition is the only way to assure that we are safe from any pitfalls to recovery.

Today ask yourself what you might be holding on to, what impediments there are to your spiritual practice. Are you ready to fully confront these challenges, and are you willing to let go?

# June 24

### *"Efforting"*

The effort required for meditation is different from the effort we are accustomed to applying in other areas of life. How do you "try" to let go of a thought or feeling? How do you "try" to pay attention to the breath? The typical effort of striving only gets in the way and makes such things harder. As we develop a meditation practice, we have to explore the subtle nuances of effort. Sometimes it's an effort to relax more.

Perhaps the most important element of effort in meditation is just showing up, as it can also be in our recovery program. People often express how hard it is to "make time" to meditate. Of course, we can't actually *make* time, we can only let go of other activities so that there is time for practice. Still, as we meditate, there can be a sense that we need to do more, try harder. We might adopt a precise meditation form, like a visualization, a mantra, or defined system. This can make us feel as if we are really doing something, and that once we master this form, we'll be successful meditators. This is another misunderstanding.

As we strive one way then another, eventually we may become frustrated and give up trying. That's might be when our practice really starts. That's when we get down to the raw material of meditation.

What is meditation but engagement with what is—with our body, our senses, and our mind—the fullness of our human experience? All the forms are simply ways to guide us to this essence. Meditation begins with being still and staying present. But in some sense, that's too simple to teach, so the forms give us something to do, something that makes us feel productive, while the real work of being still and present develops. Eventually, the stillness, the silence, and the presence manifest as a moment of actual meditation, and then we finally have a taste of what this is all about. We can still continue with the forms—or not—but we know now that the form isn't the goal or the purpose of practice. The form is just a tool. When we become too caught up in perfecting the form, that efforting blocks the natural manifestation of presence.

Today, notice how you are striving in your practice. What would happen if you didn't try so hard, but instead relaxed and let be?

# June 25

## *"Wings"*

Buddhism is said to have two wings: wisdom and compassion. These also reflect absolute and relative truths, or the universal and the personal. The wisdom side is the absolute view of reality, that everything is impermanent and empty. The compassion side responds to the fact that despite the universal truths, we must still deal with life's struggles on a personal level. Holding these two wings in balance is an important part of working with these teachings.

Most people live only in the relative, personal truth, and that gives them a limited understanding of reality. It's true that we should be treated with compassion if lose something important to us, but if we also hold the absolute truth of impermanence, it can be easier to accept. If we remember that everyone suffers, everyone experiences loss, and that pain is a natural part of life, we are able to hold the personal crises without being overwhelmed.

If all we see is the relative, then tragedy has no context or meaning. It is just random agony inflicted by the universe. When the Buddha was approached by a man who was out of his mind with grief over his son's death, he told him, "Come to your senses." In a famous phrase he said, "Sorrow, lamentation, pain, grief, and despair" come from our attachment to those we love. The man in the sutta couldn't accept this teaching and left in frustration.

The Buddha wasn't saying that we shouldn't care about people or love our children. Instead, he gave this teaching so that with greater understanding we would be comforted. He wanted us to realize we are not alone in our suffering; loss is a natural part of life; and we must find a way to continue despite it all.

Today reflect on your relationship to these two truths, the universal and the personal. Can you hold them in balance? Do you tend to see one more easily than the other?

# June 26

*"Living the Steps"*

Usually we talk about "working the Steps," which is an important aspect of our growth in recovery. Eventually, though, we need to start to "live the Steps." This means internalizing key aspects of the recovery and Step process so that we can call upon certain attitudes and behaviors when needed. This might mean making an amends or taking responsibility for some unskillful words or actions; it might mean dealing with a loss or failure by turning it over; it can be a spontaneous act of service or an intuitive prayer.

There are many ways that we live the Steps, but fundamentally it means taking in the principles of recovery as core elements of our own identity. We are no longer doing the Steps in a mechanical way or just the way someone told us to do them. They have become part of us.

What this means is that, at some point in your recovery, you start to think more about what each Step means to you personally. What does "powerless" mean? "Turning it over" to God? "Character defects"? How are your "shortcomings" removed? What about prayer and meditation? Or asking for "God's will"? All of these questions (or their answers) are intensely personal.

In the beginning of recovery, it makes sense to follow the guidance of others and just get established in your program. But if your program doesn't eventually become your own, if you are just *working someone else's program*, you are likely at some point to hit a wall.

Today begin to consider what each Step means to you. Start to do some reflection or writing on the Steps and how you are living them today.

# June 27

*"Attitudes of Mindfulness: Letting Go"*

*Adapted from* Buddhism & The Twelve Steps Workbook
"Letting go is the antidote to clinging. The simple practice of returning to the breath when you notice that you are thinking shows the power of letting go. Oftentimes we'll have a sense of relief and release when we come back to the breath. Our habitual way of being is to pursue streams of thought, to follow them wherever they go, letting them control and lock up our minds. When we start to meditate, we see how this way of handling thoughts actually causes a sense of unease, stress, or restlessness. This experience can inform our lives in important ways.

"For the addict, developing the ability to let go is key to recovery. Addiction is the antithesis of letting go, and, further, the tendency of addicts, even when not getting stuck on substances is to get attached to thoughts, beliefs, and feelings. Watching how these attachments cause suffering and learning to let go will carry us a long way in our recovery.

"When we start to examine our experience with curiosity and non-identification, we can begin to be more objective about what works and what doesn't in our life, what brings more happiness and what brings more unhappiness. We soon discover that things that might have seemed so important, like our judgments about people, are really not worth the stress they cause.

"This internal experience can also be mirrored in our external experience. Sometimes we see that things we own or activities we do are more of a burden than a blessing. The spirit of letting go is to examine our lives, inside and out, and see what is really working for us and what is not. It doesn't mean that we have to make radical changes in our lives, just that we start to question our habitual ways of being, and start making choices based on mindful observation rather than the coercive effects of internal conditioning or social pressure."

Today begin to examine the things you are attached to, both internally and externally. Notice where these attachments are not serving you and consider how you might let go.

# June 28

*"Exploring Difficult Sensations in Meditation"*

When we sit still in meditation for a substantial period of time, thirty or forty minutes or longer, some unpleasant sensations will naturally arise. Our bodies are not designed to be still for extended periods. The problem with this in meditation is that moving disturbs the development of concentration. So, we try to stay still as much as possible.

Exploring sensations with curiosity is very different from the usual response of immediately trying to fix them, our survival instinct. But in meditation we aren't in actual danger, so we can usually sit through difficult sensations with no risk. This allows us to scan the sensations mindfully, something we've probably never done. (This doesn't mean that we force ourselves to sit still. We should always be careful not to harm ourselves.)

The Buddha suggest we examine sensations through the lens of the four elements: earth, air, fire, and water. Earth element is the quality of solidity, of weight, and of density; air element is the quality of movement; fire element is the quality of temperature; and water element is the quality of cohesion and fluidity. By identifying sensations through this lens, we dis-identify with those sensations, and we see them in their raw form, not as part of the story of "me."

Even without using the model of the four elements, we can pay attention to sensations as just feelings, not messages or demands. We might discover that many sensations from which we had recoiled are actually manageable. In fact, intense sensations can become a great concentration object. While the breath is subtle and hard to be with, strong sensations can hold our attention easily. Again, be careful not to do this in a way that could cause real harm. There is no benefit from toughing it out. Only work with sensations that you can hold with mindfulness.

Today, see if you can lengthen your meditation until the body becomes a little uncomfortable. See if you can examine the sensations through the elements lens or just with more clear attention.

# June 29

*"Working with Others' Pain"*

While it's certainly difficult to deal with our own pain, when we see others suffer, a whole new set of challenges arises. We might be afraid of the feelings that come up. Or we might feel responsible and start trying to fix their pain. If it's someone close to us, our own fears about losing them may overwhelm us. How do we deal with all of this?

In the crucible of spiritual practice, we develop strength, the strength that comes from having walked through physical, emotional, and spiritual pain, and survived. This, then, gives us the strength to be with others' suffering. As we sit with a friend or dear one, we breathe into our own heart. Even as we feel their pain, we know it is not ours, so we don't have to be swept away by it. Our experience of surviving pain can then become a support and inspiration to this person. Our capacity to be there for them, to not turn away, relieves their aloneness.

When we feel ourselves getting caught in feeling like we need to fix someone else's pain, we remind ourselves of our powerlessness. We can't even make our own pain go away, so how could we eliminate someone else's pain? Instead, we try to offer love, care, and understanding, breaking the barriers of separation. Pain and loss may be inevitable, but we learn that instead of being impediments to life, they can be gateways into more connection, wisdom, and insight.

Today, notice the suffering around you and see how it affects you. Can you hold other people's suffering with compassion, without getting overwhelmed or attached to fixing it?

# June 30

## *"Spiritual Awakening"*

The spiritual awakening of Step Six is the acknowledgment of our readiness, or lack thereof, to change or do the work of transformation and spiritual growth. It's easy to fool ourselves on this account. We think we want something different in our lives, but when faced with the actual tasks involved in changing, we might balk.

Once we overcome this resistance, a world of possibilities opens up for us. Limiting ideas of who we are and what we are capable of fall away. Opportunities that seemed distant or unattainable now appear within our reach. We see that our understanding about what was standing in our way was mistaken. It was our own resistance, fear, and lack of willingness that held us back.

With this new understanding, we become excited about the future instead of fearful or despairing. We realize that, while there is no easy or simple way to solve problems or to grow and heal, all we really need is the willingness to take the next step. We may not know exactly where we will end up, but we know it will take us in a positive direction.

A sense of freedom comes with this willingness. We'd been trapped, unknowingly, in our own narrow view. With this Step, we escape that trap into the open world of possibilities.

Today, examine your own readiness to change and let go of counterproductive qualities and behaviors. Are you still holding back, or are you willing now to fully participate in your own transformation?

# July: Step Seven

*"Humbly asked Him to remove our shortcomings."*

# July 1

*"How Do I Let Go?"*

In the traditional language of the Steps, it's "God" who removes our shortcomings. Approaching the Steps from a dharma perspective requires us to interpret this process differently. If we can't simply ask God or a Higher Power to do this for us, how are we to accomplish this enormous task? How are we to let go?

The teachings of the Buddha are all about answering this question. The premise of the dharma is that clinging is what causes suffering, and that non-clinging brings freedom. The Noble Eightfold Path is designed to bring this about. So we can say the way we learn to let go, to not cling, is by practicing the Eightfold Path. But, let's start more simply with the beginning of the Buddha's teaching: The First Noble Truth.

The Buddha says that suffering is inherent to life. And he says the response to this truth should be to "understand suffering." He's not talking about an intellectual understanding, but the felt experience, the deep realization of this truth. For addicts, this realization is the beginning of recovery, Step One. In both systems, Buddhism and the Steps, this insight into suffering spurs us into letting go. We see that our suffering is caused by clinging (the Second Noble Truth), and we naturally release that which has trapped us.

This seeing is mindfulness at work. We train in mindfulness so that we gain more clarity about how we are creating suffering. We see more and more subtle attachments: to things, to people, to ideas, to self.

Today, ask yourself if you are really clear about how you tend to create suffering for yourself. Notice the subtle ways you are attached and see if you can begin to let go.

# July 2

### *"Right View to Let Go"*

Step Seven throws us into the fires of true transformation. It brings us to a crossroads that is perhaps the greatest challenge of recovery: whether to face our pain, and in so doing begin to let go of its causes, or to shrink from that suffering and relapse or fall back into numbing behaviors.

This brings us back to the original challenge of dharma and of recovery. Our addiction arose out of a desire not to feel, a desire to avoid pain and maximize pleasure. Here is the problem: to really be motivated to let go, you have to let yourself feel the pain that comes from clinging. And so, you are forced to decide whether your determination to let go is stronger than your avoidance of suffering.

Right View, the first element of the Eightfold Path gives us another way to understand this crossroads: do we want to live a life based on truth or delusion? The truth is that suffering is caused by clinging, and if we are willing to let go of that clinging, we can end suffering. The delusion is that somehow we can avoid this whole formula, that we can find enough palliatives in life to glide through, maybe not totally unscathed, but unscathed enough to make it worth avoiding the challenge of the deeper work of recovery and spiritual growth.

This would mean halting our growth on the path, and fundamentally shortchanging ourselves. Why go just halfway? Once we've begun this process, why not carry it to its end?

Today, open yourself to the suffering of clinging. Use that experience as a spur to letting go.

# July 3

*"Humbly"*

The Twelve Step literature emphasizes humility in Step Seven. This harkens back to Step One's powerlessness. It's the acknowledgment that we can't force ourselves to change, that we have to engage in a process that will play out in its own way. Further, humility is part of the Buddhist and Twelve Step agenda to weaken attachment to ego. Pride, the opposite of humility, supports the sense of ego, control, and power. It puts us on a path of conflict with the world.

Both Buddhism and recovery require us to be deeply engaged, truly committed to our spiritual growth, while letting go of the results of our actions. This is a difficult balance to achieve. In fact, we don't really "achieve," balance. Balance comes and goes. Rather it is our persistence that carries us, our willingness to fail and continue, our willingness to follow a path that makes no guarantees, but in fact, challenges us at every step of the way.

Humility, though, isn't self-deprecation; it isn't self-hatred or judgment. Going through the inventory process, and indeed, continuing that process (as suggested in Step 10) is one of facing our shortcomings in a profound way. To do this risks a lot of negative thoughts about ourselves. It's hard to see our past mistakes so starkly. But humility actually means that we see those actions as ordinary, if unskillful, human behaviors. Self-hatred is still about self; it's still egotism. This is another challenge of humility, and it brings us back to the question of balance: how to balance honest self-appraisal with self-care and love.

This balance depends upon questioning our negative—and positive—thoughts about ourselves. Oftentimes we'll need help in this from a sponsor, therapist, or understanding friend who can point out the distortions in our thinking.

Today, reflect on your relationship to humility. Do you think of it as a negative thing—as *humiliation*? Are you *too* humble? Not humble enough? Try to develop balance in your view.

# July 4

*"Interdependence Day"*

In the U.S., July 4th is called Independence Day, but in Buddhist circles it's sometimes called "Interdependence Day" in a nod to the idea that, rather than everything being separate, or independent, all things are *inter*dependent, connected and related. This truth reveals itself in our practice.

When we see the truth of suffering, we realize its universality. Looking at our own mind reveals the essential human struggle with craving. It becomes clear that this struggle is not personal or unique to us, but simply a part of being human. Thus, we come to understand that we are connected with every other person through this shared experience. Out of this sense of connection arises compassion, the wish for others to be free from suffering.

Another way we see our interdependence is when we reflect on something as simple as a meal. Looking at the food in front of us, we can see that it depends on the rain, sunshine, and the earth. It needs care and cultivation from farm workers. Before it reaches us, it is harvested or otherwise prepared, packaged, shipped, and sold to us. We are dependent upon all the natural and human factors involved in this food appearing before us. We are not separate.

The Buddha points to an even more essential quality of interdependence and relationship: the Four Elements of earth, air, fire, and water. He says that our body is composed of these and that we can explore our experience through this lens. For example, you can see your bones as the earth element; breath as air element; blood as water element; and warmth as the fire element. None of these elements are separate from the world; we are made up of the same things as the rest of nature.

Today reflect on your connection and interdependence with all things.

# July 5

## *"Intention and Renunciation"*

Intention, the second element of the Eightfold Path, keeps us on track. First it gives us a clear direction. Second, when we lose that direction, it helps us find our way back. One of the expressions of Right Intention is renunciation. This word has a lot of negative connotations in our culture. We might think we're being deprived of something or rejecting the world. Renunciation is actually about letting go or refraining from our addiction. And it's only effective when it arises as a spontaneous response to the suffering that comes from clinging, not as an act of will or self-harm.

"Sobriety itself is a form of renunciation. When we renounce our self-destructive habits and substances in the First Step, it's not a repression or a masochistic effort at self-improvement, it's a spiritual release. When our craving for booze or drugs or food is removed, it's not because we willed it or because we have a strong character. It's because we've hit bottom, seen the suffering our addiction caused, and couldn't bear anymore to continue to destroy ourselves in that way. In a 'moment of clarity,' of clear seeing, we let go... And this is why the Twelve Steps emphasize honesty and self-examination at every stage, showing us how our unskillful behavior caused us suffering. And this is why Buddhism emphasizes mindfulness. We don't let go because there is some rule or commandment which says we must; we let go because we see how our clinging is causing us pain in this very moment." *One Breath at a Time*, p. 165-66.

Today, reflect on your reasons for letting go of drugs and alcohol (and other addictions). See if you are clear that you are renouncing them wisely, not through self-will or personal effort.

# July 6

*"Letting Go of Self"*

Some Buddhists say that our primary addiction is to self. The AA Big Book hints at this when it says, "Selfishness—self-centeredness! That we think is the root of our troubles." When the Twelfth Tradition says, "Anonymity is the spiritual foundation of all our traditions," it's getting even closer to this idea. It recognizes that our attachment to our own ideas and identity drag us into painful and unskillful thoughts, words, and actions.

In Step Seven, we face this addiction squarely. Now we are asked to really change. The so-called "character defects" and "shortcomings" of Steps Six and Seven are often integral parts of our identity. They can't be surgically removed. To let them go we have to be willing to let go of who we think we are. These beliefs tend to limit the choices we make in life.

As addicts we get into deep grooves. We make choices based on what feels comfortable and convenient. We don't tend to go outside our comfort zone. In recovery we begin to see how narrowly we had defined ourselves and how small our world had become. Stepping out of that world can be frightening at first, but once we open that door, we discover a whole other realm of opportunities.

A lot of recovering addicts do things like going back to school, changing professions, and trying new hobbies. Someone who had avoided commitment because they wanted to be "free" might realize that preference was actually founded in fear of being hurt. In recovery they might discover another fear, of intimacy itself. But the Steps and the dharma help us to move through all these fears. And eventually we come to a place of *true* freedom.

Today, reflect on the self-beliefs that limit you in your life. What are you willing to do to break out of those limitations?

# July 7

*"Standing Meditation"*

The Buddha said that it wasn't enough to only be mindful in sitting meditation, but that all activities should be performed in this way, just as Step Twelve tells us to "practice these principles in all our affairs." To accomplish this, the Buddha taught four postures for practicing mindfulness: sitting, standing, walking, and lying down. By developing this range of practices, mindfulness becomes more integrated into our lives.

Each of these four postures is worth exploring as part of regular practice. Today let's focus on standing meditation.

Begin standing with your eyes closed or slightly open, feet shoulder width apart, arms at the side. Feel your feet on the earth. Notice the effort involved in standing upright.

The body will tend to sway a bit. Standing on two legs is more difficult than four.

Now begin to move the attention through the body, either from the bottom up or the top down. With the body standing we can feel all the sensations and energies in the body. Notice points of strong sensation and points of little or no sensation. Notice pulsing, tingling, throbbing; notice heaviness and lightness; heat and coolness. Notice points of tension or tightness; areas of relaxation and comfort.

After moving the attention slowly through the whole body, you can let the attention rest either on the breath or in the feet. As with sitting meditation, notice when the mind wanders and bring it back. Try to keep standing for a little while, at least ten minutes or more. Notice how sensations change. Unpleasant sensations may arise over time. Work with them for a while if you can.

Once you've learned to do standing meditation, you can apply the principles to daily life: standing in line at a checkout counter, waiting for a bus, and any other time when you are simply standing. Combining standing and walking meditation broadens even further your opportunities for mindfulness throughout your day.

# July 8

*"Beseeching the Law of Karma"*

While Step Seven says we asked God to remove our shortcomings, the renowned Thai Buddhist master, Ajahn Buddhadasa suggested we "beseech the law of karma through our actions, not merely with words."

We aren't just repeating some rote phrases. We are actively engaging in a process that goes against our long-term, conditioned thoughts, words, and deeds to bring change in our lives. By living in a new way, our life is renewed; by addressing our destructive habits and ceasing to act on those impulses, we are breaking down the power of addiction; by taking up new behaviors and attitudes, we are creating new karmic patterns that bear fruit in every aspect of our lives.

"Letting go" isn't a passive activity. When we let go of our drinking, drugging, binging, or other addiction, it's an intensely engaged, challenging, and energetic act. It takes a lot of counter-action to get into recovery—actions that go against our historical behaviors.

It's important to remember that karmic actions, meaning the behaviors that actually change things, take three forms: thoughts, words, and deeds. It's not just that we behave differently, though this is critical, but we also have to examine our thinking and our speech. This is why mindfulness is vital for change, because in order to be aware of our thinking, we must be mindful. Otherwise, the thoughts just run through the mind, triggering feelings, words, and deeds. We don't understand that the roots of all these are our thoughts.

How do we uproot our unwholesome and destructive tendencies? We think, speak, and behave differently. But this transformation isn't rapid or, in most cases, complete. Our habitual tendencies have been developed and practiced over decades of our lives and won't turn back overnight. Nonetheless, we must persist—gently, kindly—if we expect a different life. This is our work.

Today continue your work of transformation by watching your thoughts, words, and deeds and trying to make wise choices in these actions.

# July 9

*"A New Life"*

"Many of us imagined sobriety as a bleak, boring place where all the fun was sucked out of life, and we would live in an eternal purgatory of party-lessness. Instead, most of us find an entirely new life, one we couldn't have imagined. Sobriety isn't just a matter of removing drugs and alcohol from our lives. In fact, that's only a small part. Sobriety is finding a new way of living which involves engagement where there was withdrawal; generosity where there was self-centeredness; community where there was isolation; joy where there was bitterness; trust where there was cynicism.

"For some people who first encounter Buddhism, monasticism might carry the same sense of bleakness that sobriety does for the alcoholic who is still drinking. The Theravada monastic tradition is quite strict... There's little of what we would call 'personal freedom.' And yet, freedom is exactly what monastics experience. Ajahn Amaro explains it this way: 'It's not like ordinary human life with some bits cut out. It endeavors to manifest in the physical realm our innate, divine, transcendent nature. That's why many people find monasticism both appealing and frightening.' True sobriety is much the same: it's not ordinary life with the drugs and alcohol cut out. It's a new way of living, of relating to ourselves and to the world. It's not a different version of the life we are living, it's a completely new life, one which can't be imagined until you are there. And it is 'both appealing and frightening.'" *One Breath at a Time*, pp.166-67.

Today, reflect on the ways recovery has changed you beyond abstaining from addictive behavior. How are you living a new life?

# July 10

### *"Too Much Letting Go"*

"Renunciation isn't a panacea. The Buddha's own journey shows the limits of renunciation, how he realized that his austerities needed to be balanced with proper nourishment, clothing, medicine, and housing. Some of us can get caught up in this movement towards letting go and lose sight of our own needs." *One Breath at a Time*, p. 172.

Addicts tend to overdo things; that's who we are. We even find ways to overdo recovery. We might work the Steps in an obsessive and fundamentalist way; we take up exercise and workout so hard we pull a muscle; we go on a diet and become anorexic. As the saying goes, "Anything worth doing is worth overdoing."

The Buddha's Middle Way anticipated this. After living a life of luxury for 29 years, he nearly starved himself to death in his efforts to be a "good" spiritual practitioner. But then he realized that neither extreme was the answer. A balance of self-care and self-restraint created the best circumstances for spiritual growth, contentment, and insight. A patient approach to gradual transformation was the most effective strategy.

The same applies to your recovery. In the beginning of the process, you have to focus on breaking the addiction. Working all Twelve Steps in the first week of recovery probably won't help. A wholesale overthrow of your life isn't wise. When you get clean you might realize that there are many problems in your life, issues around work, relationships, family, health, and more. But you can't fix them all at once. In fact, you probably aren't in the best condition to make any important decisions about your future except that you need to work a program and stay clean and sober.

Patience and restraint aren't typical qualities of most addicts, but those are the ones that we now need to develop. We can only work our program one day at a time.

Today, notice any habits of overdoing and over-efforting in your recovery. Are you trying to rush the process? Ask yourself what you can do today to build a solid base of recovery and what can wait. It's also wise to talk with a sponsor or trusted spiritual friend to help you gauge this.

# July 11

### *"The Momentum of Desire"*

"Our gut-level feeling when we have a desire for something is that when we get it, we'll be satisfied, we won't want it anymore. And, while that makes sense logically, the law of karma, cause and effect, works differently in most cases. Instead of satisfaction, getting what we want conditions us to want more. The most obvious case of this is the addict or alcoholic. Does having a drink satisfy our craving? On the contrary, it excites our craving. That's the whole idea behind the phrase, 'One drink is too much, and a thousand isn't enough.' The Buddha understood this. When Mara the Temptor told him he should turn a mountain into gold, he said, 'And were that mountain all of yellow gold, twice that is not enough for one man's wants.' Craving breeds craving. Giving in to craving breeds more craving." *One Breath at a Time*, p. 169.

This truth, which is essentially the Second Noble Truth, is so counterintuitive that even when we understand it intellectually, it's very difficult to live by. The monastic life is built around an understanding that if I restrain my actions, if I limit how much I act on desire, that desire will decrease and have less power over me. The same thing applies to the person in recovery. When we go without acting on our addiction for a while, it tends to lose its power. Many people find that all craving for drugs and alcohol disappears.

Once again, though, we need to keep this insight in balance. If we try to become perfect Buddhists and restrain all desire, we likely will just suppress craving until it bursts out in a binge. Letting go of desire needs to be a natural, healthy response to our insight into its harmful potential. But desire itself isn't "bad," and acting on basic wishes isn't harmful. With wisdom and compassion, we begin to find a comfortable place of non-destructive living that allows for healthy desires and restrains harmful ones.

Today, begin to notice your relationship to desire. Do you act on every one? Are there some you could restrain? How does it feel when you let desire go?

# July 12

### *"Karma and the Precepts"*

Beseeching the Law of Karma with our actions is most directly done by aligning our behavior with the Five Precepts of Non-Harming. By making a commitment to live in harmony with these basic moral guidelines, our life changes in big ways and small. Adopting the Fifth Precept, to abstain from intoxicants, is what put us most firmly on the path of recovery. While many (at least Western) Buddhist practitioners seem to take this precept lightly, for those of us in recovery, it's the key to everything.

Other precepts might have less radical, but equally important effects. When we cease lying, we gain trust from those in our life. When we speak more kindly in general, we reduce conflict.

When we cease sexual misconduct, relationships change significantly, and true intimacy becomes more possible. When people know we won't steal from them and that we are not violent, they tend to trust us.

Following the precepts has outer effects like these, but the internal effects are just as important, if not more so. Self-esteem grows as we gain integrity. And knowing we are innocent of wrongdoing gives us inner joy. As we've talked about, the Buddha calls this "the bliss of blamelessness."

The sense of safety that comes with this way of living supports the deepening of serenity in meditation. This is the practical benefit of living skillfully. Westerners who neglect the precepts might not realize that the agitation in their meditation practice is often rooted in their lifestyle. This is one reason people in recovery have a head start in their meditation practice.

Today, reflect on your relationship to the Five Precepts. Consider where you are more committed and less committed. Consider cultivating more commitment where you come up short. You might also choose one Precept at a time to focus on, bringing more reflection and mindfulness to that area of your life.

# July 13

*"Elements of Cultivating Meditation"*

"Here's one way of encapsulating meditation: we need to relax, while staying alert; pay close attention to our moment-to-moment experience without judgment, grasping, or resistance; and we need to sustain our attention long enough to become deeply settled in the present moment. Blending relaxation and alertness is the realm of Right Effort; paying attention without judgment is the realm of Right Mindfulness; sustaining the attention and effort is the realm of Right Concentration. So, we can see that these three aspects of meditation aren't separate and in fact won't create real change without interacting." *Workbook,* p. 154.

People often think of Right Effort, Right Mindfulness, and Right Concentration as separate aspects of practice. They might ask how to stay awake during meditation, how to deal with pain in the body, or how to stop thoughts from disturbing their meditation. These are questions of effort. But they can't be separated from questions of mindfulness and concentration because in order to deal with sleepiness, pain, or thoughts, we need to be mindful and to sustain that mindfulness.

Sometimes mindfulness is characterized as passive acceptance of whatever is arising in our mind or body, but it's not always skillful to just "let it be." Sometimes we need to act or arouse engaged activity—make an effort—to respond to what we see with wisdom.

Finally, many meditators seek out the pleasure and peace of concentration with no particular interest in the insights that come with mindfulness. While beneficial, concentration without mindfulness limits the great potential that Buddhist meditation offers. Without mindfulness and an engaged effort, concentration can, in fact, be used like a drug, as an escape from life, rather than an opening into life.

We can see, then, that developing Right Effort, Right Mindfulness, and Right Concentration together is the most effective way to learn meditation and to derive the most benefit from a meditation practice.

Today, reflect on these elements of meditation, and consider which ones need to be strengthened.

# July 14

*"Sitting Like a Mountain, Melting Like Snow"*

In establishing our posture, a good image is sitting like a mountain, grounded, stable, immoveable. This gives us a sense of stability and helps the mind to settle. In a sense, the busyness of the mind stands out in contrast to the stillness of the body, allowing us to see and let go of the more persistent thoughts. Making a commitment to sit absolutely still forces us to be present for the restlessness and resistance that makes us want to move.

At some point, though, sitting like a mountain can become stressful or forced. That's when we want to relax. Here we can bring the image of melting like snow, imagining all the stress and effort flowing down through the body into the earth. Without actually moving, we sense the solidness of the body dissolve into a pool of ease and calm.

We blend these two images of strength and release to create a balance in our meditation. This mirrors the two elements of effort and relaxation that make for an effective practice. As we work with these images, we track the balance between the two: when the mountain image brings too much effort and constriction, we turn to the melting snow; when too much relaxation makes us drift off, we bring back the strength of the mountain.

Today work with these two images, practicing strength and release in tandem.

# July 15

## *"How We Let Go: Mindfulness"*

Over the next four days, we'll look at the methods of practice that lead to letting go. We begin with mindfulness since this is the basis of all Buddhist practice.

As we practice mindfulness, we are seeing our experience directly. A great deal is revealed that had previously been hidden or beneath our awareness. We see how thoughts create stress, anger, anxiety, and frustration. We see the belief systems, habitual reactivity, and stories that we use to define ourselves.

Through this seeing clearly, we begin to let go. We try to release counterproductive reactivity, like anger or fear. We let go of beliefs that are revealed as irrational. We let go of stress simply by relaxing when tension arises. We even let go of ideas about who we are, as mindfulness reveals the layers of conflicting identity that underlie these views.

Mindfulness lets us step out of this barrage of thoughts and feelings into the space of simply knowing. This allows us to escape the forces of compulsion that drive so many actions. It shows us exactly what we are holding onto, which is the prerequisite to any kind of letting go.

Today, bring mindfulness to bear on clinging. See if it can help you to let go in the very moment of seeing.

# July 16

*"How We Let Go: Concentration"*

The term concentration is somewhat confusing when applied to Buddhist meditation. While this can sometimes refer to a narrowly focused, laser-like attention, concentration, or Samadhi, it often refers to something more subtle and spacious. The most obvious symptom of deepening concentration appears in the body with a sense of grounded stillness and peace. As this state arises, much else falls away. Although thoughts might still be present, they don't have the same hold on us. The hindrances are largely subdued.

When the mind and body settle in this way, we discover that much of what distresses us is created internally. Remarkably, problems recede, anxiety falls away, mood lifts, and all feels well in the world. And all of this happens only because of a shift in mind state, a shift toward inner quiet. For the addict who has lived a life filled with agitation and struggles with just being in a body, this experience is a revelation, and brings an enormous sense of relief.

Ordinarily we think that letting go requires going right at a problem and figuring it out or developing a directed strategy to let it go. But when we enter a deep state of concentration, we realize that rather than focusing externally to solve problems, we can focus internally, healing *ourselves* instead of "solving" the problem. The insight that comes with this revelation can change the whole way we approach life. Now, instead of always looking for ways to control or fix the world, we simply see if we can fix our attitude toward it.

Concentration has a deeply healing quality to it. It's like whole-body, non-verbal therapy. After a deeply concentrated session of meditation, we feel cleansed, and the world looks brighter and more friendly. Nature seems more alive, beauty revealing itself in the smallest things.

Today, enjoy the benefits of concentration in your meditation. Even if you aren't deeply concentrated, see if, at the end of your session you can detect any shift in feeling and perception.

# July 17

*"How We Let Go: Love"*

"The cultivation of love and compassion is one of the practices that directly engages our negativity and helps us to let go. While mindfulness has a neutral quality, just seeing things as they are and allowing that awareness to organically help us to let go, the practice of love and compassion is engaged in intentionally developing positive qualities."
*Burning Desire*, p. 199

Love is a natural human emotion, but it often gets lost amid life's stresses, struggles, and traumatic wounds. In Buddhist practice, we address this loss directly by looking at the hardened heart and learning to soften. The initial work, then, is to confront the stuck places in us, to feel them, and to breathe into them. Then we begin to reflect on different people, offering them love with metta phrases.

As we work with the dear ones in our life, we come to realize that this specific, personal love has its roots in something more universal. This then opens the door to the broader spreading of metta to neutral and difficult people. Now we are moving away from a love based on personal preferences to an unconditional love. We let go of grudges and resentments and begin to feel the interconnection and interdependence of all beings.

Cultivation of love and compassion has these multiple dimensions: letting go of armoring, of anger, of ego, and the sense of separateness. Along with these forms of letting go comes the growth of caring, of generosity, and connection.

Today, reflect on how much you let love guide you. Do you appreciate your dear ones? Can you touch into the sense of connection with all beings? Are you willing to cultivate a broader and deeper love for others and for life itself?

# July 18

*"How We Let Go: Contemplation"*

While much of Buddhist practice encourages us to let go of thinking, contemplation, or inquiry, gives us a way to think skillfully. To effectively work with contemplative practices, we need to have developed a strong mindfulness and concentration practice first, so that we can stay on topic and notice when the mind has wandered. Contemplation, then, comes out of this place of clarity and serenity, when we turn the attention toward a spiritual question.

With contemplation, we are stepping back and looking at the big picture, seeing things through the lens of dharma. From this point of view, we try to avoid biased, reactive, and conditioned views to get at the root of a question. It's this kind of inquiry that leads to real insight and understanding. We see suffering and its causes; we see the pervasiveness of impermanence; we see the workings of karma; and we see how interdependence ties us all together.

With these and many other insights, contemplation loosens the hold of delusion and grasping. We penetrate into the deeper truths of life, of reality, no longer under the sway of the myths and illusions that society perpetuates. And finally, with this newfound clarity comes letting go.

Any meaningful transformation must include contemplation and inquiry. It is this deep reflection that brings home the truths we uncover in meditation. To fully understand and integrate the dharma into our lives we must develop a practice of contemplation.

Contemplation can be applied to universal topics like impermanence, suffering, love, or not-self. It can also be applied to more personal inquiries. Always begin a period of contemplation with some calming meditation. As you engage the topic, carefully monitor the digressions of mind.

Today consider your own practice of contemplation. Begin to experiment with intentional thought and careful reflection.

# July 19

*"The Karma of Thoughts"*

The Buddha famously said that, "Whatever one frequently thinks and ponders upon, that will become the inclination of their mind." It makes sense: if we focus on something a lot, naturally enough it will keep popping up in our thoughts. This is the essence of karma: while actions bring results, so do thoughts. Repeated actions become habits and addictions; repeated thoughts become habits and obsessions. It is for this reason that we want to watch our thoughts and learn to let go.

When we learn to meditate, one of the first things we see is how persistent our thinking is. No matter how we try, the thoughts just seem to keep streaming through. If we spend our time trying to shut them down, we'll likely just become more and more frustrated. But if we turn our attention to the content of the thoughts, we'll learn something. Now we'll begin to see more clearly what we "frequently think and ponder upon."

It can be surprising and even upsetting to start to get insight into our habits of mind. Just seeing how trivial so many of our thoughts are is deflating. We aren't the disciplined, thoughtful people we thought we were. Then when we see the negative habits, the judgments, the cravings, the resentments, the fears and jealousies, it can become truly disturbing. For addicts, this is particularly true. Just as the inventory process surfaces our past mistakes, the meditative process reveals our destructive thought patterns.

This is the moment when we need to do three things: dis-identify (not take it personally), let go, and replace the negative with something more positive. This is the work in front of us, the work of a lifetime.

The beginning of this process is the clear seeing.

Today, start to track your thoughts more closely. Notice the negative habits of mind. Tomorrow we'll talk about dis-identifying.

# July 20

### *"Dis–identifying with Thoughts"*

In the recovery world, our personal story is the starting point of our journey. We share our stories as a way of establishing connection and revealing ourselves with rigorous honesty. Coming to see how our behavior over the course of years brought us to full-blown addiction and eventually a bottom is an important part of establishing clarity in Step One. But that story can also become an albatross we carry around our necks. It comes to define us and limit our self-understanding. We become so identified with our story that we can't let go.

Buddhism suggests another way of understanding ourselves. It tells us that the events of our life do not define us, that our story of addiction and recovery is just that: a convenient way of viewing a series of events. While this story is useful in a functional way because it has given us a route out of the cycle of addiction, it doesn't mean that's who we really are.

When we learn to meditate, we begin to examine our story. We see that it is made up of thoughts, and that thoughts are unreliable. They come and go; they are conditioned by moods, experiences, and circumstances. We have thoughts that we don't like, that we don't even want to have. Finally, we come to see that we are not our thoughts. This realization opens up a new perspective in which we can view thoughts dispassionately, seeing them as simply words and images appearing in the mind. No longer a slave or victim to our thoughts, we can choose which thoughts to follow and which ones to set aside. This is the power of mindfulness to transform us.

Today, notice the unreliability of thoughts. Begin to sort out which thoughts are credible and which ones are simply conditioned beliefs. Practice letting go of negative and destructive thoughts.

# July 21

## *"Letting Go of Thoughts: Replacing"*

Many times, simply by seeing a thought, it disappears—we let it go. But when thoughts are more persistent and distressing, the Buddha offers a set of responses that can help. Over the next few days we will explore some of them.

The first of these responses is called "replacing." Here, when we see, for instance, an angry thought, we might replace it with a loving one; an anxious thought with a calming one; a sad one with something uplifting. That might sound simplistic, and, in fact, it probably won't be very effective if just done mechanically. There are some other elements to this process that help it to work.

First, of course, we must *see* the thought, bring mindfulness to it, not be swept away. As long as we are not mindful of thinking, it will just go on like a background processor, churning out words and images that keep us under their spell. Secondly, we need to bring awareness to the painful or destructive nature of such thoughts. If we think that our difficult thoughts are useful or meaningful, it will be harder to let them go. Seeing how destructive they are will motivate us to let them go. Further, we have to understand that thoughts are not facts but simply ideas. When we live under the illusion of thoughts' reality, it's as though we were in a hypnotic state, simply responding to the orders that appear in our mind. When we see through this illusion, it weakens the power of thoughts to keep us under their sway.

With this foundation for letting go, when we have a thought of anger and see it clearly, we can intentionally bring loving-kindness to mind. With an anxious thought, we might try to bring a broader perspective on what safety really is; in Buddhism, it is dharma, the truth, that is our true protector. And with sad or depressing thoughts, remembering impermanence can help; just seeing that our present-moment mind state is temporary can help us to avoid despair.

Today, begin to work with replacing thoughts. Experiment with different strategies to see what works for you.

# July 22

*"Letting Go of Thoughts: Seeing the Danger"*

Another strategy the Buddha suggests for letting go of unwholesome thoughts is to see where they are leading and to recognize their potential consequences. For an addict this can be a helpful reminder of the risks in following a craving or obsession. Knowing the trouble we can get into, and knowing that thoughts lead to actions, we realize that we need to let go.

The Buddha compares this to a young, attractive person discovering that they are walking around with a dead carcass around their neck. This suggests not only the foul nature of the thought, but that we might imagine how we'd feel if people could see our inner thoughts.

Such a radical image might not have much appeal, but it points to how the Buddha thinks of shame. While in our culture shame is seen in mostly negative terms as a form of humiliation, the Buddha talks about shame more in the sense of conscience. When we say someone "has no shame," we are talking about the same thing: that they don't feel bad about their harmful behavior.

We need to find a balance between accepting our humanness, *not* being ashamed, and being careful that we aren't following destructive cravings and resentments. When we write inventory, we are cataloguing the "danger," the carcasses we've carried around. In Step Seven we are learning to let go of those dangerous thoughts and tendencies, without judging or blaming ourselves for having them.

Today, notice the unhelpful and harmful thoughts that arise and see if you can make a habit of letting them go.

# July 23

*"Letting Go of Thoughts: Calming"*

As we develop skill and flow in our meditation practice, we can learn to settle our thoughts in a gentle way. Here we use the breath to calm the body little by little. The Buddha describes a person who is running and decides to walk; then going from walking to standing; from standing to sitting; and finally, from sitting to lying down. In the same way, we internally slow ourselves down.

For this practice, allow the breath to be deep and slow, letting the body relax on the exhalation. The distracting thoughts might be running in the background, but in the foreground you just have a sense of settling deeper and deeper. The body feels as if it's being drawn downward into the earth. Everything seems to slow down.

This, then, is an antidote to restlessness or anxiety. It gives us a sense of agency in our own mind/body state. We see that we don't have to be swept away by such feelings if we stay present and work against them.

For the addict who has lived in a reactive mode, this provides a way out. We don't have to stay caught on the treadmill of craving. Instead we can actively work to overcome negative thoughts and energies through calming mind and body. Where we might previously have viewed our mind with fear or aversion, we start to gain more confidence in our own capacity to be present for difficult states.

Today, work with calming mind and body through intentional breathing and visualizing.

# July 24

*"Equanimity"*

Equanimity appears in several of the Buddhist teaching lists: the fourth Brahmavihara, the seventh Factor of Awakening, and the fourth Jhana. It's a subtle concept, often misunderstood. It describes a balanced, non-reactive state of mind, one with clarity and insight.

Equanimity is both an effect of practice and a support thereof. As you quiet the chattering mind and still the anxious heart, you become less reactive, more peaceful. With that calm inner state, and without the emotional push and pull of ego and bias, comes the capacity to look at the world with wisdom.

Our reactivity is conditioned by *vedana*, the pleasant, unpleasant, or neutral feeling tone of any sense perception or mental state. It's *vedana* that triggers craving and aversion. If we can see *vedana*, be with it and interrupt it as a triggering force, we will experience equanimity. Instead of finding ourselves caught in craving or aversion, we will be undisturbed, even as we are aware of how these perceptions feel.

Equanimity is sometimes thought of as a detached numbness, but this doesn't capture its actual effect. In fact, with equanimity we are more fully aware because we aren't running toward or away from our experience, but standing firm, awake and present. We experience the fullness of each moment, free of the clinging and aversion that usually accompany it.

Equanimity is both an attitude and a mind/body state. We can develop an attitude of equanimity, which is some of the vital work of Buddhist practice; we can't, however, hold onto the state, since all states are impermanent.

Today, reflect on the attitude of equanimity and how you could bring it more into your life.

# July 25

*"Freedom"*

In our culture, we have the notion that freedom means you can say anything you want, go anywhere you want, do anything you want. But this kind of freedom is really the lack of responsibility. True freedom is found in our inner life, not in the outer world.

For an addict, freedom means not being enslaved by a drug, drink, food, behavior, or obsession. When we were caught in our addiction, we had to have our drug of choice. We were trapped in a cycle of craving with no way out. We often lived irresponsible lives, thinking that we were free because we didn't have to answer to anyone. Eventually, though, this thread played out, and its true nature was revealed: the cage we were locked in became more and more apparent.

When freed from the cycle of addiction, we found a new definition for freedom. No longer dependent on substances or behaviors, we were able to make healthier choices based on our values, on the needs of others, and on the wisest path forward in our lives. Our outer world might look more constricted, with responsibilities of work, school, family, and relationships, but inside there was peace. This is the freedom of recovery.

Freedom from a Buddhist viewpoint is much the same, but with even more emphasis on the inner world and the mind. The Buddha sees us trapped by our own minds—our greed, hatred, and delusion—the cycle of ego and craving that's never fulfilled. As long as we keep trying to wrest satisfaction for our craving, we'll forever be frustrated. When we finally give up this search, we find that freedom lives right here, right now in the peaceful, loving, and wise heart. There's nowhere we need to go, nothing we need to acquire. Rather, freedom comes from letting go.

Today reflect on how free you are and how much you are still imprisoned by your own craving.

# July 26

### *"Perfection"*

It's easy to turn meditation and recovery into pursuits of perfection. While it's possible to be perfectly clean and sober, very little else about these paths can be perfected. If we try to work a perfect Twelve Step program, we will inevitably be frustrated. Step Seven is a good case of this, where we discover that we simply can't permanently remove all our shortcomings. We are bound to make mistakes in life, to slip into bad habits or old ways of thinking, speaking, or acting. This is why humility is so important in our program. We need to always remind ourselves that we aren't perfect, and that that's okay.

The same applies to Buddhism and meditation. It doesn't really make sense to try to be a "perfect Buddhist." Since suffering and impermanence are seen as inevitable, how could we hold on to some perfect state? And what would perfect meditation even look like? No thoughts? What's the point of that?

No, perfection isn't the point. Ongoing engagement and vigilance is a better goal. Maintaining Right Intention is a reasonable aim. These all suggest being present, which is the fundamental commitment of our practice. Striving for some imagined perfection is actually the road to more suffering. With that as a goal we will always fall short, become frustrated, and end up judging ourselves.

A newcomer to sobriety or to Buddhism is more likely to fall into this trap than someone who has been around for a while. With the excitement of beginning, one can imagine realms of perfection, that some magical transformation is going to happen. With time, the repeated challenges of the path reveal the more complex reality that all we can do is take care of today, do our best, and let go of the results. While this may feel like surrender, it actually grows out of the wisdom that experience gives.

Today notice any tendencies toward perfectionism. Do you have unreasonable expectations about yourself or about the path? Consider what more sensible goals might look like.

# July 27

*"Letting Thoughts Come and Go"*

For addicts, "stinking thinking" is a particularly persistent problem, both in our addiction and in our recovery. To confront and abandon these thoughts will often require a strong effort. However, not all thoughts are that destructive. In our meditation, many of them may be simple distractions that can be managed with subtler means.

Thoughts are sometimes described as clouds passing through the mind. What this points to is how ephemeral and transitory thoughts can be. While troubling and sticky thoughts usually require us to apply active measures in order to let go, less difficult thoughts can often be allowed to simply come and go.

One way to think of this is that you have the breath in the foreground of awareness, while thoughts and images pass by in the background. As you sit and focus on the breath, try not to be bothered by thoughts. If you don't react to them, you won't be feeding them. As long as no really strong thoughts of desire or aversion take over, you'll be able to settle and stay with the breath in a comfortable way over time.

Because meditation is often portrayed as "stopping thoughts," it can be difficult at first to make this shift in perspective. You might think you're "doing it wrong," that if there are any thoughts in the mind you are failing. But this is not the right understanding. Thoughts have a life and energy of their own. If left alone, they tend to peter out. (Again, this doesn't apply to particularly distressing thoughts.)

Today, begin to experiment with letting thoughts simply arise and pass away. Don't struggle to stop thoughts; just let them run down on their own.

# July 28

*"Energy and Mindfulness"*

On retreat one discovers the importance of energy in meditation. As we bounce from sluggishness to restlessness, it can seem as if it's impossible to find a balance between these extremes. Sleepiness makes it almost impossible to be mindful, and agitation destroys any concentration.

These two energies undermine recovery as well. Without energy, we easily fall into states of negativity, depression, and despair. With restlessness we can't sit still or focus, caught in obsessive worries and regrets. Either of these states can trigger relapse.

Energy, then, is a vital factor in our recovery and spiritual work. How to create it?

Tomorrow we'll look at the physical factors, but today we can discuss the mental ones. Mindfulness, it turns out, has an energetically balancing quality. That is, if we practice mindfulness persistently, our energy will tend to come into a healthy state.

We discover this on retreats when beset by alternating attacks of sleepiness and restlessness. If we stay with the schedule of sitting and walking meditation, while continuing to apply mindfulness to all other activities as well, soon we'll find that the pendulum of energy stops swinging so widely. This can seem somewhat mysterious, but, again, it's the power of mindfulness that does this.

When we have this experience on retreat, we learn skills that can be applied at home. We start to see how energetic states affect moods, and we become less reactive to those swings. Mindfully working with different energies becomes a regular part of our daily life.

Today, notice how energy is affecting your attitude and mood. Bring mindfulness to those experiences as much as you can.

# July 29

### *"Energy and Health"*

Working with energy isn't just a matter of applying mindfulness. We also need to take care of our bodies. Sufficient rest, healthy diet, and a solid exercise routine all support the maintenance of energy. And yet, all three of these can be difficult to accomplish.

A culture of overwork permeates our society, making fatigue a common problem for many people. With a busy life, even having enough time for sleep becomes an issue. Then, even when there is enough time, the stress that comes with overwork and personal problems can cause sleeplessness. Meditation can help with this as it reduces stress, both physically through relaxing the body and mentally by letting go of thoughts.

Diet is a vital piece of health and energy as well. As addicts we often neglected healthy eating—or eating at all—so in recovery we need to learn new habits. If food is our primary addiction, this becomes a central part of our recovery. But even if food isn't our primary problem, maintaining a healthy diet takes a commitment. With busy lives, just finding time to shop, cook, and sit down to eat can be challenging. If finances are an issue, we have to be thoughtful about how we shop and the choices we make. All of this means taking diet seriously, not as just a side issue in our lives.

Knowing how exercise can protect against depression and anxiety is a motivator to set up a healthy routine. Here again, time and priorities come into play. Getting outside or to the gym stimulates energy. At the same time, exercise, like diet, can actually be part of our addiction, so finding healthy ways to use our body without overdoing it is another challenge. Mindfulness helps us to be more conscious of how our body is handling exercise.

Today, reflect on how you are taking care of your health and energy. What areas are working, and which ones need more attention?

# July 30

*"Daily Kindness"*

In the busyness of our daily lives it's easy to lose touch with our wish to be kind. The stresses of traffic, work, maintaining our home, family and personal relationships can create an ongoing sense of inner turmoil that subsumes our intention. If we aren't paying attention, we can suddenly find ourselves snarling at other drivers, ignoring people we pass on the street, and generally feeling agitated. Making a commitment to kindness can help us to counterbalance these tendencies.

You can set up simple intentions to carry this out. When walking down the street, keep your head up and look at people as they approach you. If they meet your eyes, you can smile and greet them. If they avoid your eyes, you can send a brief "May you be happy" metta phrase to them.

Bring this attitude into interactions in stores, cafés, restaurants or anywhere you encounter strangers. Smiling and fully acknowledging people tends to create a warm, positive mind state for both parties.

When we start looking at people, really looking, we might also see their stress and suffering. It's striking how our faces reveal our pain. Tension, sadness, and anxiety come out in people's eyes, in the set of their mouth and jaw, in the slump of their shoulders or the dreariness of their gait. When we see suffering, we can work at opening our heart with compassion. It's hard to look at suffering, but ignoring it simply shuts us off from the fullness of life.

Seeing suffering in this way can be counterbalanced by observing joy—a playful puppy, a smiling child. If we open our eyes, we discover the joys of life all around us. Taking time to soak in these moments uplifts our day, helping us to keep a bright, appreciative attitude.

Today cultivate daily kindness and awareness of all the joys and sorrows you encounter. Notice how intentional kindness and appreciation can uplift your interactions with others.

# July 31

### *"Spiritual Awakening"*

With the spiritual awakening of Step Seven comes the realization that true transformation is possible. The seemingly permanent qualities that kept us stuck in our addiction now begin to shift and change. We don't have to be slaves to our craving or to our emotional swings.

While the language of Step Seven tells us that God will remove our shortcomings, the actual experience of the Step is that our own effort in cooperation with the Law of Karma does the work. We can't expect divine intervention, or even chemical intervention, to save us or make our lives work better. We need to show up, day-by-day, week-by-week, and year-by-year, doing "the next right thing," for our lives to change.

Implied in this, then, is patience. This is a quality in short supply for addicts. We want it now, on demand—whatever it is. But as we awaken, we learn that spiritual growth has its own timetable. While we might think that thirty days of sobriety is an accomplishment, we soon realize that the work before us will be measured in years, not days. This is one of the reasons people track and celebrate anniversaries of recovery: they point to the long-term work before (and behind) us.

Another awakening in this Step is the sense of freedom that comes as we find ourselves less ruled by our "character defects" and "shortcomings." A sense of ease and confidence comes over us. We see that we can face life without intoxicants, and that we have the capacity to grow and find happiness.

The final realization is that Step Seven is not a once-and-done process. This is where humility comes in. While the Step says that our shortcomings will be removed, they have a tendency to slip back in when we aren't watching. Although our lives may change drastically over the years of recovery, we must remain vigilant to these tendencies, and continue to do the work of addressing and letting go of our destructive and addictive thoughts, words, and actions.

Today, reflect on the ways you have awakened through Step Seven.

# AUGUST: STEP EIGHT

*"Made a list of all persons we had harmed, and became
willing to make amends to them all."*

# August 1

*"The List"*

Step Eight throws us back to our inventory, back to facing up to our personal failings, our foolish and harmful actions, and the worst of our life of addiction. This means dredging up memories that we'd all prefer to bury forever. Yet the Steps suggest that buried memories are not dead. Like ghosts, they come back to haunt us if we don't fully face them and do our best to heal the wounds they have left.

There's a strong tendency when arriving at Step Eight to become concerned about Step Nine (if you haven't already started worrying about it). So, it's important to understand the purpose of Step Eight and how it differs from Nine.

The Step starts with the list. Here we will naturally look back at Step Four, which was inwardly directed at our "moral inventory." Step Eight moves the focus outward. We've gone from the personal to the social dimension of our lives. The Buddha emphasized the importance of harmonious relations with "Noble Friends." Without such connections we can have little peace and less support on our spiritual path.

At this point it becomes clear that our problems as addicts were wrapped up with our problems in relationship, whether familial, sexual, romantic, professional, or personal friendships. Even those of us who isolated in our addictive behavior did so because of our discomfort in social situations.

The list, then, opens up a range of reflections. Who did I tend to harm and why? What relationships triggered addictive behaviors? How did my addiction harm those relationships?

Perhaps not surprisingly, we may have forgotten people we harmed when writing a Fourth Step. Stay open to memories of harm so that the list can be as accurate as possible. As our recovery unfolds and clarity returns, a lot of the past tends to return.

If you have never done Step Eight, today begin to write your list. If you have already done the Step, reflect on the benefit you gained from creating the list and consider if there are any people who might have been left off.

# August 2

## *"Willingness"*

While making the list of those we have harmed is the prime action of Step Eight, willingness is the prime attitude. As we've seen, willingness is a central part of Twelve Step work, and here it holds a special place. The willingness to make amends doesn't mean that the amends will be made. Because of the boundaries of Step Nine, that we only make amends where possible and when it wouldn't harm people, we may never actually make amends to a fair number of people on our list. Of course, that shouldn't be used as an out, but it can make it easier to confront this work.

What does it mean to be "willing to make amends"? One way to approach this is to imagine the situation. Right away we'll feel the fear or resistance to facing the person we harmed. Using our mindfulness practice, we can breathe into those feelings, surrendering to and holding those feelings with kindness and gentleness.

If we consider intention to be the Buddhist corollary to willingness, we can reflect on who we want to be and how we want to live in the world. If we are living with the values of honesty and love that Buddhism and the Twelve Steps foster, then we will want to clean up our lives, to get straight with people we have harmed. We no longer feel comfortable with these skeletons in our closet. We want to bring them into the light and face them. Hopefully we will find forgiveness, if not from the other, at least within ourselves.

In fact, once we have become completely willing, once we've overcome the resistance and fear of facing our amends, the hardest work is over. It becomes possible to walk into the situation with clarity and love.

Today, reflect on your willingness to put people you have harmed on your list and to make amends. How fully have you embraced that attitude?

# August 3

## *"Practicing with Preferences"*

As meditation becomes a more integral part of our lives, we begin to recognize how different situations influence mind states in practice. Some people find it easier to meditate in a group setting where there is an agreed upon meditation period, removing the temptation to shorten the sit. The group experience has other effects as well. When we are with others it can give us more confidence in the practice, recognizing that many people find it beneficial, that we aren't alone in that regard. Some people even feel that there is some kind of energy created when a group meditates together.

Other people feel less comfortable in a group. Victims of abuse can feel unsafe closing their eyes around others. Some people feel claustrophobic when surrounded by other meditators. And there can be a sense of loss of control when you are expected to meditate until someone rings a bell.

Less troubling, but also frustrating, can be the sounds of people coughing or moving. Here's a tip: don't sit in the back of a meditation hall because latecomers and early-leavers will interrupt your practice.

Practicing alone has its advantages. You can sit as long as you like. You can pick your own time to sit. There's no one sneezing, coughing, or rustling around. On the other hand, practicing alone presents its own challenges. It's tempting to shorten the sit when no one else is around. And just getting yourself to meditate at all can be tough if there's no time frame or anyone to share the practice with.

Although you might have preferences between practicing with others or practicing alone, mindfulness suggests we simply notice these preferences and the way they make us feel. If we are going to establish an ongoing and effective meditation practice, we need to learn to practice under different conditions and work with whatever comes up.

Today, make note of your own preferences in terms of sitting with others. How do those preferences affect your experience in meditating?

# August 4

*"The Harm"*

Everyone makes mistakes in life. Everyone hurts others. However, addicts tend to make more mistakes and hurt more people than our fair share. Step Eight asks us to face this harm squarely. To finally take responsibility in this way is difficult. How are we to hold this pain?

Our first challenge is to recognize that self-pity has no place in this process. If we are taking responsibility, then we can't expect anyone to feel sorry for us. We're the ones who committed these harmful actions, no one else. While a sponsor and other recovering friends can understand and sympathize with our struggle, we have to hold this pain alone.

Our meditation practice gives us tools to feel pain without becoming overwhelmed. We learn to breathe into the painful feelings, not to run and not to succumb to despair. Pain is part of life, as the Buddha taught, and living with it is part of growing into maturity and balance.

In the recovery community, we also see that we aren't alone in the harm we've done. Knowing that others have done as much damage as we have doesn't relieve us of any responsibility, but it does put our actions in a larger context: we are neither the best nor the worst people. We are human and as such, imperfect.

Holding this harm means finding a balance between fully acknowledging our part and not wallowing in self-pity or self-hatred.

Today reflect on how you are holding the harm you have caused. Are you honest about what you've done, or do you avoid looking fully at your past? Do you have a balanced view of your actions or do you bury yourself in self-blame?

# August 5

*"Harming Ourselves"*

The thrust of inventory and amends work is the harm we've done to others, as it must rightly be. Taking responsibility for our actions is a necessary step in our recovery and our growing maturity. Our addiction was characterized by denial, blame, and avoiding honest self-appraisal. But it must also be recognized that in our addiction we harmed ourselves as well.

Just using intoxicants or living out addictive patterns causes us harm. The hangovers, the financial and professional mistakes, the damage done to relationships with family, friends, and partners, all this and more takes a toll on us. Nobody is going to feel sorry for us, given that we were the instigators of our own suffering. But in our healing process, we can still acknowledge the wounds we carry from our years of addiction.

These wounds can run deep and warp our lives in many ways. Our professional reputation might be harmed or destroyed; our savings might be gone; our family may have turned away from us. Internally, we may feel such shame and self-hatred that we find it difficult to rise out of despair. Thus, with Step Eight we must recognize that we ourselves belong on the list of those we harmed. We must make amends to ourselves.

Before we can begin such a process, we might have to overcome our doubt that we deserve such care. Didn't we bring all these problems on ourselves? Aren't we responsible for this mess? Of course, the answer to those questions is yes, but that doesn't mean that we can never be absolved of our mistakes or that we should live a life of misery. What is the point of that? What would that accomplish? In fact, we have a responsibility not to indulge in such negativity, which is really just another form of egotism, seeing ourselves as especially bad, more unworthy than anyone else.

Today, reflect on your own need for healing and care. Are you willing to make amends to yourself?

# August 6

## *"The End of Isolation"*

Bill Wilson tells us that Step Eight is the "beginning of the end of isolation," from people, and he says, from God. This speaks to the power of amends. To come out of the shadows and make the effort to clean up the mess we made of our lives can have a transformative effect. Perhaps it is because it's so unusual to encounter such honesty that people tend to respond very positively to such actions. This isn't to say that every act of amends will be met with smiles and pats on the back. Not at all. But the overall impact is almost invariably a positive one.

Shame and guilt kept us locked away from the world. Our fear of being caught, of people finding out the truth of our behavior, and further, of seeing the addicted animal in our hearts kept us at a distance. Our companions were often like us, on the run from life, from themselves, from the world. To turn and face the world with honesty and remorse opens the possibility of forgiveness and reconciliation.

This all must begin with willingness. Up to now we have been *un*willing—unwilling to face the truth, unwilling to admit our failings, and unwilling to take responsibility. When we finally surrender and make the decision that we must begin the process of making amends, we are, as Wilson says, at the beginning of the end of isolation. While there is a great deal of work ahead, we may have done the hardest part already, the internal shift that was so hard to accomplish.

From a Buddhist perspective, being isolated from God means we are not in touch with or living in harmony with the Dharma, the Truth. Living in delusion, we make choices based on Wrong View and Wrong Intention, and slide into the morass of addiction and despair. Ending that isolation means we get back in touch with our truest values and clearest vision of reality. Starting the amends process is a key part of this turning toward the Dharma.

Today, reflect on your own sense of isolation. Has your Step work brought an end to that or is there more work to be done?

# August 7

*"Attachment to Dear Ones"*

In one sutta a man comes to the Buddha in despair over his son's death. The Buddha uses this event to talk about how we suffer in relation to our attachment to others. He explains this somewhat counter-intuitive teaching by talking about how when those we love get sick or die, if they leave us or behave against our wishes, we experience "sorrow, lamentation, pain, grief, and despair."

What are we supposed to do when we hear this teaching? Does it mean we shouldn't form connections in our life? How is that even possible? Even in the monastic life monks develop close bonds with each other. Near the end of his life, the Buddha even talks about how he misses his dear friends who have died. So, the message doesn't seem to be "Don't form attachments," but rather that if we can accept reality, we won't suffer in the same way.

This points to the importance of wisdom and insight in Buddhist teachings. Much of life is out of our control. As we understand from the first Noble Truth, many forms of pain are inevitable. We are powerless over that fact. This is true about relationships as well. What makes the pain of loss manageable is our understanding. That understanding then can lead to acceptance and equanimity.

Addicts are probably more susceptible than others to experiencing a crisis after the loss of a dear one or the breakup of a relationship. In order to avoid relapse, we need to keep the wisdom of impermanence in mind.

When we can accept the truth of suffering, the truth that attachment leads to pain and a sense of loss, we are less disturbed. As the prayer says, when we accept the things we cannot change, we find serenity.

Today, begin to reflect on the challenges that come with your most important relationships. Can you accept those challenges without becoming lost in the pain of attachment?

# August 8

### *"Willing to Forgive"*

The difficulty of making amends is compounded by the fact that the harm went both ways: yes, we hurt people, but they hurt us as well. As we create our list, we might resist the idea of making amends to such people. It's easy to fall into blaming others and to overlook our own part. But Step work requires us to focus on our side of the street and put aside judging others.

And so, as we build the list, we consider the struggles and difficulties that may have led people to hurt us. Like us, they too have been wounded by life. Those wounds may have caused them to act unskillfully and unkindly. Recognizing that we too harmed others because of our own wounds, we become more willing to forgive. We develop compassion for those who hurt us.

The Buddha tells us that holding on to anger or resentment only causes us pain. By that logic, it makes no sense to hold back forgiveness. The feelings we carry within us are not felt by those we resent. We are the ones who suffer from our resentment. When we see this truth clearly, we are no longer so motivated to hold on to our anger. As the Buddha says, like someone who picks up a hot coal, upon recognizing this pain, we drop it.

Twelve Step work shows us that carrying resentments warps our whole attitude toward life. It drains our energy, undermines our happiness, and builds walls between us and others. As hard as it is, we must learn to forgive, to move on, to bring a new attitude to our life: one based in love, not hate; in kindness, generosity, and, yes, forgiveness. How can we expect others to forgive us if we are not willing to extend a hand to them?

Today, reflect on your own willingness to forgive. Have you learned to let go, or are you still holding on to resentments?

# August 9

*"Holding on to the Past"*

One of the great challenges of the inventory and amends Steps is the memories that are awakened for us. During our addiction, we often couldn't allow ourselves to recognize the nature of these events: the binges and hangovers, the conflicts with partners and family, the sleazy late-night behaviors, the lies, manipulation, and exploitation of others. When guided by the overriding principle of satisfying our own craving, many of us took actions in direct conflict with our values and beliefs, and now we have to look at it all. How are we to do that without falling into self-hatred, despair, or even relapse?

The first thing we can do is go to a meeting and hear other people's stories. This will at least assure us that we were not alone in our unwise, selfish, and unskillful behavior. We are not unique in our failings. This doesn't mean that we don't take what we did seriously. But letting the past swamp us now serves no good purpose. After all, now we are finally beginning to live with more integrity. We are ready to face the consequences of our actions, so we don't have to carry the past as a weight on our conscience.

The Buddha's teachings on the pervasiveness of suffering and craving remind us that we are all imperfect, conditioned to act out of selfish impulses. We are not unique in this.

If we are to move forward and be of service in the world, we must find a way to love and forgive ourselves, to bring compassion to our failings, as Buddhism encourages. If we look deeply into our past, we'll likely see that we were always driven by our own wish for happiness, that the child in us only craved love, care, and attention. While we certainly did harm in the world, we ourselves were wounded, perhaps by others, or perhaps just by life, the genetic or emotional cards that were dealt to us.

Finding a balance between taking responsibility for our past and not being crushed by it is a vital part of the inventory and amends process.

Today, reflect on your relationship to your past. Are you able to hold the memories of your past harmful actions with honesty, compassion, and acceptance?

# August 10

### *"Arousing Positive Energy"*

Joy is one of the Factors of Awakening. It can be helpful to make a conscious effort to arouse pleasant feelings in our meditation practice. Otherwise meditation can become dry and uncomfortable as we watch the Hindrances arising in our mind and body.

Start with a smile. Bringing a slight smile to the lips tends to brighten the mood and soften the heart. As you sit, feel the breath, relax, settle if you can, and gradually let the pleasant feeling of the smile radiate outwards.

With a sense of openness and surrender, see if you can feel the energy in the body as a positive, enjoyable sensation. Life is energy, and the body runs on the energy of the nervous system, the movement of blood, and the constant replenishment of oxygen. All of this can be felt as bright, living energy. As we smile and tune into this life force with a sense of curiosity, we can develop a buoyant, spacious mind state.

Feeling this mood in the body, we can bring a reflection of gratitude. Gratitude for life itself, for this amazing organism that sustains us; gratitude for the mysterious consciousness that allows us to see it all unfolding.

Sit with this open, bright, joyous feeling. Take pleasure in the richness of the senses, the fullness of human experience.

Once you've sustained this feeling for a few minutes of meditation, see if you can calm the body and mind, and sit with a more settled feeling.

After your meditation period, try to carry some of this positive energy into your day.

# August 11

*"Not-self"*

Both recovery and the dharma talk about the problem of self. In the recovery world the focus is on selfishness and self-centeredness, whereas the Buddha questions the whole idea of a separate self.

The word the Buddha used was "anatta," which has the root meaning of "no soul." But what the Buddha seems to be talking about is the mistaken sense that there is some permanent and fundamental core to our being. And instead of just stating outright that there is no such core, he points to all the things that it can't be.

Are you your body? No, he says, because your body keeps changing over time and eventually dies and rots. There's nothing permanent about that. Are you your thoughts? These, too, are changing all the time. There's no permanent thought, nothing to hold on to. He delves further by showing how consciousness itself is in flux. What we seem to arrive at is that it "feels" as if there is a self. The combination of having a body, a storehouse of memories, knowing other people and being acknowledged by them, and performing certain roles in the world all serve to create what's called a "functional self." This is the relative identity we operate in. When we step back and examine it, though, we see that it has no lasting substance, no stable reality.

What are we to do with this insight? Since the Buddha says suffering comes from clinging, what we can do is not cling to self, not cling to identity and roles. This is one of the routes to freedom on the Buddhist path. When we see our identity as fluid, we don't suffer so much when it is threatened. If we make a mistake or fail at something, we don't take it personally. And in the same way, when we succeed at something or get praise, we don't start thinking how wonderful we are. We accept and enjoy that experience, but we don't see it as affirmation of a fixed self.

Today reflect on your relationship to self. How do you suffer in your attachment to identify? How do you experience the freedom of non-attachment?

# August 12

*"Your Many Selves"*

With the insight into not-self comes another realization; namely that although we may have no fixed identity, we do take on many roles, many different selves. When we can see each of these clearly, we become less attached to any one of them.

For instance, if you have a job, you have an identity and role in that position. When you leave work, you are no longer that person. In your family, you might have multiple roles—for instance, mother, daughter, sister, partner, cousin, and aunt. With your friends you might be the joker or the one who holds the group together. If you have a hobby, you have that role as well. To different people, you might fill vastly different roles: neighbor, father, co-worker, partner, friend, sponsor, sponsee, newcomer, old-timer.

When shopping you are a customer; when in your car, a driver. On and on we can go, breaking down all the roles we play. We might move through our lives feeling as if we are ourselves, but if we look objectively, we see that none of those selves fully defines us.

Another one of the ways we define ourselves is through our past. We make a narrative of our lives by selectively remembering events and putting them in chronological order in our mind. When we get sober, this narrative tends to collapse. We realize that we had been dishonest with ourselves about who we were. We'd left out significant chunks of our lives so as not to undermine the sense of self that make us feel secure.

Admitting we are addicts is a huge shift in self-view. Suddenly the past looks very different; the story changes. Yet even now we must be careful that we don't become attached to another narrative, another idea of who we are. Even wholesome views of self carry risks.

Today, reflect on all the identities you have or have had in your life. Which ones do you cling to and which ones have less power to define you? Can you hold all of them more loosely? Which ones are the hardest to stop identifying with so strongly?

# August 13

*"Calming Breath"*

The breath has two major components: in-breath and out-breath. Each has an energetic quality. In yoga and other movement practices, the out breath is used to release tension and move deeper into the pose. With meditation, the out breath can have a similar effect. When meditating, if you notice an accumulation of either physical or emotional tension, you can use the out breath to calm body and mind.

Let the out breath be slow by subtly restricting the air as it leaves the nostrils. This may create an internal sound that can act as a reminder or indicator that you are intentionally relaxing. As you breathe out, feel the whole body releasing tension. Have a sense of tension moving downward through the body and into the earth.

Feel the shoulders soften and release; let the arms hang loosely; open the chest; breathe into and soften the belly.

The in-breath naturally slows as well. Feel the body filling with air, expanding, getting ready to release.

As you work with this practice, bring your attention to the belly and notice any anxiety or tension there. Open to this feeling and allow it to gradually grow quieter. Continue to soften the belly.

You can call on the calming breath anytime you feel the need. During a meditation period, you might start with calming, then go to a more natural mindfulness. Later you might find a building tension, and again call on the calming technique. There's no guarantee that this simple process will dispel all tension or anxiety, however, in many cases you will find that the release in the body results in the mind settling as well.

Today, use the calming breath at the beginning of your meditation and see how it affects the rest of your sitting.

# August 14

*"The Feeling Self"*

Our behavior and preferences are largely dictated by our reactions to pleasant, unpleasant, and neutral feelings (*vedana*). We are almost constantly moving toward the pleasant, away from the unpleasant, and unaware of the neutral. Our relationship to feeling then becomes one more way we define ourselves: "I'm a person who likes X, dislikes Y, and doesn't care about Z. That's who I am."

Just as a person might like one clothing brand, avoid certain foods, and not care about what kind of car they drive, these preferences start to look "real," substantive and meaningful. In fact, they are just conditioned responses. Our mind defines our preferences as facts: "These are good clothes, bad food, and boring modes of transport." But the very fact that other people can believe the opposite—hate those clothes, love those foods--shows that there is no absolute truth to feelings. There can't be two different absolute truths, which means they must be relative.

A primal force for each of us is seeking a life of pleasant *vedana*. Since this is not possible, the Buddha encourages us to change our relationship to feeling. Ultimately, we seek equanimity around *vedana*. We want to be aware of the range of feelings without creating attachment, without being caught in craving or ignorance.

When we sit in meditation, we are practicing being non-reactive, and this is a training in equanimity. Even though we might have an unpleasant feeling, we don't stop meditating; even though we feel happy and peaceful, we don't believe we've found the ultimate answer; and even though the breath is neutral, we don't stop paying attention to it. To find peace we must learn to be aware of feelings, accept them, and avoid grasping at them.

Today, notice feeling, *vedana*, as it arises and pulls you this way and that. See if you can step back and be less reactive or clinging.

# August 15

*"EcoDharma"*

Contemporary Buddhists with a concern for environmental issues have coined the term "EcoDharma." This comes out of an expanded understanding of the Five Precepts and reflection on the Buddhist idea of interdependence.

The first two precepts, not to kill and not to steal, have direct environmental implications. With human behavior leading to the extinction of many beings on the planet, the first precept suggests that we have a responsibility to protect these species.

The second precept, not to steal, is implicated in the developed world's exploitation of natural resources. These nations use far more than their fair share of the earth's treasures. Here the environmental movement intersects with social justice issues.

Our treatment of the environment is similar to the way an addict treats their body: we exploit it for our own pleasure with no regard for the long-term consequences. Our craving for wealth and comfort overrides any sense of responsibility or concerns for future generations. We live in the delusion that we are somehow separate from nature, not an integral part of it.

Seeing the broad-ranging effects of our individual and collective actions on the planet, we realize that we can't separate the personal from the political, the political from the moral. It's all connected.

EcoDharma points us toward personal behaviors as well as social and political responses. We try not to waste resources and reduce pollution. And we begin to support movements and leaders who understand the urgent need to change our relationship to the earth.

As we develop spiritually, our consciousness grows beyond just our personal experience and needs. We start to see ourselves as part of a larger story, just one organism in a vast network.

Today, reflect on the ways you can bring EcoDharsma into your life to help heal the planet. If you can, spend time in nature every day.

# August 16

*"Practice: Metta for the Earth"*

Just as recovery begins with a personal focus and moves toward "carrying the message" to others, so too does the Buddha's teaching on loving-kindness move from self, to other, and eventually to the whole world, including the environment.

Here is a practice for giving Metta to the earth. Slowly repeat these words in your mind, reflecting on their meaning and letting the feelings radiate outward. You can repeat the phrases two or three times to connect more deeply.

**Metta for the Earth**

Breathing into my heart, I feel my connection to the air and atmosphere all around me.

Breathing out of my heart, I radiate love to the atmosphere, seeing it protected and healed.

The sky is bright and blue; the air precious and pure.

Breathing into my heart, I feel my connection to the earth beneath me.

Breathing out of my heart, I radiate love down into the earth, seeing it protected and healed.

The earth is vibrant, green and fragrant with life.

Breathing into my heart, I feel my connection to the sea from which all life arises.

Breathing out of my heart, I radiate love to the sea, seeing it protected and healed.

The sea is clear blue, bright and shining.

I hold the entire planet and all living beings in my heart with love, care, and compassion.

May this planet be safe; may it be healed; may it be free from suffering.

Adapted from *Living Kindness: Buddhist Teachings for a Troubled World.*

# August 17

### *"Right Effort: Avoiding"*

When we first hear meditation instructions, to pay attention to the breath, we are often surprised to find that it's not that easy. As a result, we might start trying harder. But then we find that trying harder actually makes things worse. We get tense, start judging ourselves, feel frustrated, and begin to think we are no good at meditating. This is where Right Effort comes in.

Right Effort is part of the Noble Eightfold Path. The classical description of Right Effort describes four aspects: avoiding letting unwholesome states arise; letting go of unwholesome states that have already arisen; cultivating positive states that haven't arisen; and maintaining positive states that have already arisen. These are known as The Four Great Efforts.

While this is a very specific instruction, it doesn't really say anything about how to accomplish these tasks. How do I avoid, abandon, cultivate, and maintain?

Let's start with avoiding. For an addict in recovery, we need to avoid temptation, so we don't go to bars (if we're alcoholic) unless we have important business there. Likewise, a drug addict doesn't drop in on his dealer to reminisce about old times. A food addict doesn't hang around the ice cream parlor or leave unhealthy snacks on the kitchen counter. A gambler doesn't go to the casino.

In meditation this might not be so easy. How do we avoid thinking? Most of us can't. Perhaps if we are mindful enough, we can avoid letting our thoughts go in certain directions, more or less making a vow not to think about our ex or a resentment that's been nagging at us. When mindfulness is well-refined, you can actually feel the stirrings of a thought before it arises and avoid it.

Once the unwholesome thought arises, though, it falls into the realm of abandoning, tomorrow's topic. For today, begin to notice ways you can avoid falling into unwholesome or negative mind states, emotions, or thought patterns.

# August 18

## *"Right Effort: Abandoning"*

Once an unwholesome thought or mind state has arisen, we move to the second aspect of Right Effort: abandoning or letting go. To abandon requires first that we are aware of the unwholesome state, which means we must be mindful. For addicts, this is what Step One is about: understanding that we have a problem, that we have an addiction.

The key to letting go is awareness. In this case, awareness of the suffering you are experiencing by holding on. This is what eventually drives us to recovery, truly knowing and seeing the pain our addiction is causing us. So, applying this principle more broadly, if we pay attention to the pain of anger or the discomfort of craving, we will be motivated to let go.

Clearly this requires some reflection. If we believe that anger is justified or will help us accomplish something we want, then there won't be much motivation to stop pursuing it or acting on it. The same goes for craving. If we really believe that getting some thing, some experience, some relationship or anything else is going to bring some permanent answer to our problems, then we'll simply stay on that track. Buddhism, though, tells us otherwise. The Buddha's teachings say that anger just eats away at us, bringing no benefit. It's not that expressing our anger in constructive ways can't be worthwhile, but outbursts of rage accomplish nothing useful. And with craving, it's not that we shouldn't work toward a goal or acquisition, but that setting all our hopes on these things just creates a painful sense of tension and lack.

When we reflect on these ideas as well as paying attention to their real-time manifestation in the body and mind, letting go becomes easier. We let go because we don't want to feel that pain anymore.

Today, notice the thoughts and feelings that cause you pain and see if you can abandon them. Use the tools of practice to do this: mindfulness of breath, of feelings, and body; loving-kindness, compassion, and equanimity.

# August 19

*"Right Effort: Cultivating"*

With the third Great Effort we turn from the unwholesome to the wholesome. Now we are going to try to arouse some positive qualities. The simple act of applying awareness to the breath is, in fact, cultivating mindfulness. Other practices aim at cultivation as well, like loving-kindness and concentration practices.

In following the Buddha's way, we try to cultivate all the elements of the Eightfold Path, like Right Speech, Right View, and Right Intention. Cultivating is at the heart of dharma practice because it's founded in karma: taking action to develop the qualities that embody this path.

The Twelve Steps are also about cultivating qualities that transform. The spiritual awakening referred to in Step Twelve is the result of our efforts to cultivate new ways of being. And while the language of the Steps tells us that God is at the root of all this, a Buddhist view is that God refers to the power of the dharma, which rests in effort.

It must be said that while both Buddhism and the Twelve Steps offer tools and strategies for transformation, the process is neither simple nor automatic. We rarely find that we can just cultivate some quality and expect immediate results. This is where so many of us stumble. We feel as if we've done all the right things, checked all the boxes, and yet things don't work out as we'd planned. Here Step Three and the attitude it fosters can be a guide. When we "turn our will and our lives over to the care of" the dharma, we understand that we are not in control of the results of effort.

With Right Effort we learn to cultivate without expectation.

Today, reflect on what you are already cultivating in your life, what you might be wise to start cultivating, and how you handle the challenges and setbacks to cultivation.

# August 20

### *"Right Effort: Maintaining"*

Once we have cultivated some positive quality, habit, or capacity, we now need to try to sustain it. Here is where the challenging work begins. Like the New Year's resolution, the new diet, exercise plan, or meditation program, it can be easy to start something, but hard to keep it going over time.

With meditation, maintaining our practice is key to development. While we might have some powerful experiences on a retreat, consistent daily practice gives us something else, something indispensable. When we sit each day, we see the multitudes of mind states that make us up. We see the stress and fatigue; we see the anger and calm; we see the boredom and excitement. All of this shows up, day-by-day, month-by-month, year-by-year. Sitting through it—showing up and trying to be present—gives us perspective on what really makes up our mind and how to deal with the broad spectrum of experience.

Maintaining also applies to our commitment to the Precepts, to Right Speech, and to Right Action. Sila protects us. Lapses in sila can have wide-ranging, even damaging effects on our life and the lives of others. One moment of violence or sexual impropriety can tear down everything that decades of skillful action have built up.

Maintaining Right View means bringing wisdom into every situation. Remembering the Truth of Suffering and its causes frees us from unnecessary struggles with things we can't change. Remembering impermanence helps us walk through challenging moments since we know they *will* change. And keeping an attitude of compassion and loving-kindness brings peace and intimacy to our lives.

Today, reflect on the positive actions and qualities that you want to maintain in your life, in your practice, and in your recovery.

# August 21

### *"Maintaining Recovery"*

With recovery, spiritual maintenance may be the most important element of Right Effort. Because relapse is so prevalent for addicts, this aspect is the focus of much recovery work. The basic guidelines of going to meetings, getting a sponsor, and working the Steps can carry you through the initial years, which in and of itself is a significant accomplishment. Staying clean and sober longer requires even more effort, though not always in obvious ways.

What often seems to happen to people as they get deeper into recovery—say seven, ten, or more years—is that the initial motivation and excitement wears off. Then some kind of personal crisis arises, a divorce, illness, job loss, or death in the family. This puts extra stress on their program. Another common challenge is that people find that their spiritual understanding or growth evolves to a point that the language or literature of the Steps doesn't resonate anymore. Someone drawn to Buddhism can easily begin to question the God language or the classic message of redemption. Sometimes people just start to wonder if after all these years clean and sober they really have a problem anymore.

Any or all of these issues can break the back of recovery. In a single moment, like a trip to Wine Country, vacation on a cruise ship, or a festive wedding, we might pick up "just one glass of wine." A doctor prescribes opioids for post-surgery, and we wind up with a bottle of thirty by the bedside. We find ourselves turned off by meetings and decide we can do it on our own. We go on a meditation retreat and are convinced that meditation is our program now.

Ultimately, we all need to find our own path of recovery using whatever tools are available. That might mean lots of meetings, Step work, and sponsorship. Or it might look different from that. What is common to everyone who sustains their recovery for a long time is commitment. Some combination of spiritual tools is integral to their daily life. If we stop maintaining our recovery, we enter into a very risky situation.

Today, ask yourself what you are doing to maintain your recovery. What are the tools you are using?

# August 22

*"Wounds"*

Life wounds each one of us in myriad ways. Our dear ones die; we get sick; we're betrayed by a lover. We lose a job, fail at an enterprise, or suffer from bias or limited opportunities. Part of finding happiness and contentment in life is learning how to live with these losses and wounds. For addicts, these wounds are often deeper—and, sadly, self-inflicted.

When we first come into recovery, we might not be aware of the depth of pain, trauma, and wounding we carry beneath the surface. The numbness of addiction can carry over into early recovery, or perhaps we are so relieved to be free from those chains that we float free for a while. At some point—and this can certainly happen during the inventory or amends process—those wounds may resurface. This presents new challenges to our Step work and recovery. While the program asks us to focus primarily on the harm we have done to others, now we have to face the harm or personal pain that we experienced.

This presents another risk for relapse. As these raw spots are exposed, we can easily look to our old answers, seeking comfort in a bottle or a pill, in food or sex, desperate to escape the pain we have never confronted. If we are going to maintain our recovery, we will have to find a new way of living with these wounds.

Mindfulness meditation helps us develop the inner strength and balance needed to deal with our wounds. The essence of the practice is to sit, be still, and not run from whatever comes up in the mind or body. This teaches us a new way of relating to our experience. Instead of analyzing or trying to change things, we are breathing with them, allowing them space, and finding the inner capacity to hold them. This is the beginning of learning to be with our wounds.

Today, reflect on the wounds you carry. Are you learning to hold them with tenderness and compassion? Can you be with them without needing them to vanish?

# August 23

*"Feeling Fear"*

When approaching Step Eight it's natural to feel fear. We are on the verge of facing the people we harmed, trying to become willing to make amends, with no idea how that effort will be received. It's easy to see why someone would draw back from such a task.

What is it that we fear? It's unlikely any great harm will come to us from trying to make up for our mistakes. Instead, what we mostly fear is the shame and public humiliation of admitting our failings. We are afraid of the damage that will be done to our ego. But if we want to maintain our recovery, we have to be ready to accept this pain. We have earned that pain and must learn to bear it.

If we allow fear to hold us back, we will never to move forward with this work. Every big step in life presents risks, and as such, evokes fear. What we learn as we move through these challenges is that the fear itself is worse than the thing we fear. Fear is uncomfortable. Again, our practice of mindfulness comes to our aid. With mindfulness we learn to hold feelings without running or reacting. We can feel fear, yet still maintain enough balance and awareness to respond wisely.

The intense energy of fear can be used to sharpen our awareness. When these feelings come up, we breathe with them, sensing the nervous system activation they set off. If we can relax enough to take the edge off the fear, we'll find that we are awakened and enlivened by its energy.

Today, notice when fear arises. See if you can channel it into clarity and positive energy. The fear itself is not a problem. What matters most is meeting it wisely

# August 24

### *"Naming vs. Non-naming"*

Many traditional Vipassana meditation techniques involve naming experiences as they arise. We might name thoughts as "thinking," sounds as "hearing," sensations as "feeling." We might be more precise by naming thoughts "planning," "remembering," "judging," or whatever other form they take. The value of this practice is that it encourages us to be more precise in our noticing. Without naming, our mindfulness can become somewhat vague and distant. Naming emotions can be an important part of this—though it has risks.

Knowing what we are feeling—being able to understand that we are sad, angry, scared, or anything else—is an important part of recovery and emotional maturity. This is why therapists often emphasize this idea, so that people can become clearer about what is going on inside and why they are acting the way they are. Unraveling our emotional makeup and its roots is a vital part of psychological healing.

In meditation, however, we see the limits of this practice and its potential negative effects.

When we are meditating and we name a specific mood or emotion we've noticed, it might also trigger a corresponding reaction. This might be a judgment such as, "I shouldn't be feeling this fear/anger." It might be a fear such as, "Oh, no, I hope I'm not falling into another deep depression!" Now we've reified our experience, making it more solid. We see ourselves in a "state" something static, unmoving. This is the risk of thinking about our feelings.

Mindfulness asks us to simply feel emotions. We see that they are less solid or specific than any name we give them. When we stay on the felt level, without trying to categorize feelings, we experience them as energy: fluid, dynamic, and unnameable. They might be pleasant or unpleasant, but they don't carry the weight of "sadness" or "fear."

Today, see if you can feel your emotions without naming or judging them. How does this change your experience of your emotional life?

# August 25

### *"Naming Our Condition"*

Many people struggle with the idea of saying they are alcoholics or addicts, as is the tradition in Twelve Step meetings. There are various reasons for this resistance. Sometimes people simply don't feel that "alcoholic" accurately names their behavior, especially if they were periodic in their abuse. Others feel that it goes against the Buddhist idea of "not-self," that it's taking on an identity when Buddhism suggests we do the opposite, let go of identity. And some people feel that it unnecessarily stigmatizes them, as society can still do.

These are all legitimate concerns, but they miss the more important point. The idea isn't to take on an identity, to shame us or to define our exact behavior. We call ourselves alcoholics or addicts as a reminder of the problem we had with alcohol and drugs (food, sex, gambling, co-dependence, etc.) and of our need to avoid using them. If we are committed to living a clean and sober life, we need to put up a pretty strong wall around our addictive behavior because that addiction itself is powerful and will try to pull us back in. By fudging on our condition, claiming that "It wasn't that bad," or worrying about our self-image, we put a crack in that wall that can, over time, broaden enough to give us the idea that maybe we can have "just one." And just like that a relapse begins.

Ultimately, saying you are an alcoholic or addict in a meeting is not a diagnosis. Here's what it means: "When I was active in my addiction, I had problems, but I couldn't deal with them. Without that behavior, I still have problems, but now I can deal with them one day at a time." As Step One says, our lives were unmanageable. Recovery made them manageable. If that's not true for you, maybe you aren't really an addict—but be very careful before you make *that* diagnosis. It's a mistake many people have made, and a lot of them have died trying to prove they were right.

Today, reflect on your relationship to calling yourself an "alcoholic" or "addict." Is there resistance to those terms? Can you let go of that resistance and appreciate their value?

# August 26

*"The Practice of Non-naming"*

For this meditation, try to move out of the realm of words and thoughts, and into the direct perception of experience.

Begin by establishing your posture. Feel the body finding its balance and alignment. Come into stillness.

Scan the body for points of tension or discomfort, and relax and release through those points.

Feel the whole body as a single object. Feel all the different sensations happening at once within that single object.

Without ceasing to feel the body, open to sound. The mind will try to name what you hear. Let go of those names. Listen closely to the tone and quality of sounds. With steady sounds, notice if there are multiple frequencies in a single sound.

Notice your mood. Without naming the feeling, open to and allow the mood to be fully there, to take up as much space as it wants.

Breathe with the mood.

Breathe with the sounds.

Breathe with the body.

Let the breath come into focus as a primary object, letting body, sound, and mood move into the background. Feel the breath coming in and going out. Just feel without thinking about the experience.

If a sensation, sound, or feeling gets strong, let it take over as the primary object without naming or thinking about it.

If thoughts, words, or images draw you in, just notice that and come back to the breath.

Sit in this open, spacious, and non-verbal realm for as long as is comfortable.

# August 27

## *"Thoughts Aren't Facts"*

"With mindfulness, it's not so much that we try to stop thoughts—although that can happen at times—but more that we try to change our relationship to them. One way we change that relationship is to question them or to take them less seriously.

"A current bumper sticker says, 'Don't believe everything you think.' And that's it. But we do believe our thoughts, don't we? We're so used to these words and images passing through the mind like a CNN scroll bringing us facts, updates, comments, criticism, that we rarely step back and realize that these 'objects of mind' have no authority. They're just spit out over and over based on past conditioning. They may contradict themselves, they may have no basis in reality, but they don't care.

"As Wes Nisker, the author of *Buddha's Nature,* says, 'Your mind has a mind of its own.' Once we actually start to look at the content of our thoughts, to question them, we start to change our whole way of being. Our basis for decision-making changes; our understanding of reality changes. What we had taken for facts are now called into question. In Twelve Step programs they say, 'Feelings aren't facts,' and they might add, 'Thoughts aren't facts either.'" *A Burning Desire*, p. 32.

Learning to questions our thoughts is a breakthrough that resonates on both the psychological and spiritual levels. Psychologically this realization can help us to avoid falling into emotional spirals based on our distorted thinking. This includes the type of self-destructive thoughts that lead to relapse. Spiritually, questioning thoughts is part of the process of disidentifying with personal experience. Our thoughts are tied up with self-image and ego. As we disconnect from them, we become less bound to ego as well, which frees us from habit of seeing everything from the limited perspective of "I."

Today, reflect on your relationship to your thoughts. To what extent do you view them as facts? Can you shift that perspective?

# August 28

*"Do Addicts Fit into the Buddhist Community?"*

The mainstream Western Buddhist world isn't focused on recovery. When we come into a meditation hall it can feel quite different from a Twelve Step meeting. Here there's a lot of silence, not the chatter we're used to at meetings.

The teacher is the authority, not the group conscience. And the teachings are broad, complicated, and sometimes confusing or even paradoxical. There's no "How It Works" or Twelve Steps to guide the way, just a jumble of what can often be confusing lists.

While we in recovery might see the direct parallel between the Buddha's teachings on suffering and attachment with addiction, somehow, many mainstream Buddhists often don't get it. Teachers sometimes see us as outsiders or some special subset of their communities, not natural allies in the quest for freedom.

Besides this, many Buddhists don't understand that the Twelve Steps can be adaptable to Buddhism—and vice versa. Put off by the God language, they might make assumptions about the Steps without investigating, thus missing a valuable spiritual resource.

Finally, there are a number of people who come to Buddhism as a way to obscure, suppress, or overcome an addiction problem that they don't want to fully face. We may be surprised to discover that these seemingly spiritual people have stubborn elements of dysfunction in their lives that have never been fully acknowledged.

None of this is to say that we, as Buddhists in recovery don't have our place in the sangha. We do, and we must assert that place. We can bring the values of openness and honesty, morality and ethics, not to mention sobriety and clarity to our community. The spirit of service from the Steps can be of great benefit to a Buddhist sangha as well.

Today, if you aren't already part of a sangha, make a point of becoming involved with a local Buddhist group and encourage the teachers and members to make recovery one of the values that guide the community.

# August 29

*"Love, Love, Love"*

In the stress and challenges of our daily lives, feelings of aversion towards others and ourselves can arise with persistence. Even with the best intentions, we can find ourselves muttering about jaywalkers and baristas; we can get angry with ourselves over perceived flaws or silly mistakes. Further, the news cycle and social media can stir up angst and agitation. All in all, we can wind up swamped with dukkha. At such times, one of the best resources can be a simple phrase or a few prayer-like words.

In Buddhist teachings, the antidote for anger and aversion is metta, loving-kindness. Phrases of loving-kindness are recommended as both a meditation practice and a reset in the midst of a challenging day. You might say to yourself, "May I be happy," if you are feeling stressed or upset. Or, if the challenge is with another person, "May you be happy." If you want to evoke compassion, "May you be free from suffering and the causes of suffering" is a direct way of addressing pain.

Perhaps the simplest and most direct metta phrase takes the Beatles' "All You Need Is Love" opening: "love, love, love." Repeating this word three times can break up some of the harshness of our inner world. It reminds us what's really important and who we want to be.

It's interesting to see what happens to the mind when we say something kind to ourselves in response to our own aversion. There is often a sense of lightness that comes with such a shift.

Today, try out a couple different blessing phrases to use in times of aversion. Find one that feels comfortable and begin to make it part of your daily practice.

# August 30

### *"More on the Fifth Precept"*

The Fifth Precept traditionally focuses on substances, intoxicants that cause heedlessness. But many Buddhists expand the meaning of the precepts to include more subtle areas. For instance, Thich Nhat Hanh, the Vietnamese Zen master, encourages us to see the way we intoxicate ourselves with television and the Internet. Today, of course, so-called smart phones are perhaps the most widespread addiction in our culture—or maybe the world.

For something to be an addiction, though, it must have harmful effects, otherwise we'd say that humans are addicted to air. With smart phones, thousands of people are killed in their cars every year due to looking at their phones rather than the road. That should qualify them as addictive. And these devices have many more insidious addictive effects such as the games we habitually play on them, the obsessive checking of social media, and the apparent need to constantly stay in touch with others.

This points to the idea that the Fifth Precept isn't a moral issue, but a practical one. Buddhist practice is about waking up, and addictive behavior is about escaping, falling asleep to the world. Developing a mindfulness practice means learning to hold all of life's experiences with openness, balance, wisdom, and love. Addictive behaviors, whether consuming drugs and alcohol or staring at your phone as you walk down the street, are about shutting out the world and controlling or numbing your mood and mind state.

This, then, points to why mindfulness and recovery go hand in hand: they are both about welcoming life.

Today, consider the ways you seek comfort and escape in your life. Which ones seem to be harmless and which ones carry risks?

# August 31

## *"Spiritual Awakening"*

In Step Eight we awaken to all the people we have harmed. It may come as a shock to realize how widespread the damage really was. When we're active in our addiction we tend to downplay our unskillful actions, but in recovery, the truth is revealed if we are willing to look at it.

The freedom that comes from this awakening is knowing that we now have the potential to clean up what might have seemed a permanently polluted past. If we can actually get to a point where we have a (relatively) clean slate, we can get a second chance at life, and this is what recovery is all about.

In our addiction we walk around with a shadow, the hidden or denied parts of our thoughts, feelings, and behavior. To shine light on those hidden places, as we do in the inventory and amends process, is to awaken from the fear, shame, and wounds that kept us trapped in our addiction. However, this description might make it sound easier than it is. There's a reason why we hid from these truths for so long. They are painful to acknowledge.

This is what makes the path of recovery heroic. Not that we need to get puffed up about how wonderful we are for quitting our destructive behavior and trying to make up for our mistakes, but there's no doubt that facing these things takes courage, and few muster such will.

As we make our list, though, the feeling of freedom comes as we can now see the end of this painful journey just ahead. And further, we've gained an invaluable skill, the capacity to admit we were wrong and try to make up for it. This newfound ability will carry us far beyond our initial passage through the Steps and serve us for the rest of our life.

Today, reflect on the benefits you have derived from working Step Eight and confronting the list of those you have harmed. Take joy in the courage and steadfastness you have applied to this journey.

# September: Step Nine

*"Made direct amends to such people wherever possible, except when to do so would injure them or others."*

# September 1

*"Making Amends"*

Making amends is perhaps the most frightening of the Twelve Steps. Much of the work up to now has been internal, and even sharing the Fifth Step is done in a fairly safe way with someone who you know is trying to help. With Step Nine we enter into the unknown. How do I make amends? How will they be received? Where do I start? There's no user guide to tell us how to perform this task. Each amends is unique and has to be addressed carefully.

The first, most important thing we need to do is talk to someone else, preferably a sponsor, about the amends before embarking on them. It's easy to get confused about what we should do and wind up doing even more damage. The combination of guilt over our actions with the anxiety that comes up when considering making the amends can muddle our thinking about what we are doing. The wish to get it over with can make us rush into an ill-considered amends.

A key principle of Buddhism is to "do no harm," and this directly applies to the risks in making amends.

The first mistake is to think that a particular amends is absolutely necessary for our recovery and our serenity. What's truly *necessary* is the willingness that comes in Step Eight. But there are many circumstances where you either can't make an amends or it won't help anything.

The amends process is neither simple nor guaranteed to solve anything. Rather, it is meant to reinforce and solidify the emphasis on honesty and openness that the Steps foster throughout. Here we find the essence of Step Nine.

If you have never made amends, begin today to work on that process. Contact your sponsor and go over your Eighth Step list.

If you have made amends previously, now can be a time to review whether they are complete and what you have learned from making amends.

# September 2

*"Wherever Possible"*

Step Nine provides a couple of escape hatches from making amends. The first is "wherever possible," a phrase that can relieve us from the responsibility of carrying out an amends if someone is dead or disappeared from our lives long ago and can't be found. Other circumstances might also arise that render it impossible to make an amends. Here we once again want to consult what the Buddha calls "a wise person," who might be a sponsor, mentor, spiritual guide, or trusted friend. We want to guard against the natural tendency to avoid facing the person we harmed and be sure that it truly isn't possible to make the amends.

What should we do if we can't make amends?

Once you've started this process and begun to see the benefits and relief from cleaning the slate with people, the realization that some of these issues will never be resolved can be distressing. If you imagine that you are in the process of bringing closure to your past, you now realize that in some cases you will never reach such finality.

If you have reached such a level of commitment to moral accountability, you can take joy in realizing that the Steps have truly changed you in deep and fundamental ways. While you may be blocked from completing your amends, you can take solace and even gain self-respect in the acknowledgment of this sign of spiritual growth.

Some people choose to make a kind of symbolic amends at this point. They might, for instance, volunteer for an organization or donate to a cause the person they harmed would appreciate. This can bring a certain amount of closure to the amends. At least they are able to feel that they've made a sincere effort and taken some action to compensate for past wrongs.

Today, consider if there are amends you have not been able to complete. How could you bring some sense of completion or closure to that process?

# September 3

## *"Injuring Them or Others"*

One of the most critical questions to address when preparing to do Step Nine is: "Will any additional harm come through my effort at amends?" There are many circumstances where simply contacting someone will open old wounds. This particularly applies to ex-partners, lovers, and friends.

When considering contacting an ex-partner, the first question to ask is, "Will they be happy to hear from me?" The next question is, "Do I have any hidden agenda in contacting them?" For instance, do I want to get back together with them? Or perhaps I want them to know how great I'm doing without them. Reflecting on our intention, as Buddhism encourages, will help us to be clear about what is behind this impulse.

On the other hand, if we are still with a person or the relationship is damaged but not ended, an honest admission of our failings and sincere apology can be the beginning of healing—but only the beginning, because real healing depends upon real change in our behavior, and that only happens over time.

This brings up the broader question of what value amends might have. Simply saying, "I'm sorry" can be a pretty lame statement. Generally, there needs to be more to it than that. With friends, family, or professional relationships, a new attitude and new patterns of behavior, as well as a full and complete accounting of our failings, is needed to truly repair the damage we've done.

It's this new behavior that ultimately makes the difference. In some sense, we can never truly make restitution for our past. Certainly, we can never go back and fix what we've broken; we can't take away the pain we've caused. Rather, what amends are ultimately about is becoming a person who takes responsibility, who admits their mistakes, and who tries to live with kindness and integrity. These outcomes reflect the highest values of Buddhist morality as well.

Today consider how Step Nine has impacted who you are. Have you let the lessons of this Step penetrate and change you?

# September 4

## *"Buddhism and Amends"*

The term "amends" isn't a common one in Buddhist texts. However, it does appear in several suttas, including one in the Anguttara Nikaya. Here a young monk accuses an older monk of striking him. When brought before the Buddha to address this charge, the older monk refutes it in the strongest terms. Eventually the younger monk admits that he lied and apologizes. The Buddha then tells him, "Since you see your transgression as a transgression and make amends for it, we accept it." He then says that you grow on the path when you see your mistakes, make amends, and "undertake future restraint."

What we learn here is that the Buddha values honesty and is willing to forgive if you understand what you've done was wrong and make a sincere vow to do better. Ultimately no amends is worthy that isn't followed by "future restraint." If we simply go back to the same old behavior, we've accomplished nothing in our amends. Amends are only meaningful as part of the whole change in attitude and actions that come along with the Steps and with Buddhist practice.

Though the phrase "see your transgression as a transgression" is an odd one, it points to an important idea. Namely, that we actually know right from wrong. As addicts we often lost our moral compass and forgot or simply became cynical about morality. The Steps bring us back to living in accord with basic moral principles, and demand that we see where we have gone wrong with our "searching and fearless moral inventory."

We can see clearly that the teachings of the Buddha echo the work of the Steps. Forgiveness is at the heart of both. We shed the weight of past actions so that we can move ahead in our spiritual development. While Buddhism encourages us to let go of the past, the Steps show that such letting go isn't meaningful if there are unresolved issues lingering there. We certainly don't want to stay stuck in these memories, but if we are going to be free of them, we must confront them honestly, with a willingness to do what we can to heal any harm we have done.

Today, consider if the work of amends is complete and if your life is now truly guided by the highest moral values.

# September 5

*"Asking Forgiveness"*

As with much of our Step work, there are no guarantees when we make amends. We do it because it's the right thing to do, and also because it can help us to forgive or accept ourselves and our past. While amends are usually done outwardly to another person, Buddhism offers meditative practices to heal inwardly.

Here is a practice from the *Buddhism & The Twelve Steps Workbook* (p. 193):

**"Asking Forgiveness**: each of us carries a burden of guilt from our addictive and selfish behaviors. Step Nine is about doing something about those unskillful actions. Forgiveness meditation allows us to do the inner work of accepting forgiveness, whether or not we actually receive it externally. For this part of the exercise, think of the people on your Eighth Step list and the ways you harmed each one. Bring each person to mind and say to yourself, *For all the ways that I hurt you, through thought, word, or deed, I ask your forgiveness. Please forgive me.* Again, it can be difficult to accept that we are forgiven, but this is a form of internal amends, admitting responsibility and asking if we can move on."

This is especially helpful for the amends we cannot make. It can help soften our attitude toward ourselves. While there is no way to reverse the damage of our past, carrying it forward day-by-day is useless. Once we have taken full responsibility for our actions, we need to find a way to let go, and that's what a practice like this can help with.

This is not a quick fix. Guilt and self-hatred don't disappear just because we say a few words to ourselves. But to complete the healing of the Steps, we need to embark on this journey of self-forgiveness. We need to find a way to hold our past so that it doesn't remain a burden in our efforts to become a more loving and productive person.

Today, reflect on where you stand in relation to self-forgiveness. Consider making a practice like this part of your daily spiritual work.

# September 6

*"Our Side of the Street"*

One of the challenges of amends is sticking to our responsibility and not taking someone else's inventory. Relationships are a two-way street, so naturally we don't always carry the whole blame for painful situations. But the job of amends isn't justice, it's examining our side of the street, and only our side.

Before we make any amends, we need to be clear about this. We may have real grievances toward the person we are making amends to, but those need to be shelved for this Step. Instead, we need to bring the greatest humility to the situation.

At first, taking this stance of humility may feel belittling, like we are somehow lowering ourselves. But with time we see that it is, in fact, freeing. A great deal of the work of the Steps is about learning to stop protecting the ego. We get a taste of real serenity when we don't have to settle scores, be right, or come out on top. It turns out that being wrong is not so terrible.

This work starts in Step Four, but at that point it is more theoretical. Writing about our mistakes and sharing them is very different from confronting another human being. The temptation to backtrack, to justify our behavior, or to spread blame can be very strong. Our Step work is meant to prepare us for this moment, to teach us to avoid blaming or striking out at others.

When we see how much peace comes from this new stance, a real shift in our attitude can occur, a true spiritual awakening.

Today, reflect on your willingness to stay on your own side of the street in making amends, and in relationships in general. Have you developed the humility to not need to protect your ego anymore?

# September 7

*"Not a Theory"*

Many people are drawn to Buddhism for its elegant philosophy and straightforward thinking about life. Some are drawn to the simplicity of Zen, others to the mysticism of the Vajrayana (Tibetan Buddhism), and still others appreciate the asceticism of Theravada. However, to get caught up in these images and external qualities is to miss the point of Buddhist practice. The dharma is meant to be experienced directly, not studied like some artwork in a museum.

This idea is echoed in the AA Big Book when it says, "the spiritual life is not a theory. We have to live it."

The hardest part of any spiritual path is doing the daily work of awareness, compassion, and balance. It's one thing to go to a retreat and get inspired by the wonderful dharma talks, but it's something else entirely to come home and deal with the challenges of day-to-day life.

For those of us in recovery, this truth is even more evident than for the ordinary Buddhist. Living our path means more than studying a philosophy, or even meditating. Rather it requires that we live differently—that we stop acting on our addiction—and that we maintain that way of living over time.

Life is hard. We all know that. Inevitably there will be ups and downs, and those downs can take us pretty low. It takes tremendous determination to maintain sobriety, to stay on our path of recovery without relapse. Sometimes it might not be pretty—it might not look very "Zen"—but if we are able to maintain our commitment to our bottom line recovery, somehow things will tend improve.

No, it's not a theory. We do have to live it.

Today, remind yourself of all the ways you are "living it." No matter how high or low you are today, remember that sticking with your program and your practice is an accomplishment in itself, one to appreciate in yourself.

# September 8

*"Painstaking"*

When it comes to Step Nine in the AA Big Book, there is famously a list of what have become known as" The Promises." These are introduced with this sentence: "If we are painstaking about this phase of our development, we will be amazed before we are half way through."

Rarely has a spiritual text offered a more enticing introduction to a set of propositions. The idea that we'll be amazed by the results of our Step work is very intriguing. But perhaps we should focus first on the earlier part of the sentence, the requirement that we be painstaking.

The demands of the Twelve Steps can start to seem onerous, as we pass from admitting powerlessness and turning it over to a Higher Power into the deeply challenging inventory and amends process. These are not tasks that anyone would take on voluntarily. In some ways, this is what sets Twelve Step work apart from ordinary spiritual practices, including those of Buddhism.

Painstaking it is. And in truth if this isn't undertaken painstakingly, not much will come of it. A half-hearted inventory isn't worth much. To hold back or be dishonest in that work makes it pointless. And to shy away from directly addressing those we've hurt means we've completely missed the point and lost out on the potential benefits of making amends.

Many addicts have probably tried to get through life by cutting corners. With a goal of self-satisfaction, we might never have seen the point of doing a good job just for the sake of it. With the Steps, we are learning that we can't risk that attitude anymore, that there are real life implications to taking shortcuts. Here, it's either engage wholeheartedly or risk the consequences of relapse.

Today, consider if your Step work has been painstaking. This doesn't mean you have done them perfectly, but rather that you have done your best and stayed honest and consistent in the process.

# September 9

*"Do Not Be Bothered"*

Many of us come to meditation hoping for a pleasant experience of peace. How to achieve this serenity and calm is the great question for beginning (and sometimes experienced) meditators. What we soon discover is that, ironically, trying hard to achieve a tranquil meditation actually gets in the way of that happening. Then we are left with the question, how can we achieve something without trying?

Perhaps the most useful advice comes from Suzuki Roshi who says, "When you are practicing zazen [meditation], do not try to stop your thinking. Let it stop by itself. If something comes into your mind, let it come in and let it go out. It will not stay long. When you try to stop your thinking, it means you are bothered by it. Do not be bothered by anything."

This is pointing to an attitude of meditation, rather than a technique. We often come to meditation practice with the idea that there is some form, some technique that is the key, as if we are learning to throw a ball or tie a shoelace. But form is not the point.

There are many techniques of meditation, as we've seen throughout this book. Perfecting any of them will not create effective meditation. Rather it's the attitude Suzuki points to that brings real impact in our practice. And this attitude is subtle and counterintuitive. It's not exactly *not*-trying, but it's also not exactly *trying*.

The key is, "Do not be bothered by anything." This is the attitude that creates a pleasant and productive experience of meditation. To achieve this, we have to let go of goals and expectations. We have to let go of self-judgment and fear of our own mind. We might say, "acceptance is the answer."

Today, work at shifting your attitude in meditation. Practice not being bothered by anything that arises, internally or externally.

# September 10

*"A New Freedom"*

The "Promises" begin: "We are going to know a new freedom…" What is this freedom?

Perhaps we need to first ask, "What was the old freedom?" For many of us, it was the freedom to be loaded, to act on our craving. All we wanted was to be left alone to get as high as we wanted (or to eat, gamble, or act out). Essentially, freedom for us was about control—being able to control our circumstances, our mood, and the people around us. Sadly, freedom is also associated with having lots of money. But this kind of freedom is not a path to happiness. No amount of money, power, or control can create happiness or end suffering. And, for addicts, the freedom to act on our craving led inevitably to the prison of our addiction.

A new freedom is diametrically opposed to all this. It's the freedom of release from the prison of addiction. It's the joy of living in harmony with the universe, and more practically, in harmony with those around us. Free of conflict, free of longing, free of obsession. While addiction and cultural messages depict freedom as resulting from things we can acquire, recovery sees it as resulting from letting go—in Buddhist terms, "renunciation."

Our minds were enslaved by our addiction. We couldn't go a day without thinking about, if not obsessing about, our drug or behavior of choice. Strategies for using consumed us.

Every day we had to satisfy that need. Our very lifestyle was defined by our craving. Plans had to include the need to fit in or satisfy our need for a drink or a drug. Work, play, social life—all of it had to fit into the necessity of using. On top of this, we had to lookout for arrest, as many of us were breaking the law by using illegal drugs or driving under the influence. The idea that we were free in any way is laughable, seen from this perspective.

Today, reflect on the freedom in your life that comes from recovery.

# September 11

*"A New Happiness"*

The second Promise, "a new happiness," is pretty enticing. Who doesn't want happiness, new or otherwise?

But what could be new about happiness? If we look at the "old happiness," we can get some insight. For an addict, happiness was having a good stash and no responsibilities. That way, you could get as loaded as you wanted without having to worry about the consequences. Unfortunately, there were always consequences, whether physical, emotional, social, professional, or otherwise. Our so-called happiness was always short-lived and often came with a big price.

The happiness of recovery has none of these drawbacks. It's the happiness of clarity—waking up and remembering everything about the night before. It's the happiness of honesty, no secrets to protect or lies to cover up. It's the happiness of connection, letting people know who we are and learning to know them in meaningful ways; going through your day without guilt, shame, or regret; knowing that even if we make a mistake, we can own up to it and move on.

As addicts we associated happiness with ecstatic moments, and exciting events. We wanted to heighten our experience of life. In recovery, we learn to appreciate the quiet moments, the moments of serenity and peace. We take joy from a walk in the woods, a meal with a friend, a job well done. We discover that life itself is enough without the enhancements of intoxication or adrenaline rushes.

Today, reflect on what brings you happiness in recovery. Take joy in your new happiness.

# September 12

*"Not Regret the Past"*

The past is a big deal for addicts. Many meetings are consumed with people talking about their past. We all know that we made serious mistakes, that we harmed others badly, and that we harmed ourselves. The Twelve Steps are designed to help us come to terms with that past. By taking and sharing an inventory, trying to change or let go of our negative qualities, and finally by making amends, we are coming to grips with all that damage. Though we know we can't turn back the clock, as much as possible we want to resolve things and move forward. Moving forward means that we can't carry that burden with us.

Regret, like guilt, is a pointless emotion. Buddhism, with its emphasis on present moment awareness, puts a fine point on this idea. There is only this moment. The past is irretrievably gone, out of reach of any effort to change. To rehash past mistakes is a fruitless exercise. This doesn't mean the past is forgotten. We learn from the past, try to correct our mistakes and grow. But to continue to berate ourselves is useless.

When we come to this insight, it can be freeing. Somehow, we'd felt that we deserved to continue to suffer, and that by carrying around regret and guilt we were paying the price for our behavior. But when we see that regret serves no function but to sustain our own pain, we realize the fallacy of this stance.

The gift we give to the world is our recovery. If we can move forward with kindness, generosity, compassion, and wisdom, we are doing all we can to compensate for our past mistakes. Regret cannot add anything to that.

Today, consider if you are still carrying the burden of regret. What would it mean to let go of that burden?

# September 13

*"Knowing Peace"*

The Buddha said that the highest form of happiness is peace. For addicts, this takes some time to understand. We sought something more wild, frenzied, and blissful. We wanted peak experiences and rapturous pleasure. Peace seemed a little too flat.

As we become more mindful and gain more clarity in recovery, we discover the underlying discomfort of that frenzy. It always contained a bit of fear and a sense that it was never enough. We were constantly chasing something, always looking for more, more, more. When we finally landed in recovery, it might have seemed a little boring at first. But that was because our awareness wasn't subtle enough to appreciate peace and serenity. With time, however, our awareness grew until excitement and thrills began to lose their allure, and quiet, stillness, and calm drew us in.

Now we aren't chasing so many things. We aren't on the prowl for thrills and chills. We discover that life as it is, simple and clean, is actually fulfilling. A job well done, a meaningful conversation, a meal shared with friends—these simple pleasures become not just *enough*, but truly joyful events.

The Steps have gotten us here. First by confronting our addiction and letting it go; then finding a new way of living in harmony with the Dharma; and finally, by honestly reviewing and trying to heal our past. We have arrived at a place where life is no longer so complicated. Sure, we have our problems, but they're no longer insurmountable.

Buddhism gives us guidelines for understanding experience: everything is impermanent, no need to fight with change; there is an unsatisfactory quality to experiences, and that's okay, we don't need perfection; when we lead with love, compassion, and forgiveness life unfolds without a lot of stress.

Today reflect on the level of peace you have in your life. What could you do to enhance your serenity?

# September 14

## *"Our Experience Can Benefit Others"*

One of the core principles of Twelve Step recovery is "carrying the message," a term found in Step Twelve. Here in Step Nine it appears as one of the promises. That's because this stage of our Step work is so challenging, and it's important to feel that there is a purpose in it beyond our personal recovery.

It's hard to look back at our lives as we do in a Fourth Step inventory, making an unvarnished examination of all the mistakes we made. It's easy to fall into despair, guilt, and regret. We can get the idea that we've wasted years of our lives chasing a high or running from reality. The Promise that those mistakes may ultimately help someone else can be a source of comfort and help pull us out of negativity.

The truth of this claim is self-evident. Every time we share with a newcomer; every time we work with a sponsee; every time we tell our story in a meeting, we are validating it. Further, our encounters with suffering softened our hearts and made us more compassionate, understanding, and forgiving.

The Buddha, too, made unwise choices that informed his teaching later. His spiritual journey took him down the self-destructive path of extreme asceticism. The description of his efforts to, for instance, limit food intake sounds like anorexia. And in his earlier life, he had pursued sensual pleasure as the key to happiness. He discovered that neither of these extremes brought true freedom, and thus described his teachings as "The Middle Way" between these two poles. Had he not gone to those extremes he would never have formulated this wise model for spiritual development. He would never have had a message to carry.

Today, consider the ways that your experience has been and could be of benefit to others.

# September 15

*"Uselessness and Self-Pity"*

The sense of uselessness and the feeling of self-pity are pointless attitudes. They grow out of a misunderstanding of life and undermine our happiness.

The Steps help us to build purpose in our lives and culminate with service. In this way, they undermine the sense of uselessness. By giving us energy and engagement, recovery helps us to find value in our lives.

Self-pity comes out of a sense that we are suffering in a unique and unfair way. We feel as if no one else is having this pain or this problem. It suggests that somehow this shouldn't be happening to me.

No one's suffering is unique. This is the Buddha's First Noble Truth: we all suffer. If we look around, we see the truth of this teaching. There is so much suffering in the world, and ours likely pales compared to some of the hunger, abuse, and trauma that many people experience. At the end of the day, everyone gets their share of suffering, some greater, some lesser.

As for fairness, the Law of Karma tells us that what has arisen always has a cause. It's not a special punishment or curse we are experiencing. It comes as the results of actions and conditions, some of which we are directly responsible for, some of which grow out of situations we were placed in. It's not random.

Do Buddhism and the Steps actually protect us from the sense of uselessness and self-pity? Perhaps not, but what they do give us is a way of seeing ourselves differently, of changing our perspective. By taking responsibility for our behavior, they help us avoid blaming others and feeling sorry for ourselves. By inspiring us to embrace our lives more fully, they infuse our life with meaning.

Today, reflect on the real ways you are useful in the world. Dispel self-pity with gratitude for the ways your life has changed with Step work and Dharma practice.

# September 16

### *"Gaining Interest in Others"*

Addiction is selfish. It's all about satisfying our own craving and controlling our circumstances. Other people are there to satisfy our needs, and if they don't, we want them out of the way. Recovery breaks us of these selfish ways.

When trapped in addiction, all your energy focuses on your self-centered craving. When you are no longer in that trap, you discover the joy of focusing on others. One Buddhist monk says, "Whenever I think of myself, I get depressed." Taking our attention off our own problems can actually be a big relief.

Getting clean and sober is a little like coming out of hibernation, blinking at the light, and seeing that there's a big, wide world out there. We aren't alone, and it's time to engage with others for more than purely self-centered reasons.

When we're not so concerned with satisfying every craving, it becomes possible to care about other people. When we aren't lost in our own suffering all the time, we can use some of our energy to reach out and help others. As the Big Book says, "We will lose interest in selfish things and gain interest in our fellows."

In both Twelve Step work and Dharma practice, community or sangha is central. In recovery we depend upon meetings, sponsors, and friends in the program to be with us in the tough times and to share the good ones. In Dharma practice, we depend upon teachers to guide us and peers to support us. Few people can learn and sustain a meditation practice alone. And over time, as our recovery and Dharma practice ripen, we naturally begin to look for ways to share with others.

Today, reflect on your relationship to this teaching. Have you "lost interest in selfish things and gained interest" in others?

# September 17

*"Compassion for Those Who Do Harm"*

Perhaps the most difficult amends to make are to people who have harmed us or others. While we may have had a part in harming such a person, we might want to justify that by pointing at their behavior. Here we can draw upon Buddhist principles of compassion. These teachings say that everyone is the "owner of their karma," that sooner or later they will bear responsibility for their harmful actions. If we have seen them act in unskillful ways or break precepts, we know that they will suffer at some time. However, because of the unknowable timing of karmic results, it may appear that they have avoided responsibility. According to the Buddha, that is an illusion.

Here is a practice for spreading compassion to people who have done harm:

Settle back into your meditation posture, closing your eyes, connecting with the breath, and opening your heart. Let your body settle.

Bring to mind this difficult person. Remember the unskillful actions they have done. Feel the pain of those actions whether directed at you or others.

Now consider how it feels to do such actions. Even someone who tries to justify their harm can feel its repercussions inside. The effort to avoid responsibility itself creates inner stress.

Now reflect on the ultimate karmic consequences that must come out of this behavior. This person will suffer. They may not even know why they are suffering, so they may also be confused in that suffering.

Recognize that they acted in ignorance of the consequences, driven by their own grasping and aversion. Remember that you, too, have acted out of ignorance, grasping, and aversion.

Try using the simple phrase, "May you be free from suffering," repeating these words with your breath.

Offer this person your caring and kindness. Try to arouse a sincere wish for them to be free from suffering.

# September 18

*"Amends for Ourselves"*

"Clearly, making amends to others is a subtle and complex process. We can't always be clear about who we should make amends to. But one person who was there for every mistake, who suffered every time we used, who took the brunt of all our selfish, foolish, and destructive behavior, was us. We are the ultimate owners of our karma, the ones who carry the burden of our past, and as we move forward in our lives and in our recovery, we are the ones we owe the greatest amends to.

"Of course, simply getting clean and sober is a huge start in healing our past. But I think that many of us have to learn to be more kind to ourselves. As selfish as we might have been, addicts are also terribly self-destructive and full of self-hatred. While we may have been seeking pleasure in our addictive behavior, we may also have been trying to harm or even kill ourselves. Now we have to learn what might be the hardest lesson: to love ourselves. This is an inside *and* outside job.

"Mindfulness teaches us how to see our own thoughts, and this is where our amends begin. We need to listen inside and try to change that voice. We don't have to beat ourselves up or take the negative view on everything. Humility is one thing, but self-abnegation is quite another. The Buddha encouraged us to give love to all beings, *including ourselves.* We are all human and equally valuable. Can we take that in? Can we start to treat ourselves as if we believed that?" *Workbook,* p.198

Part of recovery is learning to treat ourselves with more care and understanding. This is something we addicts cannot be reminded of too often. Are you truly remembering to make amends to yourself today?

# September 19

*"The Practice of Amends to Ourselves"*

"Making amends to ourselves starts with getting clean and sober, whatever program or addiction we are working with. True recovery, though, demands that we continue to take care of ourselves through all the challenges and opportunities life presents us.

"For this exercise, ask yourself what you are doing for yourself today. More generally, what are you doing for yourself in your life right now. Are you taking care of your body with food, rest, and exercise? Is your work life satisfying? Your family life? Social life? What opportunities do you have for fun and pleasure? Do you have a creative outlet?

"Sometimes recovery, or just trying to live a spiritual life can become a kind of grind as we try to live up to some high standards or always do the right thing, be of service, work hard, and be responsible. Sometimes when we get into recovery, a sense of guilt combined with a newfound energy and engagement turns us into workaholics...

"It's vital, if we are to sustain our recovery that we be kind to ourselves, that we take time to enjoy ourselves. Just learning how to have fun in recovery is a big challenge for many of us, but an important one to accomplish.

"Consider all of this as you move into making amends to yourself."
*Workbook*, p. 199

# September 20

*"Fear of People"*

It's an interesting and comforting comment in the Big Book that "fear of people" will leave us. That fear might take different forms.

One is simply a shyness and isolating tendency that some addicts have. Alcohol, cocaine, speed, and even rave drugs could help us in social situations. A pill, line, or a few drinks would free our inhibitions and self-consciousness enough to have fun at a party or other social event. But, of course, our addiction repeatedly pushed that behavior over the line, so that some of us became persona non grata at those events.

The Steps help us get to the root of this shyness and insecurity. We learn to let go of the egotism of separation. Our low self-esteem was just another way of feeling special, and recovery wipes that away. The support and unconditional acceptance of the Program further allows us to come out of that fear.

Meditation practice doesn't exactly make us less shy or fearful of others, since it's done in silence. But what it can do is reveal the underlying emotions and thought patterns that such fear was built on. Buddhist meditation undermines the stories we tell ourselves about being different, less than, or otherwise an outsider.

The Steps also force us to interact more with others. In Step Five we share our inventory, here in Step Nine we make amends, and finally, in Step Twelve we carry the message. These functions of the Steps often push us out of our comfort zone where we learn things about ourselves that we would never have seen otherwise. We discover our capacity to connect, to reveal ourselves, to be humble without humiliation, and to serve. Ultimately, all these actions make us more comfortable in our relationships with others.

Today, reflect on your own comfort level in social interactions. Have you let go of "fear of people?" If not, what other work might you do to further that healing?

# September 21

*"Fear of Economic Insecurity"*

This Promise doesn't say that we won't have financial problems, only that we won't be swept away with fear. As we move through the Steps and deeper into our recovery, our relationship changes not just toward our past as it's uncovered in our inventory, but to our future as well. We learn to trust that if we continue our work of recovery and take actions based on our highest values, that things will work out. We understand that challenges are part of life. Financial problems may arise, but now we have the right attitude and approach to handle whatever comes our way.

Fear implies a lack of faith. Steps Two and Three begin the process of developing faith in the program. As we see the results of this faith over time, we gain even more trust. Before we came to recovery, we thought we had to fight with and conquer life's challenges through sheer effort and force of will. The Steps teach us that far more is accomplished in the long run by living in harmony with the truth, with the dharma. This doesn't mean that we don't make an effort—we absolutely do. However, we always try to align that effort with spiritual values, not just material ones.

In our addiction we chased long shots and short cuts. We looked for quick success and magical solutions. Real change takes time. Recovery shows us how to appreciate and value each day without being in such a hurry.

This principle accords with Buddhist mindfulness practices as well. These teach us to be present for our lives, not to live in the past or future. Our relationship to money was defined by past regrets and future hopes and fears. We may have been driven by a sense that material belongings defined us and gave us value. Buddhism teaches that freedom comes from letting go, not acquiring and trying to hold on. With this spirit, there is nothing to fear.

Today, reflect on your relationship to financial insecurity. Have you let go or do you still carry fear in that regard?

# September 22

### *"Intuition"*

Intoxication blurs all the senses. We're in a fog, two steps away from reality, uncomprehending and thoughtless. Just giving up that behavior clears up our thinking. As we move through the Steps, more and more obstructions are removed. Our anxiety and stress are reduced as we work Step Three and become more trusting. Defensiveness and shame fall away with Steps Four and Five. Underlying habits of negativity, judgment, anger, and depression begin to be uprooted as we engage Steps Six and Seven.

All of this brings more and more clarity to our thinking. Less caught in inner drama, our natural wisdom begins to shine through. While we still ask for feedback and guidance from sponsors and trusted friends, we aren't dependent upon those suggestions. We've learned to listen inside.

Mindfulness, of course, is the art of listening—inside and outside. As we deepen our meditation practice, we become attuned to the nuances of emotion, habitual thought patterns, biases and preferences that appear in the mind. This understanding helps us to distinguish true wisdom from ego-driven beliefs. Now we aren't simply under the sway of our cravings but can make sensible choices and clear decisions.

Our recovery depends upon persistent efforts to maintain clarity. As addicts, it's easy for us to fall back into habits of anger, judgment, and craving. Intuitive wisdom isn't a given; it requires vigilance. A daily meditation practice is an important foundation for maintaining our most beneficial mind states.

Today reflect on your capacity for intuition. Do you trust your intuition? Could you cultivate deeper intuition?

# September 23

### *"What We Could Not Do for Ourselves"*

The language and literature of the Steps often brings us back to theistic concepts, such as "God is doing for us what we could not do for ourselves." From a Buddhist standpoint, this doesn't quite make sense, so it's helpful to try another lens.

If we substitute "Dharma" for God, we can tease some meaning from this statement. What this would mean is that by taking Refuge in the Dharma and trying to live by its principles and practices, transformation is possible. One Buddhist teacher says, "The Dharma takes care of those who take care of the Dharma." This has a similar tone to the Big Book's claim.

With faith that we'll benefit from living in this way, we reject our habitual impulses and turn to the Dharma for guidance. Here, we are encouraged to be present and accepting of things as they are. The Dharma also reminds us that everything is impermanent. This truth, then reveals the unsatisfactory quality of life, that nothing lasts, nothing can be held onto. And yet, with this difficult revelation, we finally see the importance of caring and compassion over self-centeredness and blaming.

The "ourselves" of the Big Book is that self-centered person. In aligning with the Dharma, we are turning away from that orientation and taking guidance and cues from the Buddha. This demands that we first study the Dharma enough to know what he taught, and then that we continually choose that guidance over the persistent craving to satisfy the "self."

Today, reflect on how your Step work and Dharma practice have transformed your life.

# September 24

## *"Healing the World"*

As we deepen our recovery and dharma practice, we can't help but become aware of the suffering and dysfunction in the world around us. We know through personal experience the scourge of addiction that crosses all social, economic, religious, ethnic, gender, and racial boundaries. Coming out of the fog of our own stuff, we are struck by how pervasive these problems are.

In the Buddhist world, broader issues of suffering are starting to be addressed as well. Many leading teachers are addressing the climate crisis, racial oppression, economic inequality, and many other issues in their talks and writings. Over time the specific issues may change, but the emphasis on addressing suffering remains.

Dharma and recovery are both about healing. They begin with personal and spiritual healing, but as we grow on the path, we find that we can't turn away from the greater suffering around us. It's not enough to simply meditate and work the Steps for our own benefit. We must find ways to reach out and help the world we live in.

The Traditions of the Twelve Steps say that groups shouldn't be involved in "outside issues," but this certainly doesn't apply to individuals. This isn't to say that we should engage in any particular stance, but rather that we have an obligation to give back. Step Twelve has a direct way to do that in the Program by "carrying the message." That's certainly vital work, but our involvement in helping others doesn't have to stop there.

Today consider ways you might be of service in the world, whether through your recovery, your dharma practice, or other community service.

# September 25

*"Refresher"*

Today we'll get back to basics in meditation.

Begin by establishing a solid, stable posture. Find a place of balance and alignment so that you are upright yet relaxed. Try tipping side-to-side and back-to-front to find the place where you feel centered. Then come to stillness, closing the eyes or lowering the gaze.

Now scan the body to make sure there is no tension or tightness in the body. Relax the jaw; soften the eyes; relax the forehead. Release the shoulders; soften the belly; open the chest.

Feel the body as a field of energy, an array of sensations from head to toe.

Now notice sounds in your environment. It doesn't have to be silent to meditate; just listen with openness and receptivity. Know that hearing is happening.

Check in on your mood. How are you feeling? Is there a pleasant, unpleasant, or neutral tone to your mood? Meet the mood with curiosity and acceptance.

Finally, connect with the breath. Notice the sensations at the nostrils as you breathe in and out, the touch of air. Notice the feeling of the belly rising and falling with each breath. See which area is easiest to pay attention to, then make that your primary concentration point.

Begin to bring awareness to each breath, in and out.

If the mind wanders, that's natural and normal. When you notice that happening, just gently come back to the breath. Doing this is a moment of mindfulness.

This is the basic framework of mindfulness meditation practice. Make a habit of coming back to this structure whenever your meditation loses focus.

# September 26

### *"Looking Up"*

Many years ago one of my teachers pointed out a simple thing. When walking down the street (or anywhere else) there's a tendency to look down. While this might simply be an effort to be careful and not trip on anything, in many cases it's not necessary in terms of safety.

What happens when you look down when walking? There is a tendency to go into your thoughts. You're not really looking at anything, but wind up ruminating. Oddly enough, the tilt of the head tends to put the mind in a downward posture as well so that thinking becomes more negative or circular. Besides this, we pass through the world without really seeing it.

When we look up, we start to see a different world, one filled with interesting sights. Buildings, trees, flowers, birds, and, yes, other people appear. This takes us out of our own head and into appreciation of the world around us. It also tends to lift the mood.

Addiction is like that downward, inward posture. All we can think about is ourselves—what we want, and how to maintain our high. We develop a narrow view of the world, a self-centered and lonely view. It leads nowhere and has no jumping off point. It's just a circular life of highs and lows, of cravings and attempts to satisfy them.

Recovery is like looking up and realizing there is a whole world out there, an alternative to the life of addiction. We simply need to lift our eyes and engage more with it.

An essential part of mindfulness practice is also this larger scope, being aware of the world around us. With clear seeing, we move from rumination to wisdom, from self-absorption to a spacious awareness.

So, walking with your head up is both a practical approach and a symbolic one.

Today, notice how you walk through the world. Try lifting your eyes to see what is around you.

# September 27

*"Attitudes of Mindfulness: Acceptance"*

"When we come to meditation it's often with the hope of accomplishing something, whether we want more peace in our lives, to let go of stress, to feel more connected, more wise, or to develop an open-heart. But we can't make these things happen. If we are always trying to change the way we feel, then we'll never find peace or connection. The attitude of mindfulness is, 'What is happening right now? Can I just be with this without trying to change it?' This attitude of open acceptance points us back to the present moment and to letting go of goals, judgments, and striving.

"It's very common in meditation to fall into traps, though. Even though in principle we agree with the idea of being accepting, something might happen that doesn't seem right. Maybe someone comes in the room and slams a door. We think, 'Don't they know I'm meditating? Why don't they quiet down.' A mindful, accepting attitude might be more like, 'That was an unpleasant sound,' and then noticing the irritation and the desire for things to be quiet.

"Acceptance says, 'Things are as they are. If you fight that, you just cause yourself more stress and discomfort; if you can accept things as they are, many of your petty irritations will just fall away.'

"Be careful, though, because acceptance isn't the answer to every situation. Some things shouldn't be accepted, and as the Serenity Prayer says, we need to learn to discern the difference between what should be accepted and what we should work to change. Mindfulness isn't about passively accepting everything, but rather getting a more accurate understanding of what's happening. Nonetheless, learning to accept things as they are is an important starting point because of the tendency to try to control everything." *Workbook*, p. 44.

Today, try to cultivate the attitude of acceptance. Notice where and when you have the urge to control or resist things that are happening. Practice letting go in those moments.

# September 28

*"Routine"*

One of the hardest things for many people is to establish a consistent meditation routine. Daily practice requires a willingness to set aside time, to sit when you don't feel like it, and to continue to practice even when nothing seems to be happening in your meditation. However, without this persistence, it's very hard to develop a meaningful meditation practice and derive the benefits.

Most regular meditators have a set time each day when they sit. In monasteries and meditation centers, the daily schedule rarely varies. This kind of approach makes practice easier to do because it's simply built into the day. You don't have to think about it or make time. The time is already set aside.

When this isn't possible, we have to be more intentional in our daily practice, making the commitment to put in time sitting no matter what. This can mean simply sitting for one minute on days when it doesn't seem to fit. That's fine. Maintaining the daily consistency is ultimately more important than putting in a specific amount of time. That's not to say that a more robust practice isn't important. You certainly will want to sit for at least twenty minutes as your regular schedule. The point is that we don't use limited time as an excuse to skip meditation altogether.

Routine is important in our recovery as well. The lives of addicts tend to be chaotic and undisciplined. What we might have thought of as freedom may end up simply being a messy, disorganized way of living. Learning to live more structured lives is part of returning to normalcy. While it may not provide the thrills and spontaneity of our previous life, we'll wind up being happier and more productive in the long run.

Today, reflect on your routine or lack thereof. Do you need more routine? Less? Are there things you should change about your daily schedule?

# September 29

## *"Retreat"*

Taking time away from your ordinary daily life to reflect on spiritual matters and reset your mind state is a practice found in virtually every spiritual and religious tradition in the world, including the Twelve Steps. Buddhist meditation retreats can be particularly rigorous and demanding, but offer special benefits.

In the Insight Meditation tradition of Buddhism (which derives from the Asian Theravada tradition of Burma, Thailand, and Sri Lanka), the retreat form is quite simple, and mostly involves sitting meditation and walking meditation. A typical retreat is ten days (some shorter, some much longer), and is conducted primarily in noble silence. Each day there is meditation instruction, Q&A, and a dharma talk. Every couple of days participants meet with a teacher, either one-on-one or in a small group for practice discussion.

Out of this form one can develop much deeper concentration than in daily practice and a range of insights that reveal truths both personal and universal. The form is challenging, to say the least, but the rewards are remarkable. People often come out of retreat with renewed energy and inspiration. Clarity about goals and ambitions as well as appreciation for life itself are typical outcomes.

Retreat can also bring up intensely difficult feelings, memories, and past traumas, which is why it's important to practice with an experienced teacher. These challenges themselves can often be used as spurs to growth, insight, and compassion.

Retreat brings inner healing, renewal, and deeper understanding of life and dharma. Many Buddhists consider yearly retreat practice fundamental to developing their spiritual path.

Today consider looking into going on retreat. Because of the time and cost involved, you usually have to plan anywhere from six months to a year ahead. Many retreat centers have wait lists, as well. It's worth the effort to make this happen. Online retreats can be more accessible and less costly. They can be of great benefit if we take them seriously and use our time diligently.

# September 30

## *"Spiritual Awakening"*

Step Nine awakens us to the freedom of imperfection. No longer bound by the need to be right or flawless, we learn the joy of confession and amends. Our delusion was that such admissions, apologies, and self-revealing would cripple us, that somehow owning up to the harm we had done would diminish us. Instead, we find that it lifts the burden of self-protection and self-centered defensiveness.

The Promises enumerate many elements of this freedom. The essence is the newfound capacity to confront those we've harmed with humility and fearlessness. This points to the fundamental spiritual awakening that the Steps build toward: the emptiness of ego, awakening to "not-self." When we stop protecting this illusory self, a weight is lifted, and we discover how unnecessary and useless it was to avoid admitting our failings.

Now we can live a more transparent life—one informed by honesty and kindness. This creates the potential for healing in our interpersonal lives. We are viewed differently by others, with more trust and respect. We were never fooling anyone anyway, so now we're free of both self-deception and trying to deceive others.

Step Nine opens the heart through the surrender of amends. We can't approach this Step with armor. It forces us to lower our defenses, so naturally we become more vulnerable. This leads to, perhaps the core purpose of this Step: healing our relationships.

Making amends is an act of compassion, saying "I care about the pain I caused you, and I want to try to make up for it." Such compassion naturally spreads to other relationships and situations, and becomes an organic, integral part of our lives.

Today, reflect on and appreciate the benefits that have come to you from practicing Step Nine.

# OCTOBER: STEP 10

*"Continued to take personal inventory, and when we were wrong promptly admitted it."*

# October 1

## *"Continuing Inventory"*

Step Ten essentially reiterates Steps Four through Nine. Several things are implied by this fact. First, that a one-time only inventory-amends process isn't sufficient. We will continue to make mistakes for which we need to make amends. That understanding should help us be more forgiving of ourselves, not to expect perfection just because we've worked some Steps.

Another message from this Step is that we need to be careful going forward. We see that letting resentments and conflicts build up without examining our part and making amends leaves us vulnerable to relapse, as the emotional burden of these issues trigger a wish to escape our feelings.

Step Ten begins the maintenance part of the Steps. While Steps Four through Nine are meant to address the past and bring some closure to our destructive, addictive behavior, Steps Ten through Twelve are guides to living a clean and sober life. The Steps aren't just something we do and then move on with our lives. They *are* our lives.

The dharma makes the same supposition. The Buddha says we should be mindful in every posture, every movement, and every behavior. We should practice Right Action, Right Speech, and Right Livelihood. Mindfulness and the teachings of Buddhism aren't just things we practice while sitting in meditation or in special situations. They're meant to be followed all the time.

Clearly Buddhism and the Twelve Steps agree on the need to live our lives fully engaged with the present moment and our spiritual principles.

If you aren't already, begin to integrate Step Ten into your daily life, being careful to make amends whenever needed. And try to make mindfulness and the guidance of dharma a regular part of your day.

# October 2

### *"Promptly"*

The distinct difference between Steps Nine and Ten is the immediacy of Step Ten. Step Nine's amends come after what can be a long, arduous process of inventory work, making the list, and discussing how to move forward with a sponsor or trusted advisor. Step Ten is much more on the spot.

Here, we might find ourselves getting frustrated with a customer service person, realize we're off base, and quickly apologize. We might get angry at our partner, but after simmering down, suddenly realize that we were being defensive or reactive. We can then quickly go and make up. Such a willingness to act is fundamental to the health of any long-term relationship. Without it, small daily conflicts can build into a pattern of alienation and finally breakup.

Mindfulness of the body and feelings are the direct feedback mechanisms that tell us when we're acting unskillfully. Anger, irritation, and impatience show up in the body. We get tense, tight, and anxious; we feel the toxicity of those emotions in the body. If we stay mindful of these sense experiences, we'll quickly know when we're behaving harmfully. At that moment, we need the willingness to counter this energy and reverse the behavior.

This takes us back to Step Six, the willingness to change. Again, these Steps must become part of our repertoire, ways of acting that are integrated into our lives. Often our tendency when we feel anger or impatience is to strike out at someone, so the Steps are trying to help us to alter these patterns in constructive ways.

Today, make the commitment to promptly admit you are wrong. Keep track of your feelings so that you can pause when triggered, not react on impulse.

# October 3

*"Self-Reflection"*

Coming to understand ourselves is one of the great tasks of the Twelve Steps and of dharma practice. Step One is a big acknowledgment that we didn't know ourselves, that we were unaware of living in an unwise way. The inventory process is also one of very specific self-discovery. It seems that we keep realizing that we aren't who we think we are. This process of looking into ourselves is one of the most difficult and at times painful parts of the Steps. But over time we can learn to take what we find less personally and be more forgiving of ourselves.

The practice of mindfulness meditation is clearly one of self-reflection, as well. With a less specific agenda than the Steps, meditation examines the heart and mind, and shows us who we are.

There is also the positive side of this process, whereby we discover our innate goodness, our longing to love and be loved. Beneath the surface of fear, ambition, and jealousy lies this core human wish for connection. Buddhism sees our nature as essentially good, something that is covered over by the cruder impulses, but which, when given a chance, will lead us toward kindness, caring, and wisdom.

While dharma practice has a somewhat more circumspect approach, the Steps seem to throw us into a confrontation with our demons. Together, though, they can help us to move beyond these negative qualities and cultivate healthy behaviors and mental states. The inventory process and the practice of mindfulness act as guardians, keeping watch over those destructive impulses and guiding us back to our better selves.

Today remember to keep up the practice of self-reflection, cultivating the positive and abandoning the negative.

# October 4

*"Balanced Inventory"*

At times the Twelve Step literature emphasizes taking our own inventory to an extreme degree. In fact, the whole Twelve Step culture often takes the perspective that we should only ever consider our own part in conflicts. While there is clearly a value in being completely honest about our mistakes and failings, if we look exclusively at our own issues, we can develop a negative and skewed view of ourselves, one that can lead to painful self-judgment.

Dharma teachings have a different emphasis, but one that can lead to similar problems. Here the focus tends to be on the judging mind. We're taught to take less seriously the critical and evaluative thoughts that appear. We see how the tendency to label everything as good or bad, right or wrong, traps us in a limited world view, one bounded by our conditioned beliefs, often unquestioned and unseen. Learning to see these judgments and let them go is a significant step in the development of a dharma practice. However, like the over-emphasis on inventory, it can have a downside.

If we cease to take any of our judgments seriously, we become wishy-washy. We can't take a stance or assert any truth or value on anything. The key with both Step work and dharma practice is to learn to distinguish judgment from discernment. Judgment is conditioned, biased opinion based on unexamined beliefs and reactions. Discernment is wise understanding based on mindful reflection, consideration, and accumulated wisdom. A sincere practice of mindful self-examination gives us the clarity to see the difference.

Today, consider where inventory and letting go of judgment have become out of balance in your program and your practice. Start to bring honest evaluation and discernment to such situations so that you can have a more accurate understanding of yourself and others.

# October 5

## *"Maintenance"*

In meetings we recognize and celebrate the amount of time someone has been clean and sober. We don't demand that they prove how well they've worked the Steps or how the rest of their life is going. The belief is that with time, everything will work out. While this isn't true in all cases, what we do know is that if we relapse things will almost certainly get worse. So, maintenance becomes, in some ways, job number one after our initial recovery.

How do we maintain our recovery, besides working Step Ten? There are some obvious supports we all know about: going to meetings, working with a sponsor, sponsoring others, and continuing to work the Steps. For many of us, we also need to address emotional challenges and health challenges, as well as relationship and career challenges. The program and our community can help us to face all of these problems, but our recovery also means that we are learning to handle things as mature adults. We call upon therapeutic and medical help when needed. We learn to network and develop professionally. We are able to ask for help, but we are also able to take care of ourselves when appropriate. This is all part of thriving in recovery.

Our dharma practice also requires careful tending to sustain it. Daily meditation is a must for any serious practitioner. Sitting and studying with a group is also vital. More intensive practice on retreats takes us deeper into meditation and an understanding of the dharma. And study through books, audio, and video is an important source of growth.

If we aren't growing in our program and our practice, we risk relapse and regression. Maintenance doesn't mean staying where we are, but rather continuing to deepen our spiritual lives.

Today reflect on how you are maintaining your program and your practice. What could you do to grow and sustain your recovery and your meditation?

# October 6

### *"Keep It Simple"*

It's easy to get tied up in knots with our meditation technique. The more we learn about meditation, the more elaborate it can seem. While it's useful to study the nuances of practice, at times it's best to return to basics.

One of the most basic elements of mindfulness meditation is paying attention to the breath. Once you choose where to pay attention to the breath, usually either at the tip of the nostrils or the belly, get very familiar with that experience. Examine the details of sensation. Get in the habit of taking the mind to that place. Throughout your day, come back to the breath.

Another basic element is stillness. Work at maintaining a balanced, upright posture that you can hold in stillness for sustained periods. Try not to move while sitting.

The third basic element is returning to the breath. You can't force the mind to stop wandering, so that is an inevitable part of practice. Sure, there may be times when the thoughts quiet down, but much of the time we'll find our attention to the breath interrupted. We need to get into the habit of coming back without adding commentary or judgment. It's easy to get frustrated with the wandering mind, but such frustration only creates more of a problem. Work at letting go of self-evaluation in your meditation, just accepting what arises.

Today, focus on the basics of your practice. Strip it down and only add elements that are useful.

# October 7

*"Daily Practice Inventory"*

When you have a regular daily meditation practice, you might become frustrated with the frequent or persistent distractions that come up. You sit down to get some quiet time, and instead you are barraged with distracting thoughts and feelings. If you have had experiences of quiet on retreat or at other times, this can be particularly frustrating as you try to get that serenity back. However, there is another way to look at it.

What comes up in your daily practice can be your Tenth Step. It can point you to the things that are out of balance, any issues that need attention, and the unskillful actions that might need amends. If we take these seeming distractions as a form of inventory instead, they become important road signs for our actions. This is a place where Twelve Step work intersects our meditation practice.

You might remember something you said yesterday that was hurtful and realize you need to make amends. You might get some clarity about a difficult decision you are trying to make. You might uncover painful emotions that you have been trying to avoid. All this and more can come up in daily practice. Rather than ignoring or fighting all of this, if you take it as guidance and inventory, it can be utilized in fruitful ways.

At times it can be helpful to let the mind process such issues as you sit. Once resolved, you might find that your meditation returns to a more stable state. It's just important to avoid rumination or circular thinking. Once something has come up a number of times and you've processed it to some degree, then it's best if you can try to let it go.

Today, notice what is coming up in your meditation and consider if there might be any skillful response to those thoughts and feelings.

# October 8

*"Stale"*

When we first get fully engaged in recovery, we often find a lot of energy and inspiration carrying us forward. The same can be true of meditation and dharma study. It feels as if life has opened up for us with a whole new realm of possibilities. Over time, though, things can become stagnant. We go to the same meetings day after day, week after week. We get to a point where we've heard everyone's story, and it starts to feel like the same thing repeated over and over. Meditation, too, can get routine and seem tedious. This is why we need to keep our spiritual practice alive and engaged.

In recovery, this often means looking for opportunities to be of service. Helping others takes the spotlight off our problems and allows us to bring forth our own love and compassion. Caring for others gives us energy and a sense of connection.

We can also review the Steps to see where we might have drifted away from the principles. Are we really working our program? Have we forgotten our powerlessness, the nature of our disease? Is self-will taking over as we forget our Step Three commitment to turn it over? And finally, are we in need of inventory? Have we let resentments build up or left conflicts unresolved? An occasional Step check-up can help us to address these problems.

With our meditation, there are always opportunities to go deeper. Try adding ten minutes to your usual time frame. Listen to dharma talks or attend a sitting group. Go on retreat, whether for just a day or longer. Sign up for a dharma study course either in person or online.

There are many ways to revitalize our recovery program and meditation practice. It's vital that we keep them both alive and well. Our life may depend on it.

Today reflect on how engaged you are with your program and your practice. If things are slipping a bit, consider recommitting to one or both and putting more effort and time into them.

# October 9

*"Fresh"*

In recovery we're reminded to take it "one day at a time." In mindfulness practice, we are encouraged to stay in the present, to "be here now." Both traditions are encouraging us to engage in this day, this moment, this breath. With this approach, we can feel the immediacy of life. It's not something out there, or something in the future or past. Life is here, right now, to be felt, to be known, to be loved. All we really have is this moment.

When we take this attitude, each day is fresh. We see that even the most routine, mundane tasks like doing the dishes or taking out the garbage have richness within them. Life is defined not by drama, excitement, or stimulation, but simply the consciousness and the senses allowing us to be awake and aware. When we stop looking for some big moment to bring meaning to our life, we discover that joy and fulfillment are right here in front of us.

As addicts we were always looking for the next thrill, for a better high, a bigger rush. In recovery, we discover the joy of simplicity. We find the comfort of being a "worker among workers," of showing up and taking responsibility. We take pride in doing the next right thing, in being of service, and in living with integrity. We learn that being part of a community of recovery can fill our lives with purpose and connection.

The dharma gives us tools for enriching this sense of connection. We train the mind to be here; we enliven the senses; we open the heart. All of this means that being present isn't just theoretical or aspirational, but something we can know directly for ourselves.

Today remember to stay awake and aware to each moment. Enjoy the simplicity of mindful recovery.

# October 10

*"Showing Up"*

With recovery and dharma practice we can get tangled up in all the information and challenges. The Steps can feel daunting, and Buddhist teachings can seem complicated. Sometimes it helps to remember that the essence of both is showing up.

In recovery showing up starts with literally showing up at meetings. Doing this on a regular basis helps establish us in the program. A lot unfolds from just showing up. We make friends who support us; we learn how people handle the challenges of not drinking and using; we hear stories of how to deal with the greater challenges of life; we find a sponsor; and eventually we start to be of service. All of recovery unfolds from this simple daily effort of showing up. Without it, nothing happens; with it, everything becomes possible.

With meditation, it's much the same. We can read all the dharma books in the world, but if we don't show up on the cushion (or chair), nothing much happens. We have to show up for meditation. And like recovery, it's not about getting it perfect or right, but just about being there. Everything unfolds from the simple act of sitting down and trying to pay attention.

Showing up is the essence of mindfulness. We show up for the present moment. We aren't avoiding our feelings; we aren't trying to escape reality. We are here, now.

Sometimes it's hard to trust that showing up is enough. We want things to happen more quickly. But showing up allows the process of growth and change to unfold in a natural way. We can't rush things, but we find that if we stick with our program and our practice, big things eventually happen.

Today just focus on showing up for your practice and your program. Take it easy, one day, one step, and, yes, one breath at a time.

# October 11

*"Able to Be Irritated"*

One of the descriptions of the alcoholic in the AA Big Book is, "restless, irritable, and discontent." To be irritable means you are "able to be irritated." Notice how one day someone might cut you off on the highway and you let it go—you're not "able to be irritated." On another day, you might fly off the handle, swearing at them and honking your horn. Why? Because you are irritable.

Moods like irritability infiltrate our thinking and behavior. Without understanding the underlying causes, we react negatively to situations that might otherwise not bother us. Mindfulness helps us to both avoid irritability, and, when we do get irritable, be more aware of what's behind it, and thus be less reactive. We often discover that something like hunger, fatigue, or stress is triggering these feelings.

Moods like this can cause problems across a wide spectrum of our lives, from our intimate relationships to our work life and ordinary interactions with strangers. Flashing anger can create blowback and broad problems that could have pretty easily been avoided with a more rational response.

Of course, we can't always maintain equanimity. Everyone is susceptible to moods, and even if we are in recovery and practicing mindfulness, we can have lapses. That's where honesty, humility, and willingness to make amends comes in. When we can recognize and admit our mistakes, we cut short any potential expansion of blowback. People can be very forgiving when we are willing to admit we are wrong.

As part of your daily mindfulness practice, track your moods, being especially attentive to irritable and negative states that can create conflict with others. When these do arise, make extra effort to avoid reactivity and make amends quickly.

# October 12

## *"The Cycle of Depression"*

Many of us in recovery suffer from bouts of depression. We often wonder why these feelings arise. Debates about the causes of depression have gone on for a long time, and they continue today. Some researchers believe brain chemistry is the culprit, while others point to childhood trauma or genetics. Whatever the causes, it seems apparent that some people are more susceptible than others. For them, breaking the cycle with mindfulness can be an indispensable key to recovery.

When someone feels a painful emotion, they naturally try to figure out why it's happening and how to get rid of it. They start to think about it, often incessantly. However, instead of eliminating the feeling, thinking about it actually tends to exacerbate it.

That's because now not only do you feel bad, but you've engaged in a struggle with the feeling. In Buddhist terms, you have *aversion* to the feeling. You now feel bad about feeling bad. That just gives you something else to think about. This thought-to-feeling-to-thought cycle continues, and as it does, the feelings themselves invade the body. Further, the feelings trigger memories of other past depressive feelings of the same nature. In this way, your consciousness seems to become enveloped in the negative, painful feelings: your thoughts, emotions, sensations, and memories are all about the pain, the depression.

It would be irresponsible to suggest that mindfulness or Buddhism is always going to be sufficient to counter such an all-encompassing experience. Professional and sometimes medical help might well be called for. But understanding this cycle, seeing the chain of causality, the karmic process, can help us to reframe our experience. Rather than seeing it as a solid and, indeed, mysterious mind state, we deconstruct depression into its components, breaking apart the illusion of inevitability that it projects. Now, although we might still feel sad, down, or drained, we see that those feelings do not define us, are not permanent, and are, in fact, manageable.

Today, start to notice the component parts to difficult mind states and watch how they become constructed through cause and effect.

# October 13

*"Identifying with the Body"*

At the heart of the Buddha's teaching is the idea that what we call "the self" is an illusion. This illusion starts with our relationship to the body.

We experience the body as something that belongs to us—"my body"—and something that is part of "my identity" and "my responsibility." The Buddha questions all of these assumptions. He points out that if the body belonged to you, you would be able to make it behave just as you wanted. You'd never get sick, grow old, or die. You would look the way you want and be able to make the body do anything you want it to. Since this is obviously not true, then we can't actually claim that the body is "mine."

When we look in the mirror we think, "That is me." But Buddhism contradicts this belief as well. We see that what we are looking at is impermanent. The "me" in the mirror is only temporary. Years ago we looked and felt completely differently, and years from now we'll also look quite different. Internally as well, everything is changing as we age. If this body is in constant flux, how can it be "me"?

We also look to the body as a source of pleasure. As addicts we discovered the limits of this strategy. While moments of comfort are possible, no lasting satisfaction can come through the senses. Comfort and pleasure always pass—often quite quickly—leaving us with more longing. It was the misunderstanding of this truth that led us to seek relief through our addiction.

Today, notice your attachment to the body, and recognize its impermanent, unsatisfactory, and empty nature. Notice how fleeting moments of pleasure actually are.

# October 14

*"Mudita: Sympathetic Joy"*

*Mudita* is the quality of taking joy in the happiness of others. The third of the four *Brahmaviharas*, mudita is perhaps the least understood and least addressed. In English, we don't really have this concept, even though we certainly experience it. When our child scores a goal or our friend gets a promotion, we are happy for them, we experience mudita. But certainly, most of us don't take joy in all of the successes and joys of those we know. Envy erodes this capacity. When our friend gets the job we wanted, or our neighbor's child scores over ours, mudita can be a distant thought.

Most of us have to learn to cultivate and recognize mudita in order to make it a regular part of our lives. When we are taking joy in the baby we pass in a stroller, we are feeling mudita. When our friend gets some good news, we may have to remind ourselves that the happiness we feel for them is a form of mudita. The magic of mudita is that someone is almost always happy about something, so there are many opportunities to feel it if we look for them.

Mudita is sometimes called "appreciative joy." This alternative definition broadens its meaning to include enjoying natural beauty, art, or anything that touches our heart. Looking for opportunities to appreciate life can break the negative habit of always looking for challenges and obstructions. This isn't a question of being in denial or not recognizing dukkha in the world, but rather one of bringing balance.

Today, begin to look for the joy and beauty around you. Take time to practice mudita, sympathetic and appreciative joy.

# October 15

### *"Daily Review"*

One of the standard suggestions for working Step Ten is to review your day at bedtime. Taking time to reflect on any negatives or positives from the day is a helpful way to grow, trying to learn from your mistakes and build on your successes. You don't want to make this into another self-judgment where you just feel bad about yourself, but if you can review your day with an attitude of curiosity and willingness to change, it can be of real benefit.

True development in recovery is a long-term project. We come into the program broken to a greater or lesser extent. For many of us, we aren't just suffering from addiction, but we're also dealing with emotional problems, relationship problems, and work or career problems. Quitting drinking and drugging and other addictions and going to a few meetings doesn't begin to fix all this. Getting clean is just the prerequisite for dealing with these broader problems.

Daily inventory is a way of carefully looking at our lives and teasing out the issues that need attention. We don't conquer depression or anxiety in a day, but we can find a therapist and start that work. We don't fix our relationships overnight, but we can bring a different attitude to our interactions. And we can't build a career with the snap of a finger, but we can reach out and make a couple of contacts each day. After such a day, we can look back and see that we are doing what we need to do little by little. That's how real change happens.

Recovery isn't about big, world-changing events. It's built on the small steps we take to gradually bring about change in our lives. It takes time, usually years. That's one reason why we count days, months, and years of recovery, because time is what it takes to change.

If you don't already, start to make a daily review or inventory part of your program. Look for the small steps you can take each day to work towards big change.

# October 16

### *"Meeting Deep Suffering"*

In Twelve Step meetings we find real life, and part of real life is deep suffering. People bring their greatest sorrows, losses, fears, and resentments to meetings because they know people will listen. Every person who walks into an AA, NA, or any other kind of recovery meeting knows suffering, and that gives us a sense that we will be understood. But even further, we believe that the group, the fellowship, will be able to hold our suffering without being overwhelmed.

In the suttas, the Buddha talks about how a spoonful of salt in a glass of water makes it undrinkable, but a spoonful of salt in the Ganges will be absorbed with little effect. In the same way, the group can contain the pain of an individual.

Each of us as individuals also needs to be able to meet this deep suffering. Oftentimes people need more than just sharing on the group level. They also need one-on-one time. We have to learn to listen. This isn't easy. There's a tendency to want to fix people. Just listening doesn't seem like enough. But listening is the starting point, being able to hear someone's pain without moving away or trying to do anything about it.

When we are able to listen deeply, we can respond with real compassion and wisdom. We don't have to think of an answer or a solution, because our hearts will guide us. More than anything people want attention, to have someone listen who genuinely cares and understands.

It can be scary to listen to someone's deep suffering. It's as though we're afraid it will rub off on us or we'll be swamped by it and wind up in our own state of despair. But that is just fear talking. Suffering isn't contagious. In fact, listening to a person talk about their pain tends to open our hearts and make us feel more alive. Pain is so palpably real that it wakes us up to the preciousness of this moment and opens us to love. This is one of the mysteries of compassion.

Today, let yourself be open to the suffering around you. Try to hold it with care, kindness, wisdom, and genuine interest.

# October 17

### *"Elements of Self-Care"*

An important part of our daily program and practice is self-care. This has many dimensions beyond just avoiding our addictive behavior.

One of the first things we need to address in recovery is diet. When we're caught in self-destructive addictions, healthy food is often a low priority. To get well and to feel good, we need to establish healthy eating habits. For those with eating disorders, obviously this is even more important.

Regular exercise is also key. Again, in our lives of addiction, getting exercise could easily be ignored. A solid exercise routine benefits not only our physical health, but our mental health as well. Aerobic exercise especially counters depression and anxiety.

Psychotherapy is a tool that many people in recovery find beneficial. This allows us to deal with emotional issues that meetings and the Steps don't necessarily address. While not a solution to addiction, therapy can be an important supplement to our recovery.

Meditation is another vital element of self-care. Although meditating won't cure your addiction or solve your emotional problems, once abstinence is established and acute mental states are addressed, daily meditation can be a big maintenance tool for sustaining emotional balance. It also supports physical health by alleviating stress.

While recovery can seem like a fulltime job, finding time for fun is also important. Try to find activities that bring you joy: biking, swimming, or other sports; pursuing a hobby, a creative project, or simply going to the movies. Remember that life isn't just about self-improvement.

In many ways, though, self-care begins and ends with our own thoughts. What am I thinking about myself? What are my self-beliefs? These ideas can undermine all of our attempts at self-care. Throughout your day, notice the thoughts that persist. Learn to talk back and let go of the negativity.

Today, consider what ways you are caring for yourself. Could you do a better job of bringing these tools into your life?

# October 18

*"Inventory Risks"*

Daily inventory has many benefits, but it can also carry risks. Persistently looking at our failings or weaknesses can undermine self-esteem. It's important to maintain balance in this regard and another reason why positive inventory is a useful part of recovery.

The orientation of the Twelve Steps is toward undermining egotism, self-centeredness, and resentments. While these are certainly common problems for addicts, there are also many people who suffer from low self-esteem and whose problems aren't so much outer-directed as inner. Such people can actually be harmed by an overemphasis on personal inventory. Instead of undermining their egotism, it supports their lack of self-worth. This can trigger depressive states and a narrative of self-criticism. The question is, how do we determine the appropriate level of inventory versus positive support?

Such a question is difficult for the individual to answer for themselves, at least initially. This is where sponsors, friends, therapists, and others in our support network can be helpful guides. These people can help us to develop a more realistic view of ourselves, our shortcomings and our assets. They can give us feedback on our self-view. They can give more objective advice on our behavior.

With time, we can internalize their guidance. Gradually our thinking starts to change so that we don't automatically assume that we are in the wrong or that we have failed. We develop a broader, more detached view of ourselves and of the world.

Today, consider whether your self-view reflects the way others see you. Make it a habit to check with others before assuming you are at fault or bear responsibility for your life's challenges and conflicts.

# October 19

## *"Metta: The Difficult Person"*

Often the most challenging aspect of loving-kindness meditation is offering positive thoughts to the so-called "difficult person." Here we are asked to send thoughts of loving-kindness to someone who has personally hurt us or to some other figure who arouses enmity in us. This is never simple.

Typically, we come to this aspect of metta practice after sending love to self and benefactor, working with friends and dear ones, and then a neutral person. By this time, we have, hopefully, cultivated a positive feeling inside so that we aren't just plunged into facing the difficult person unprepared.

To be motivated to offer metta to the difficult person, we need to understand the essence of the practice. We aren't doing this just to feel good or to open our hearts, though both of those things may happen in the course of the meditation. Rather, we are trying to shift our entire view of living beings from one of separation and conditionality, to one of connection and unconditional love. We appreciate that every being wants happiness, comfort, and safety. Everyone wants love. No one wants to suffer. When we fully embrace this understanding, we are meant to be inspired to open our arms to even our enemy.

A further understanding, when looking at someone who has harmed people or done destructive acts, is that their behavior came out of their ignorance. They believed that doing those things would bring them happiness—or resolve something in their lives. This points to their lack of understanding of the Law of Karma. The Buddha taught that such ignorance inevitably leads to suffering, if not in the present then in the future.

It is with this spirit of wise understanding that we reach out to the difficult person and offer love.

Today, reflect on the understanding of why we give love to the difficult person, and begin to include them in your metta practice.

# October 20

*"Risks of Meditation"*

Meditation is usually depicted as a respite from life's stresses and a chance to connect with your spiritual essence. But that's not always what happens. In fact, just sitting down and closing your eyes in a quiet place can trigger difficult feelings.

Most of us aren't used to shutting out the world in this way, and it can feel awkward at first. This is usually overcome fairly quickly, but many addicts have underlying tendencies that can get exacerbated in the openness of meditation.

In recent years more attention has been paid to the potential for silent meditation retreats to bring up past trauma or cause dissociating, the tendency to get disconnected from our ordinary perception of mind and body. When we remove distractions, close the eyes, and go inside, sometimes we meet up with buried memories and wounds that can't always be managed simply with meditation.

Some strict meditation teachers will insist that such feelings can always be dealt with simply by returning to the breath and toughing it out. This seems like dangerous advice. If panic attacks, dissociation, or painful memories of abuse or trauma come up in meditation, it is much wiser to address these with a therapist. These days there are more and more professionals who understand the interface between addiction and trauma, as well as those who are familiar with the risks of triggers from meditation.

Fortunately, many of these issues are actually addressed in Step and recovery work. Inventory, especially, helps to bring such wounds into the light where they can be healed.

Today, reflect on your own challenging experiences with meditation. If any of these feel unmanageable, consider seeking out a skilled therapist who can help with the feelings that are coming up.

# October 21

*"Why Am I Doing This?"*

If there are all these potential risks in meditating, is it really a good idea to do it? Is it just a coincidence that Step Eleven (next month) comes late in the process? Is it best to hold off on this part of the program until you are stabilized in your recovery?

There is no simple answer to these questions. Some people are ready, willing, and able to engage in meditation from day one. In fact, many people have experience with meditation even before coming into recovery. For them, it can be very helpful to pick up their practice right away. For others with no background in spiritual practice, it might feel awkward and even overwhelming to jump right into periods of silence. For them it might be best to wait a little while.

Nonetheless, truly problematic experiences in meditation are not that common and mostly happen on longer silent retreats. The practice has so many potential benefits for the addict that it's worthwhile bringing it into your life as soon as possible.

Just being still is a good practice for addicts. To sit and do nothing with no distractions or entertainment brings you face to face with yourself. Right away this is like an inventory where you are forced to look at what is appearing in your mind. This helps you to see the fears, obsessions, and distractions that consume you, and allows you to begin the process of letting go.

Sitting with ourselves develops the capacity to calm our own body and mind. This then helps us to manage emotions, becoming less volatile and reactive.

And finally, our meditation practice draws us in to our spiritual depth and intuitive wisdom. We connect with the world, with others, and with ourselves in ways we never could when active in our addiction. A new sense of clarity and capacity for reflection arises.

Today, consider the benefits you derive from your practice. Remind yourself why you meditate. If you haven't started meditating, ask yourself why not?

# October 22

*"Not–Self"*

One of the most profound teachings of the Buddha is that of "anatta" or not-self. He says that the body is not the self, and neither is the mind, consciousness, nor perception. Our name does not define us, and neither does our family or our profession. Because everything is constantly changing, there is nothing permanent to point to as "me."

Nonetheless, on the relative level, here we are. We have our lives, our memories and plans, our resume, and our social security number. We have to take care of ourselves.

Spiritual maturity involves moving gracefully between these two realities. The understanding of not-self helps us to be less attached to identity, to success, to our place in the world. We realize that on the absolute level, we are only playing a temporary role. When we are attached to identity, we will suffer, because identity isn't stable. Our kids grow up, we lose our job, we get old and lose our looks; it all dissolves. If you depend on any of these things for your happiness, you will inevitably face loss and pain.

Loosening attachment to self doesn't mean you won't feel something when things change, but hopefully with this acquired wisdom you will not be overwhelmed or confused. You'll be able to hold change with understanding and acceptance.

In the Twelve Step tradition, anonymity is the corollary to not-self. Anonymity is said to be the "spiritual foundation" of the program, encouraging us to place "principles before personalities." In a Twelve Step meeting we are putting aside our worldly identity to connect on a basic level with other human beings. We don't see ourselves as unique or special, just one of the group. Addiction is a very self-centered condition, one that seeks to both comfort and glorify the individual. Letting go of the need to be different and stand out is one of the elements of freedom that come with anonymity and not-self.

Today, reflect on the ways you are attached to your identity. Start to notice how that attachment causes suffering and consider how you could let go.

# October 23

*"Mantra Meditation"*

A mantra is a word or sound we repeat silently while meditating. Many traditional practices depend on mantras, though mindfulness doesn't emphasize this form. The advantage of a mantra is that it makes your practice very simple. It's so easy to get tied up in knots while meditating, especially when trying to follow complicated instructions. With a mantra you simply repeat the mantra, and when the mind wanders, you come back.

One mantra used in the Thai Forest Tradition is "Buddho." This is, of course, a variant on Buddha. The word is divided into two parts to go with the inhalation and the exhalation: "Bud-dho." You can stretch each syllable for the length of each part of the breath. In this way, the syllables might change in length as the breath changes. This is perfectly fine.

Don't try to control the breath, just let it be natural. Feel the sensations and let the mind become absorbed in Buddho.

Anytime you find the mind wandering, don't worry about it, simply come back to Buddho.

You don't need to analyze Buddho. You're simply letting the sound of the word repeat in the mind. Nothing to figure out, nothing to accomplish. Just an easy, rhythmic repetition with the breath.

Mantra can be very relaxing, so try to stay upright and alert while working with Buddho. Try to sit for twenty minutes or more.

The mind might become quite still, which is one of the potential benefits of mantra practice. Don't try to make this happen; don't worry if it doesn't happen; and resist thinking about it if it does happen.

Your mind might also fight back against getting quiet and start throwing up more and more agitated thoughts and worries. Just continue to breathe and recite Buddho. Eventually the mind will tire of distractions and settle into the simple calm of Buddho.

Today, experiment with using Buddho as a mantra during your meditation.

# October 24

*"Domestic Harmony"*

One of the great challenges for each of us is maintaining a harmonious home life. Many addicts have struggled with intimacy, and in recovery we may find that we don't have great relationship skills. For many of us, this is the final challenge of recovery, and the one that needs the most ongoing work.

Addicts tend to be defensive and over-sensitive to criticism. We need to be able to hear our partner without being reactive, otherwise our relationship will be one long battle—followed by a breakup. The inventory and amends Steps can help us to become less sensitive and more willing to hear criticism.

Self-centeredness is another failing of addicts that undermines relationships. The attempt to control others or think only of our needs is alienating. No relationship can survive when these are dominant qualities.

It takes great commitment to change our relationship patterns. These habits are deeply conditioned. Only by bringing the tools of mindfulness and recovery can we begin to overcome them. With mindfulness, we start to see more clearly how these emotions and behaviors are automatic and unconscious. When we bring consciousness to them, we can choose to respond differently.

Now we begin to be open and accepting of criticism (not that we like it). We see that a few suggestions or observations about our behavior aren't insults or meant to harm us. We can listen and appreciate that this person might have a point. We might even benefit from their ideas.

We also start to think of the needs of others. Before taking actions or speaking, we consider the effects they will have on someone else. We realize that simply satisfying our own wishes doesn't make us happy. We need others to be happy as well.

Today, reflect on the harmony or lack thereof in your closest relationships. Are you willing to make changes to your attitude and behavior to heal them?

# October 25

### *"An Archetypal Path: Steps 1–3"*

While the Twelve Steps use Christian-influenced language, they can also be viewed as something more universal, an archetypal spiritual path.

This path starts with suffering, darkness, and confusion. This is the condition of the addict before recovery. Step One is the admission of our failure to overcome these forces ourselves: a surrender. This surrender is essential to any path because we must be willing to look outside ourselves and our habitual responses to find a new path forward.

Once we have surrendered to our condition, we must also have confidence that there is some way to heal. This is the promise of Step Two. If we remove the idea of religious belief from this Step, what is left is trust in the possibility of recovery and of our capacity to realize that possibility. The Third Noble Truth in Buddhism, that freedom is possible, says the same thing in different language and in a more general context, not just around addiction.

Step Three is the commitment to the path, the "decision." While much emphasis is put on the God part of this Step, in fact, it is the commitment to live in harmony with spiritual values and to accept the results of our actions that truly define the Step. We must step out of our personal preferences and find a higher reference for our actions, including our thoughts. When we live by this commitment to spiritual principles, our life begins to change in radical ways.

Today, reflect on the ways that the first three Steps inform and guide your life.

# October 26

*"An Archetypal Path: Steps 4–7"*

On a spiritual path, self-examination is vital to any progress. Without such careful reflection we can't truly change because we don't actually understand ourselves. Step Four requires us to dig deeply into our past before moving forward. From a simplistic view one might think that we should just forget the past and move on, focusing solely on the present. But the past lives inside us and informs our thoughts and actions in this present moment, and until it is seen clearly, we are simply repeating conditioned behaviors.

Sharing what we uncover about ourselves as we do in Step Five is part of the confession found in many traditions. It's not enough to admit our failings to ourselves. They must be revealed; they must come out of the shadows. Here comes the possibility of ending shame and guilt. Our inventory is a description of our human failings, or more essentially, our humanness. When we see them in this light, we are able to forgive ourselves more readily, to have compassion for our own suffering, and further, to clarify what needs to be addressed in the succeeding Steps.

Step Six is the beginning of transformation. Having seen the nature of our suffering and our failings, we are motivated and ready to change. Step Seven is where this process activates. The God language of the Steps serves to obscure the actual work here, which involves changing our karma through thoughts, words, and deeds.

Up to now, much has been revealed in our Step work, but actual behavioral change has been limited. Now, with the inventory to guide us and the clarity of intention, we make a concerted effort to take up new behaviors, to learn Right Speech, and most of all, to investigate our thinking so that it becomes more aligned with truth, with love, and with wisdom.

Today, reflect on the ways Steps Four through Seven have changed you.

# October 27

*"An Archetypal Path: Steps 8–9"*

Before we can complete our job of healing the past and moving on, we must revisit those we have harmed to make amends. This is the final agonizing stage of the middle Steps, Four to Nine. No longer theoretical or limited to words on a page, our work now is to confront, to apologize, to ask forgiveness, and do what we can to make up for the harm we have done. Fully exposed and vulnerable we learn the power of amends and self-forgiveness.

At this point, we also learn the limits of amends. For those who have passed away or who we know will be hurt by any contact or revisiting of the past, we must hold back. This denies any closure and means that we will have to carry our sense of grief and regret with us in our lives. But as we face the truth of the harm we have done, we realize that these wounds can never be fully healed.

This is the spiritual maturity that comes to understand that life involves carrying loss, scars, and grief forward with us, not as burdens but as emblems of having lived. We all harm others, just as each of us is harmed. The process of these middle Steps isn't ultimately one of going beyond that pain, but learning to hold it with kindness, wisdom, and compassion. We see ourselves as human beings, not especially good *or* bad. Just human. And this insight in itself is freeing. No longer striving for perfection or wallowing in failure, we can accept and love ourselves just as we are.

Today, see if you can hold your past with kindness and forgiveness, seeing mistakes as natural and human.

# October 28

*"An Archetypal Path: Steps 10–12"*

The final three Steps take us into the realm of the future. Having made our peace with the past we now set our eyes on the path forward, setting up guidelines and boundaries so that we can continue to grow and heal.

With Step Ten, this involves a commitment to honesty and humility, the understanding that, even though we've completed our inventory and amends, we still make mistakes that need to be addressed. Without this commitment, we risk falling back into the same habits or even relapsing.

Step Eleven describes the overtly spiritual elements of the path, the practices of prayer and meditation that train the heart and mind and lead to the truly revolutionary awakening promised in Buddhism and the Twelve Steps. We are reminded that this path is not a selfish one, that we must listen for the wisdom that will bring the highest good.

Step Twelve points to the transformation that this path has created, asking us to appreciate how far we have come from the degradation of addiction to the heights of awakening. And again, we're reminded that we do not practice for ourselves alone, but that we have a responsibility to carry forward what we have learned to try to heal the world.

Finally, we are told that there are no boundaries around this path, that it's not limited to some esoteric spiritual philosophy. We are responsible at all moments in all situations. This is the essence of the path.

Today, consider how you are living the Steps in your life. How could you more fully embrace their principles?

# October 29

### *"Friends"*

The Twelve Step program depends, as much as anything, on fellowship, the community of addicts, while Buddhism is supported by sangha, the community of practitioners. These are indispensable elements of spiritual practice that keep the traditions alive and give a social setting for our work.

Besides these communities, we need friends, individuals who we personally connect with. It's not enough to be a member of a group. We need to find people with whom we can share our personal struggles and challenges. While the community tends to focus on the general teachings and accepted practices, our friendships give us a place to explore the reality of our day-to-day lives.

Buddhism has a word for this relationship: kalyana mitta, or spiritual friend. In the Twelve Step world, we have a sponsor, who is less a friend than a mentor. In some ways, though, the most important support in recovery comes in the coffee shops and diners after meetings. There we chat and bond with the people who become our closest friends in recovery.

Isolating is one of the symptoms and causes of addiction. We can even isolate in our recovery, which becomes a risk for relapse. Making an effort to stay connected with friends in the program is vital both to maintaining our recovery and keeping our spirits and mood in good shape.

Our Buddhist practice can also become isolating, just meditating at home or even with groups doesn't give us much contact. It's important to find people who can become our kalyana mittas with whom we can talk about our practice and more.

In the larger society being a recovering addict or a Buddhist can make you a bit of an outsider. Being both puts you in a pretty small niche. Finding ways to connect with others in that niche will enrich both your practice and your program.

Today, make sure to reach out to a friend who supports you in your practice and your program.

# October 30

*"Sickness, Old Age, and Death"*

The Buddha, in his usual unvarnished way, reminds us that part of the challenge of life is the inevitability of sickness, old age, and death. His path helps us to live with this reality—and in some sense, transcend it.

Addicts, sadly, often make themselves sick and even kill themselves, accidentally or on purpose. We are lucky if we get to experience old age. To maintain some equanimity through these challenges is an important part of living in recovery.

What the Buddha offers us is a way to acceptance. By asking us to keep in mind that our health, youth, and even life itself are all temporary and contingent, he helps us to navigate the changes in our lives. If we live in denial about these truths, we will be shocked and devastated when their reality becomes unavoidable. But by holding them as normal parts of this brief life, our minds are not confused or disturbed as they arise. This isn't to say that we enjoy these changes, or that we don't feel grief, loss, and pain, only that those emotions are not compounded with the delusion that what is happening is unnatural or surprising.

Recognizing that these truths apply to everyone helps arouse compassion and a sense of connection with others. We are not alone in our suffering—or in our joys. Everyone, from the most powerful and wealthy to the downtrodden and impoverished is leveled by these realities.

Remembering these facts can also help us to value what we have today. When we don't take our lives for granted, we can appreciate the simple joys we get to experience. Life is precious and fleeting. It is a rare gift.

Today recollect your own frailty and mortality. Breathe with those realities. See if you can hold them with equanimity and acceptance.

# October 31

*"Spiritual Awakening"*

The spiritual awakening of Step Ten is the realization that our path of recovery is ongoing. We no longer seek quick answers or instant solutions. We don't see the Steps as a once-and-done event, but a lifetime's work. We understand that, despite our commitment to live more wisely, we will still make mistakes, probably lots of them.

When we let go of the idea of perfection and accept that it's okay to fail, to slip up, and stumble in our lives, we can be less judgmental of ourselves. We can bring more kindness to what is simply our human nature, not a personal flaw.

This doesn't mean that we give up on trying to avoid harm. We certainly strive to be the best people we can be. It's simply the recognition that even with the best of intentions, our humanity can't help but lead us into certain pitfalls. Even with the greatest effort to work the program and to follow the principles of the dharma, we are still somewhat driven by the underlying habits and conditioning of a lifetime, not to mention the genetic drives built into everyone.

A great freedom comes from not having to be perfect. We can take more risks, be more vulnerable, and give more of ourselves. Seeing our own imperfection is also a reminder that others are imperfect and shouldn't be judged for that. And, if no one is perfect, that includes our teachers and those who inspire us. If we don't put them on a pedestal, we can have a more healthy relationship with such people.

Step Ten is a doorway into a different future, one characterized by honesty, responsibility, and compassion.

Today, reflect on the awakenings that have come to you through your practice of Step Ten.

# November: Step 11

*"Sought through prayer and meditation to improve our conscious contact with God as we understood Him, praying only for knowledge of His will for us and the power to carry that out."*

# November 1

### *"Sought"*

The search that Step Eleven describes highlights how recovery is a spiritual journey of discovery. Beyond overcoming our addiction, the task before us requires an engagement with the most profound questions we can ask. We find a new way of living, discovering deeper truths about ourselves and ultimately about life. If recovery ever settles into a routine of abstinence and nothing more, we risk not just relapse, but falling entirely away from the path of awakening.

The seeker is a human archetype, someone who believes there is more to life than pleasure and accumulating wealth and power. While our primal impulses drive us toward these worldly gains, our spiritual vision reveals something deeper and more meaningful. As we let go of our efforts to control and conquer the material world, our hearts open in compassion and caring. The gentleness we uncover within ourselves brings a new perspective toward all beings and nature itself, a wish to heal and comfort the suffering of the world and an aspiration to help everyone achieve their highest potential.

With Step Eleven, then, we explicitly turn toward deepening our spiritual life, and toward developing greater wisdom and the capacity to act on that wisdom. We now see that this is where the Steps have been heading all along.

Today reflect on the nature of your spiritual journey. If you haven't already, make explicit your commitment to an ever-deepening awareness, compassion, and wisdom.

# November 2

*"What Is Meditation?"*

Meditation can take many forms: it can still the mind, connect us with our spiritual nature, and open the heart. It can help us to develop emotional balance, personal understanding, and universal wisdom.

In English, meditation usually refers to deep thinking on a profound topic. Thus, Bill Wilson suggests, in the *Twelve and Twelve* that we "meditate" on the St. Francis Prayer. Buddhists would, instead, call this "contemplation."

In other traditions, meditation is more about developing concentration, quieting our thoughts.

In Buddhist Insight Meditation, the goals and means are different. Here we combine a concentration practice, like focusing on the breath, with a mindfulness practice that seeks to understand the deepest reality.

While there are not rigid borders between these different approaches, Buddhists view the other forms as limited in their benefit, even as Buddhist meditation might draw from them.

With contemplation, the limiting factor is that of our thinking mind. Any spiritual growth that depends on thought is necessarily bound by the capacity of human logic and conditioning. We simply can't think our way to a spiritual awakening.

With the concentration practices, many people will certainly find comfort. But this can be a little like taking a pill. Once it wears off, there isn't much left to help you.

With Insight Meditation we can gain the benefits of these other two, while adding a third critical piece: a deeper understanding of ourselves and the world that comes from observing impermanence, discomfort, and attachment. We see how we create suffering by chasing pleasure and resisting pain; we see how the illusion of permanence creates a disconnect with the reality of constant change; and we develop real insight into how we cling to and protect our ego.

Today, reflect on your own meditation practice and what elements you rely on.

# November 3

*"What Is Prayer?"*

Many people who come to Buddhism from the Twelve Steps wonder how a Buddhist would pray. Since Buddhism doesn't posit an intercessionary God, one who steps into our lives to help us, then how does a Buddhist pray?

This begs the more basic question of "What is prayer?" For instance, when you repeat, "God, grant me the serenity to accept the things I cannot change..." do you really think that some external force is going to step in and make you serene? Is that what happens? It seems that this prayer is really a prayer to ourselves, a reminder that we shouldn't waste our time and energy fighting with things we can't control. When we are reminded of that fact, we tend to relax and let go—and thus become more serene.

Other prayers could be considered setting of intentions. Some are reminders to be grateful, while others evoke love and devotion, while still others point to the mysteries of existence.

In a way, what all of these prayers are doing is snapping us out of our self-centered mind state, our anxiety, anger, ego, and wish to control. They are familiar reminders of what is really important and what is really true.

Buddhists have similar practices. The "Refuge" chant states our intention to live in harmony with the Buddhist teachings and community. With loving-kindness and other similar meditations, we try to open the heart and feel our connection to the rest of the world. The Five Daily Contemplations remind us of impermanence and our responsibility to live with integrity.

While none of these practices suggest that the Buddha or anyone else can accomplish these things for us, the end result is probably the same as that of prayer.

Today reflect on your relationship to prayer. What is your understanding and what are your expectations of what your prayers accomplish?

# November 4

*"Conscious Contact"*

Step Eleven's admonition that we seek to improve our "conscious contact" with God suggests some mystical experience, going to the mountain top and receiving a secret message from the Divine. From a Buddhist standpoint, this phrase can be understood in a much simpler way: improving our mindfulness.

After all, what is mindfulness but conscious contact with the present moment? The whole path of mindfulness is one of cultivating a deeper and broader experience of reality. First, we work with mindfulness of the body and senses. Then we learn to notice the "feeling tone" of our sensory and mental experiences. This helps us to interrupt the flow of conditioned responses and bring more intentionality to our actions.

Next, we work at bringing mindfulness to our mind states, our emotions, and our thoughts, again, breaking the habitual patterns that tend to control our lives.

Finally, we try to view our experience through the lens of the Dharma, seeing how suffering is created and how it ends; how we create a sense of self; and how we attach to pleasure and avoid pain. We learn to cultivate kindness and compassion toward others, as well as emotional balance and non-reactivity.

All of this work is focused on improving our awareness—our conscious contact with life, with the mind, and with reality. Buddhist practice gives us these powerful tools for a lifelong effort at growing more conscious.

Today reflect on how conscious you are in your life. What areas would benefit from more effort to be aware? When do you tend to go more unconscious?

# November 5

*"As We Understood It"*

While the word "God" can be interpreted in many ways, , the word "him" in the Steps is hard to reconcile with an impersonal power. As we see more and more the damaging effects of sexism, misogyny, and toxic masculinity in our culture and around the world, calling God by a masculine pronoun only seems to perpetuate ancient patriarchal biases. Instead, we might call God "it" or even "them" if you prefer.

The point of the phrase, "as we understood Him" in the Steps, is to allow a very open interpretation of the word God. The founders of AA who wrote the Steps were first and foremost concerned with helping alcoholics recover, not putting forward a particular religious belief. Nonetheless, their own backgrounds as primarily Protestant Christians was bound to influence their use of language. But rather than squabbling with their words, it's more helpful to consider what they were trying to say.

Clearly they realized that religion and God are profoundly personal issues and that how people viewed them wasn't really important to the overall project of helping people get sober. Rather, what the Steps were saying is that *some* kind of spiritual life, some connection to something beyond self, beyond ego, beyond the grasping mind of the addict, was vital to sustaining sobriety and recovery.

Alcoholism and addiction are materialistic and hedonistic ways of addressing life's suffering. Spiritual teachings say that suffering can never be solved through material means because it's the very greed and aversion behind this strategy that causes our underlying suffering. Whether we take a theistic approach or one more like Buddhism's path of wisdom, one way or another we are going to need something that is not self-centered, that doesn't rest in the satisfaction of ego.

This might be God or Dharma or something else. What's important for recovery is the connection itself.

Today, reflect on how you understand Higher Power in your life.

# November 6

*"The Will of God"*

For a Buddhist, one of the most confounding phrases in the Steps is "knowledge of His will for us." This makes it sound as if we're going to get direct divine guidance. Again, from a non-theistic viewpoint, this makes no sense.

Meditation does, however, give us a way to think of this. As we let go of ego-driven thinking—as the Five Hindrances fall away (at least temporarily) and the mind settles down—our capacity for intuitive wisdom begins to shine through. This very idea is referenced in the *Big Book* when it says, "We find that our thinking will, as time passes, be more and more on the plane of inspiration." Whether we believe this thinking is coming from the outside, from God, or whether we understand it on a more earthly level as intuitive wisdom, the result is probably the same: clearer thinking, wiser decision-making, and less confusion.

Even without such inspiration, though, the Dharma gives us guidance. Right View and Right Intention make clear how we should think and act in the world. The Five Precepts themselves are guides to living. The instructions on mindfulness give us an approach to engaging our experience on every level. The teachings of the Brahmaviharas—loving-kindness, compassion, joy, and equanimity—offer more principles to follow. The understanding of the Three Characteristics—impermanence, suffering, and not-self—provide a lens through which to understand life and ourselves. So, there is no lack of help in finding out how to align ourselves with the Dharma, or the "will of the Dharma," if you prefer.

We have to tune in to know this will in each moment. We need to be awake and aware to activate our intuition. And we also have to study the Dharma so that we understand how it applies to a given situation. It is through this work that we will come to feel more confident that our actions are in alignment with the wisest path in our lives.

Today, reflect on your own intuitive wisdom. Are you cultivating the clarity and attention that allows this to arise? Do you understand the Dharma enough to apply its principles to your life?

# November 7

### *"Power"*

The Steps have a lot to say about power: our powerlessness over our addiction; the Higher Power we need to connect with; and now, the power we need to carry out "God's will."

What Step Eleven is trying to do is keep us from using prayer and meditation for selfish purposes. It points us toward God to take the focus off self. In the theistic framework, power comes from God, so that's where we are told to seek it. In Buddhist terms, we find power in a variety of places, not centered in one entity.

Certainly we as individuals have power, but the Steps display a lot of skepticism about the addict's capacity to use that power wisely. So they point us toward God. For a Buddhist this can have many aspects. Mindfulness is powerful, so we try to develop that. Love is powerful, so we cultivate that. Wisdom is powerful, so we seek that. Following the Precepts has powerful karmic effects, so they are our guides. And in fact, the entire Eightfold Path is powerful, so that is also our guide.

We might want to refer back to Buddhadasa Bhikkhu's words about prayer that "we beseech the law of karma through our actions, not merely with words." So, if we want to tap into the power of the Dharma, it is through the three forms of action: thoughts, words, and deeds.

What this all means is that when we pray for guidance and strength, we are not just sitting back waiting for results, but actively participating in the development of these qualities. This Buddhist interpretation of the Step is more complicated and subtle than a theistic version, but ultimately empowers us more than a passive relationship with an external power.

Today, reflect on the ways you are utilizing the power of the Dharma. How could you cultivate that power more?

# November 8

*"Choiceless Awareness"*

Mindfulness meditation instruction begins with very specific guidance, to pay attention to the breath, the body, to thoughts, and feelings. We might do a noting or concentration practice. All of these practices and others have clear forms and structures. However, at a certain point we might want to let go of these forms.

This calls to mind the Buddha's analogy of the raft. He says that, while someone might use a raft to cross a river, once across, you don't need to carry it with you. The implication is that the meditation forms are not the essence of what he teaches. The forms are meant to help us develop awareness and wisdom, but once we find that space of clarity, we don't have to hold to them.

Choiceless awareness is a way to step out of the box of form. In this approach, rather than directing the mind to a certain focus, whether the breath or anything else, you simply watch what is arising in consciousness. If a sensation is prevalent, you follow that until it passes; if a sound, you do the same. Or you might sit back and just watch the flow of experience as you would a scenic vista, not jumping on any particular object of awareness, just taking it all in.

This is a subtle practice, one that requires a certain amount of existing mental stability. If you try to jump into it too quickly, you are likely to space out, since there's no anchor for the awareness. You might try this approach halfway through a meditation period, once you've settled in. It can also be used on retreat when the natural concentration has developed.

Today, at some point in your meditation, try dropping the intentional focus on the breath and just watch what is arising and passing in consciousness.

# November 9

*"The Experience of Insight"*

*The Experience of Insight* was the title of the first book from the noted Western Buddhist teacher Joseph Goldstein. "Insight" is a common translation of the Pali term *vipassana*, but it doesn't capture the exact meaning of that word. In English, insight is an idea, thought or realization, something that we figure out, so it doesn't make sense to call it an "experience." However, *vipassana* points to something else.

In Buddhism, an insight is an understood experience, something we intuit. For instance, while we might logically get that clinging causes suffering, when we have a direct experience of that process, we gain real clarity and true understanding. With insight or mindfulness meditation, as we watch our own mind, we see the agitation that thinking often causes—this is the suffering. With sustained attention, we start to see how that agitation is really caused by the underlying impulse behind the thought, the grasping or the wish to control the ways things are. That's the clinging.

When we see that suffering clearly and then return to the breath, we notice how the agitation and suffering fade away. And we realize that it was through our mindfulness, focus, and engagement that this all happened.

When we see this process clearly, we are seeing the Four Noble Truths: suffering, its cause, its end, and the way to its end. And that is insight, the felt experience, the known experience. No longer theoretical or simply logical, we now know the Buddhist teaching for ourselves, in our own life, here and now. This is the "experience of insight."

Today, notice how the experience of insight manifests in your own meditation.

# November 10

*"The Steps Through Meditation: One, Two, and Three"*

While meditation is not mentioned until Step Eleven, it can actually be part of every one of the twelve. Using meditation and the Steps together in this way helps create an integrated practice. While this approach has limits because of the solitary nature of meditation, it also allows you to have a sense of ownership of your recovery, not always dependent upon meetings or other people in your program.

When we take the attitude of Step One into our meditation, it helps us face the torrent of thoughts, feelings, and sensations that often assault us as we begin to practice. Rather than immediately trying to control this flow, as with our relationship to our drug of choice, we come into acceptance of this powerful force. This doesn't mean that we don't engage in an effort to let go, but that this effort comes from a place of non-resistance rather than struggle. We can see this as "powerlessness" over mind and body.

Step Two tells us to trust that the practice will help us. Without some faith, we'll never be able to withstand the challenges we inevitably face. As we sit with the thoughts and feelings that arise, we lean on this faith to carry us through the difficult times. We sense that transformation is possible.

Step Three is the commitment to follow this path of meditation wherever it leads. When we begin to feel the power of practice and its capacity to heal, this commitment becomes wholehearted. Now we are willing to trust whatever outcomes result from any sitting or retreat, knowing that we are being carried in the right direction.

Today, notice how Steps One, Two, and Three are manifesting in your meditation practice.

# November 11

*"The Steps Through Meditation: Four and Five"*

Step Four is typically written down, but meditation offers us a way to reflect on our inventory internally. In fact, the torrent of thoughts and feelings that we've seen in Step One of this process contain much of that inventory. This is not a substitute for a written moral inventory, but something that enhances and reframes our self-knowledge.

As we've seen, Buddhism gives a variety of opportunities for what could be called inventory. In meditation the Five Hindrances—desire, aversion, sleepiness, restlessness, and doubt—are the most obvious of these. We watch them come and go in our meditative inventory.

The Five Precepts are another lens for this work. Here we see the explicit ways we have broken moral boundaries.

A more positive approach would be to look at how the Seven Factors of Awakening are manifesting in our practice and our lives. These include applying mindfulness and investigation; cultivating energy and joy; and developing calm, concentration, and equanimity. It's important to include this positive inventory so that our self-view doesn't become self-judgment.

While we don't want to make our meditation into a rumination on our flaws or even our assets, it's valuable to notice when these things appear in the mind and use the tools of practice to work with them.

In meditation, while we can't, as Step Five requires, admit our wrongs to another, we can become clearer about what needs to be shared. This can become part of any work with a meditation teacher who can help us to understand what we uncover in our meditative inventory.

Today, notice the opportunities for self-examination in your meditation practice. Make this a regular part of your practice.

# November 12

*"The Steps Through Meditation: Six and Seven"*

Ultimately our meditation practice is all about what happens in Steps Six and Seven. Here we do the work of letting go.

Step Six is about getting ready to let go, which is the first work of meditation. By watching our minds and seeing how we create suffering, we are motivated to stop following those destructive paths. The insights into impermanence, suffering, and not-self lay the groundwork for transformation.

Step Seven is where we take the action to change. While this happens in a number of ways, not just through meditation, our meditation is an essential part of the process. That's where we learn to let go, first by seeing more clearly what is going on in the mind and body, and second by utilizing the various techniques of meditation to effectuate this release.

In meditation we not only let go of thinking, but try to alter our deluded or distorted thoughts. Here the connection with cognitive-behavioral therapy appears again, guiding us to question the factual nature of our thinking. If we meditate regularly, we'll see the patterns that emerge, and discover how they diverge from reality. With mindfulness, we don't simply accept the thoughts that appear in the mind, but try to look at them as an impartial observer. This allows us to take a more objective stance and not be so caught by them.

Steps Six and Seven are also about being with feelings and letting them go. Our awareness reveals the nature of our emotional states and helps us interrupt the thoughts that spring from them. Sitting with the feelings, just as they are, allows those emotions to pass in a natural fashion, instead of feeding them with rumination.

Today, watch the process of letting go. See how it works for you, and try to make it part of your daily life beyond your meditation.

# November 13

*"The Steps Through Meditation: Eight, Nine, and Ten"*

Meditation doesn't appear to offer the opportunity for making amends, but these three Steps are actually supported meditating.

First, as our hearts open through practice, the wounds we caused bubble up from our memory, invited or not, helping us with our Step Eight list. Even those who didn't make it into our inventory will often come back to us. Further, the willingness this Step talks about is touched in the silence of meditation. Here we feel any resistance, and we learn to gently walk through that fear.

While we cannot make direct amends to others during meditation, we may find that for those who have passed, a loving-kindness or forgiveness meditation helps us to bring some sense of closure and healing.

Perhaps more to the point, meditation is an amends to ourselves. While we may have hurt other people in our addiction, there's no doubt that we also hurt ourselves. We abused our bodies and polluted our minds. We allowed our worst impulses to guide us. Meditation can be deeply healing on an ongoing basis, and so becomes a core part of our recovery.

Step Ten's admonition that we continue to take inventory and make amends is also supported by meditation. While busy and turbulent days may rush by, obscuring the underlying emotional effects of various thoughts, words, and actions, taking time to meditate often brings damaging actions into the foreground. Right in the midst of our meditation we might be struck by a memory of yesterday's behavior that requires amends.

Today, notice how your meditation practice weaves into your practice of inventory and amends.

# November 14

*"The Steps Through Meditation: Twelve"*

The three elements of Step Twelve are all developed and supported by meditation: spiritual awakening, carrying the message, and practicing the principles in all our affairs.

The insights and freedom that come from a committed meditation practice are the essence of spiritual awakening. Meditation opens our heart in a remarkable way that gives us access to feelings of love and connection otherwise lost to us. And the clarity that comes from simply quieting the mind reveals depths of reality that hide from ordinary consciousness. Meditation is the very tool for spiritual awakening.

With that awakening naturally comes the impulse to share our experience with others. Even as meditation points us inward, the greater sense of connection we feel, combined with the quieting of ego and preferences, all conspire to point us outward to caring more for the world. Love and compassion, wisdom and insight are not things one tries to hoard, but radiate to those around us and the world at large.

The training in mindfulness we receive in meditation isn't meant to be limited to times of quiet and stillness. Rather it becomes a model for how to be present throughout our lives. We develop the skill of mindfulness in the controlled environment of meditation, but then we learn to apply that skill in a broad range of activities. Further, the sensitivity that mindfulness evokes changes how we want to interact with others. Integrity, clarity, and kindness become not just pleasant goals, but deeply felt needs. The dissonance of unskillful actions becomes unsustainable, and we are driven to live a spiritual life wholeheartedly.

Today, reflect on the ways you are spiritually awake, how you share that awakening, and how you live it.

# November 15

*"Challenges of Meditation: Stillness"*

In some ways, meditation is quite simple. Just sit. But when we try to do it, we learn that it's not so easy. To sit still is the starting point—and in some ways, the end point—of meditation. What is the special value of sitting still?

Stillness of the body supports stillness of mind. When we hold the body still, it's easier to notice the movements of mind; they stand out in contrast. As we sit still, we become more aware of the subtle sensations and energies coursing through the body. We feel the body more as object than subject. In this way it's more like observing the sensations than being inside them.

But what makes it so hard to sit still?

Our bodies aren't designed for stillness. Even in sleep, we move. When we hold the body in one position for a long time, it starts to hurt. We are habituated to react to these unpleasant sensations by adjusting our posture. This happens throughout our day and throughout our life, unquestioned and often unnoticed. When we come to meditation, we are challenged to respond another way.

As discomfort arises from sitting still in meditation, instead of trying to fix it, we explore it. Maintaining posture as best we can, we point the mind to the sensations, all the while breathing and relaxing. We notice that sensations aren't stable, but rather are constantly shape-shifting: pulsing, moving, growing, and shrinking. They are dynamic and alive, and this makes them interesting subjects for investigation.

We also notice the mental reaction, the drawing away from sensations that happens as we try to move toward them. We feel the resistance, and as with the sensations themselves, we breathe into those feelings and release.

Today, try to sit with perfect stillness in your meditation. Notice the subtle ways the body shifts and tilts with no intention. Notice how the mind reacts to the body in stillness.

# November 16

*"Challenges of Meditation: Rushing Thoughts"*

When people first sit down to try meditating, they're often overwhelmed by the busyness of the mind. Without guidance, instruction, and support, they're likely to call off the entire experiment. At this point they might think that they have an unusually busy mind or that they need to find another technique that will stop their thoughts. This idea is based on the fallacy that the goal of meditation is to stop your thoughts. Instead, it's more helpful to see what you are doing as *changing your relationship to thoughts.*

This change begins with just noticing thoughts. We start to see both the content and the process of thinking. With content we see what our habitual concerns, interests, fears, and judgments are. This gives us insight into ourselves and the ways we operate in the world. With process, we start to see how habitual our thinking is, how persistent yet ephemeral. There's not much to our thoughts, just words and images passing through the mind with no substance and often with no basis in reality.

These new ways of seeing our thoughts allow us to relate to them differently. Now, instead of getting caught up and following every stream of thought, we can detach and just let them come and go. So, while the primary way that mindfulness meditation is taught encourages us to note the thoughts, to watch each one, an alternative is to see if we can experience the thoughts as something like clouds passing through the mind. In this way we aren't giving attention to the content of the thoughts, but just letting them float by. We stay connected to the breath as we expand our attention into a spacious awareness that has room for thoughts, sensations, sounds, and feelings. The thoughts become more like a background noise, like the distant sound of a train passing or the refrigerator humming in another room. We are grounded in the stillness of the body, undisturbed by the changing elements of experience.

Today, see if you can allow thoughts to simply come and go like clouds in the mind. Don't be disturbed or concerned with thoughts, just see them as a natural part of your moment-to moment-experience.

# November 17

*"Challenges of Meditation: Anxiety"*

There may be times when simply closing your eyes and sitting still evokes or reveals feelings of anxiety. You might get caught in a cycle of fearful thoughts as you meditate. It's helpful to have tools for when such feelings might arise.

The quickest way to break the cycle of anxiety is to open the eyes and essentially stop meditating, though you might continue to sit and feel the breath. However, the tools of meditation can also be used to stay with and work through such feelings.

You can approach this challenge both cognitively, by challenging the thoughts, and through the body, by exploring the sensations.

The cognitive approach asks us to question the anxious thoughts, to see whether they are based in reality. Often such thinking is driven by underlying false beliefs which, when exposed to the light of awareness, lose their power.

So, as you're sitting, if you find yourself stuck in an anxious cycle, ask yourself, "Are these thoughts true?" and "What is another way of looking at this situation?" Such questions draw from the practice of cognitive-behavioral therapy.

Working with anxiety in the body means stepping out of the thoughts themselves and intentionally feeling the anxious sensations. It's important to breathe with this experience, and often you'll want to deepen the breath as you follow the uncomfortable streams of energy through the body. Feel the feelings in the chest and belly, in the arms and legs, in the shoulders, the face, and wherever you find them. Breathe in, and with your exhalation, relax. See if you can just be with the feelings and allow them to settle.

Today, notice if feelings of anxiety are appearing in your practice and work with these strategies for dealing with them.

# November 18

*"Challenges of Meditation: Boredom"*

If you practice meditation regularly, go on retreats, join a meditation group, and generally make it part of your life, sometimes it's likely to seem boring. Just sitting there and paying attention to the breath can get pretty tedious. How can you stay engaged?

Usually feeling bored means that your attention is lagging. Without close attention, thoughts, feelings, and sensations can seem like a repetitious droning. Here we need both more energy and more purpose.

First of all, we try to look more closely, feel the details of breath, notice the sensations in the body, observe the meanderings of mind, and track emotional states. This push to engage more directly will arouse energy and interest.

Secondly, we utilize the Buddha's guidance on exploring the dharma. He encouraged us to see how experiences arise and how they disappear—in other words, the arc of experience. This reveals the changing, impermanent nature of everything, and guides us to the insight that there's nothing you can hold on to. The letting go that comes out of that insight brings serenity and equanimity to our mind and body. This state is not boring. In fact, it offers some of the richest fruit the practice bears.

Our investigation continues as we observe how suffering arises and how it ends—the Four Noble Truths. And finally, we start to see how ego arises, how attaching to self causes suffering. Again, we are motivated to let go and feel the freedom that comes from that release.

It's hard to be bored when we engage the dharma in this way. And the joy that comes with this connection inspires us to go even deeper.

Today, notice if your practice is becoming stale or boring, and bring effort to engage the attention in more determined ways.

# November 19

*"The Habits of Mind"*

When we meditate, we become acutely aware of how we are using our attention in our daily life. Whatever we've been focusing on comes right up when we sit. Stress at work? Here comes the boss and the project. Binge watching a TV show? The characters, plot, and images come through the mind. An argument with your partner? Like a GIF playing over and over, you get to hear the same words backwards and forwards.

For addicts, such thinking can lead to dangerous places. Our mental habits have been persistently destructive and driven by craving. Nonetheless, our meditation practice can help us to break these patterns.

One of the hardest parts of meditation is the unruliness of the mind. When we see how consumed we become by such thoughts, we begin to understand why the Buddha said to be careful where you put your attention. As addicts we had the habit of putting our attention in just the wrong place.

First of all, we look at how we are using our attention. Our meditation will reveal much of this and give us a chance to consider ways we might want to focus differently. In our daily lives, we apply mindfulness in the same way, noticing where we are expending our mental energy.

Secondly, we learn to be less bothered by that which appears in the mind. We take a perspective of observing from a place of non-identification. Thoughts do not belong to me. I am not my thoughts. We can see them as just a passing show, energies running through the mind.

Today, reflect on the ways you are using your attention and what that brings into your meditation. Consider ways you might focus differently in your life.

# November 20

*"The Spirit of Recovery"*

The Twelve Steps are a spiritual program. They encourage us to look beyond material and intellectual solutions to our problems and cultivate inner strength and wisdom. They ask us to develop a radical honesty about ourselves, and they push us to connect with others to support and be supported on this journey.

It's not enough to practice abstinence or to simply show up at meetings. To uproot the poisonous habits of addiction might take years, or even a lifetime's commitment to self-examination, surrender, and letting go, because addiction isn't just a behavior but an expression of deeply rooted emotional tendencies. Selfishness, fear, and pain-avoidance drive us. These must be addressed through the tools of the program in an ongoing way.

The rigorousness of inventory work is vital in this process, as is the willingness to turn things over. We find that the Steps aren't just a linear process, but a web of interwoven elements to be drawn upon when needed. First, we work them in order, but over time, we start to call on them and delve into them on demand. At one moment remembering powerlessness is key, at another, self-examination. Still other moments call for making amends, trusting our Higher Power, or letting go. And, of course, we often find the need for quiet meditation to bring calm and clarity to our agitated minds.

For our program to carry us over the long haul of recovery, we need to come to understand the Steps in their fullness, to know what's needed at a particular moment, to be familiar with the nuances of each Step so that we can easily and naturally work with it.

Today, reflect on your familiarity and understanding of all the Steps. Do you know them well enough to carry you through the many challenges of recovery and of life? Are there Steps that you need to study and work on more deeply?

# November 21

*"Keep Going"*

Time is a vital part of meditation. One of the reasons we go on retreat is to spend more time in practice. Time is one of the key elements in developing calm, concentration, and insight. We keep peeling away the layers of noise, distraction, and agitation to get to the essential clarity at the center of the mind. But this peeling isn't easy.

First we are faced with restlessness. It's one thing to sit still for a minute or two, but when we start to practice for twenty or thirty minutes or more, we find that a lot starts to happen that's not so easy to face. The body wants to move and fidget, and the mind wants entertainment. Then there are the demons that start to appear—the fears, sorrows, regrets, and resentments, some long buried, that burrow up out of the subconscious when typical restraints and distractions are put aside. These make it even more challenging to continue.

If we can find our way through the blocks and hindrances, we may finally arrive at a place of true peace. There we discove a quality of calm joy that's almost heavenly. We feel as if we've finally got it, that we now know how to meditate, and perhaps even how to be happy.

But this isn't the end. We carry on with our practice, and things continue to change.

Even on long retreats, these periods of serenity pass, and we find ourselves back in some mental cul de sac or emotional treadmill. Where did that lovely peace from yesterday go? Frustration grows, along with irritation and a sense of failure. We had it, but we lost it. What did we do wrong?

As it turns out, nothing. We remember that change is constant, that there's no arriving, no permanent place of comfort in the mind, in the body, or in our lives. And so, we continue to practice.

Today, notice your relationship to time in your meditation practice. Try to let go of the obstructions to longer sits. You might even try to sit longer than you ever have before.

# November 22

*"Outside Issues"*

In recovery meetings, we're asked to disregard "outside issues" that might distract from the central focus of dealing with addiction. This suggestion comes out of the early growing pains that AA experienced, and it has stood the program in good stead for a long time. In the Western Buddhist world, however, there is an increasing awareness that we can't simply turn our backs on the problems in society, that we have a responsibility to bring our spiritual values to bear.

How to skillfully respond to the suffering in the world is a perennial question. Buddhists have been asking this ever since the time of the Buddha, and they continue to ask it today. The issue isn't so much *what* we should do or say, but *how* we do it. If we are acting out of fear, anger, or aversion our response will be poisoned by those attitudes. The challenge is to act out of wisdom, compassion, and kindness, even as we call out the power structure and systems of oppression. This is, of course, the work of Dr. King and Mahatma Gandhi, the work of non-violent resistance.

For a recovering addict, there is an underlying risk to such engagement, and that is the threat to our recovery. If our work on outside issues comes to dominate our life and our psyche, we risk getting triggered to relapse. Balance here is key.

The problems of the world aren't always solvable, at least not by us right now. The frustration and despair that might come out of a social or political struggle can easily start us down the slippery slope to using again or acting on addictive impulses. It's vital that any work like this be held in balance with our inner life and our serenity. Without that, our efforts will always be tainted by aggression and grievance.

Today, reflect on your own engagement with social and political issues. How do you hold them? Are you doing your part? Are you overextending yourself or succumbing to anger and frustration?

# November 23

### *"The Next Right Thing"*

One of the typically enigmatic phrases we hear in recovery rooms is that we should do "the next right thing," as if this were always evident. When faced with big decisions, we simply may not know or sense what the next right thing is. What this phrase may be pointing to is not so much the big decisions, but the small ones.

Often the next right thing is actually quite simple. It might be getting something to eat, going to a meeting, showing up for work, or resting. As addicts we tend to get ahead of ourselves, thinking we need to figure out our whole life, or at least some large segment of our life, *right now!* This is why we have the saying "one day at a time," so we don't get ahead of ourselves.

This impulse to have all the answers immediately comes out of fear. It's uncomfortable not knowing what's going to happen, so we want to figure it out, make some timetable, some plan. But making decisions out of fear rarely leads to a good place. We wind up making decisions before we actually have to, which means we don't have all the potential information we might want. Instead, waiting until a decision is necessary allows other factors to unfold. We'll often find that the decisions make themselves, that it becomes apparent what the wisest course is.

Just doing what's in front of us, making a small, wise choice now, leads to better results in the end. Our small decisions build towards a positive outcome without us having to do it all at once.

Today, focus on the moment-to-moment choices and let the bigger issues take care of themselves.

# November 24

*"Being a Friend"*

Our connections with others form the basis for our spiritual growth. From the Buddha's statement that noble friends are the whole of the spiritual path, to the emphasis on helping others in the Twelve Steps world, we know that these relationships provide us with the human contact, care, and support that make all of our work worthwhile.

Listening to a friend, sponsee, student, or just an acquaintance who wants to share gives us an opportunity to be of service. The first way we serve is by listening. It's so easy to want to jump in and fix others or take care of them. If someone comes to us for help, our ego wants to prove that we can help, so we might shift into "know-it-all" mode. Besides that, it can just be painful to listen to someone else's suffering, and if we haven't got enough inner balance, we can wind up wanting to put a band-aid on their problem so that we don't have to deal with it further. And then there is the co-dependence that makes us feel that we are somehow responsible for someone else's pain, so we must fix them in order to be okay ourselves.

All of these tendencies need to be put aside if we are actually going to help. That's why the first gift we give others is our silence, listening fully. If we do so with an open heart and quiet mind, we'll likely find that a natural, supportive response will emerge. If it doesn't, we can simply say that we don't have the answers, but let our friend know that we love and care for them. That's probably what they really want and need anyway.

Today, notice how you respond to other people's suffering, and try to lend an open, caring ear to them.

# November 25

*"Attitudes of Mindfulness: Non–identification"*

"We tend to take things personally. 'My thoughts, my breath, my feelings.' Mindfulness encourages us to take another view: just thoughts, breath, and feelings—not mine, not me. This radical shift in perspective helps us to maintain an objective viewpoint. Every time we take things personally, we're adding a layer to our experience that tends to complicate matters. If you think a thought is 'yours,' then you tend to judge it more; you think that you have to do something about it; you think that you are either 'good' or 'bad' based on whether it's a good or bad thought.

"Of course, we are deeply conditioned to identify with our thoughts and feelings—as well as our physical sensations. We can't just turn conditioning like this off. But we can start to notice how we identify. Bringing that investigative curiosity to our experience helps us to begin to break the habit of conditioned response." *Workbook*, pp. 45-46.

One of the quirks of the Step process, the program, and meetings, is that hearing people's stories, we become less attached to our own identity. After a while, nothing we did seems so exceptional. Ours is just another story among thousands, nothing unique. This then begins to free us from the "bondage of self" the Twelve Step literature refers to. We have less to defend, less to prove, and less need to stand out as someone special.

Now we are getting a taste of "not-self."

Today begin to notice how you identify with your thoughts. See if, at least occasionally, you can let go of that view and take them less personally.

# November 26

## *"Perspective"*

How we respond to experience is largely determined by our perspective, how we see and understand what we are experiencing. As active addicts we often thought of our using as normal, and so didn't think we had a problem. In recovery our perspective has shifted significantly.

The Buddha's three key teachings on impermanence, suffering, and not-self help us to gain perspective. If we are surprised by change, it disturbs us; when we remember that everything is impermanent, we gain perspective on change and are less upset by it. If we are surprised by suffering, we can get overwhelmed; when we remember that *dukkha* is a natural part of life, we gain perspective on our struggles and can hold them with acceptance. When we cling to an identity, any threat will agitate us; when we remember that self-view is a construction, we don't get caught in this delusion.

These changes in perspective, what can be called "seeing things through the lens of *dharma*," allow us to move through our lives with less reactivity, more wisdom and balance. This is the quality of equanimity that the Buddha so values. It is a capacity to see the world with clarity, to understand how things work, to not be confused by all that arises and passes.

Maintaining perspective and equanimity requires mindfulness. We need to consistently remind ourselves of what is real and true, waking up from the illusions of permanence, satisfaction, and self that lull us into a dangerous dream. These tendencies, these false perspectives, are a kind of default for humans. We need the intervention of awareness to break them. With mindfulness we can remember, over and over, to step back into the perspective of wisdom and out of delusion.

Today, practice looking for a wise perspective in every situation you encounter. Remember impermanence, unsatisfactoriness, and not-self.

# November 27

## *"Meditation Is Not a Recovery Program"*

Despite the broad applications of meditation to the Steps, it is not a program in and of itself. It can be tempting to think we can take care of our recovery work solely by this practice, but that leaves too many gaps in the process, primarily the ones that involve other people.

Between the need for social support and that of feedback and guidance, a recovery community is the glue that holds our program together. The tendency to self-delusion and justification is too strong if not met by some outer response. At meetings we get reminders of how the program works and how sneaky and subtle our addiction is. Left on our own, these things can easily be forgotten as we build a wall of defensiveness and arrogance to block out any challenges to our preferences.

Addicts are often isolators, and using meditation as our whole program just feeds that tendency. We can fall into a pattern of solipsism, depending solely on our own thinking to guide us. This might be quite comfortable, but that's exactly the danger. The real work of recovery, the deepest and most vital work is not comfortable. Especially in the beginning, we need to have our beliefs questioned; to have our decision-making challenged; to be pushed to look more honestly at ourselves and our behavior. Otherwise, we will simply be continuing the folly of our addiction, the delusion that we don't have a problem, that a few lifestyle tweaks will solve everything, and that people who challenge us should be pushed out of our lives.

Obviously, this book is largely about the value that a serious meditation practice can bring to the process of recovery. However, please don't use that as an excuse to avoid the rest of this rigorous work.

Today, reflect on how you might over-emphasize meditation in your program. Would you benefit from more interaction with others in recovery?

# November 28

*"The Practice of Study"*

We put a great deal of emphasis on meditation in Western Buddhism. And there's no doubt that a regular practice has tremendous, often transformative impact on our lives. But to meditate without an understanding of the teachings can be a limited way to develop a Buddhist practice.

The teachings on the Four Noble Truths and the Eightfold Path give meaning to the experiences of meditation. They explain what the Buddha saw as the source of suffering and the way to freedom. Without grasping this essence, we are, to a great extent, practicing in the dark. Uncovering their wisdom opens new vistas in our lives.

The teachings on the Five Hindrances explain and help us navigate many of the challenges in meditation and in life. Conquering them frees us from mental bondage.

The wisdom to be gained from studying the Three Characteristics of Existence—impermanence, suffering, and not-self—can have boundless effects on our understanding of the world and our place in it. What had once seemed mysterious about life, now reveals its truth.

The beautiful lessons found in the Brahamviharas—loving-kindness, compassion, sympathetic joy, and equanimity—can transform our whole experience of life. Our relationship to others and to ourselves blossoms with kindness.

In order to fully benefit from your Buddhist practice, you need to study these and other Buddhist topics. Part of your regular practice should be reading and listening to teachings. Start with one book that resonates with you and look at the bibliography or recommended readings that the author offers. Find talks online on Buddhist topics from the teachers who inspire you. Keep exploring and pursuing knowledge of Buddhism, just as you do on your recovery path.

Today, begin to make dharma study part of your practice. Start simply, with one topic, and keep exploring and expanding your field of interest over time.

# November 29

*"Heir to My Karma"*

We can't control everything about our lives: we don't get to choose our parents or the circumstances of our birth; historic and cultural forces are largely out of our control; and other people's actions can have direct effects on our lives. It's not that we are responsible for all these things, but we are responsible for the way we handle them.

Many addicts have a genetic predisposition to addiction as well as an upbringing by alcoholic or addict parents or family members. Trauma and mental illness are common elements of our history. In the course of our addiction, we might have used these things as an excuse for our behavior. And there's no doubt that these types of circumstances are difficult to deal with. But what we are still responsible for is how we behave today.

We can't change the past. That karma is there, and we have to live with it. The only time we can change our karma is in the present moment. That's where we are responsible—and empowered. No matter how much pain or how many problems we've had, if we expect anything to be different in the future, we have to change today.

Our karma is determined by our thoughts, words, and deeds. Meditation helps us to change the karma of our thoughts, letting go of delusion, anger, and grasping. We start to see the world differently and respond differently. With mindfulness, we choose our words more carefully, knowing the impact they have on people will inevitably come back to us. And we make different choices in our behavior, understanding the long-term consequences of selfishness, destructiveness, and irresponsibility.

It's easy to dream of some better future where we won't have problems, where we'll be happy and at peace. But that future will never come if we don't change our karma.

Today, consider how your thoughts, words, and actions are creating your future. Reflect on how you could act more skillfully in these three realms of karma.

# November 30

*"Spiritual Awakening"*

The essence of spiritual awakening is the understanding that true happiness and value in life don't come through the material world. We see that acquiring possessions is ultimately unsatisfying; that power and control over others only leads to more conflict and frustration; and finally, we realize that it's our inner life that creates the circumstances for happiness and satisfaction. Meditation helps bring us to these insights and gives us a tool for living out this realization.

When we first learn to meditate, though, we come with the same acquisitive nature that society has taught us. We think we're going to "get something," become peaceful, control our minds, or perhaps heal some wound. With proper guidance and a sincere intention, we soon learn that this is the wrong approach to meditation, that it only leads to more dissatisfaction. This is the essence of the Second Noble Truth, that craving causes suffering.

With this spiritual awakening, a whole row of dominoes falls as we begin to be guided by new principles. Rather than grasping, we learn to let go; rather than controlling, we learn to accept; rather than resenting, we learn to love; rather than chasing stimulation, we learn to seek peace.

Step Eleven brings us to this climax of spiritual awakening. By thrusting us into the fires of inner work, we're taken to the graduate school of recovery, where we move beyond simple abstinence and Step work to the realm of the Great Path that so many humans have followed throughout history. We find ourselves drawn deeper into this journey. As our meditation deepens, our capacity for wisdom and insight, compassion and kindness grow. This is the "knowledge and power" that the Step refers to. The potential for a freedom previously unimagined, opens to us.

Today reflect on the ways that your meditation has transformed you. Take time to appreciate the work you have done in recovery and in the Dharma, taking joy in your own efforts and the awakening that they have revealed.

# DECEMBER: STEP 12

*"Having had a spiritual awakening as the result of these Steps,
we tried to carry this message to [addicts, alcoholics, etc.]
and to practice these principles in all our affairs."*

# December 1

*"Spiritual Awakening"*

Each month we've looked at the spiritual awakening associated with the Step of that month. Now we look at the very idea of spiritual awakening.

In the various Buddhist traditions, we see different definitions of enlightenment. Its essence seems to be non-attachment, either to the material world and its sense pleasures, to beliefs and ideas, to other people, and ultimately to self. The Steps parallel these ideas with the need for non-attachment to our addiction and the recognition that self-centeredness is at the heart of our problem. This means that spiritual awakening is having a clear understanding and direct insight into the need to let go on multiple levels.

Once again, we come back to the simple idea at the heart of all spiritual practice: letting go. This is the essence of the Four Noble Truths and the Twelve Steps. It runs counter to the human tendency to cling, one that's reinforced by economic pressure and social conditioning.

As addicts, we cling to our substance or behavior. In recovery we discover the freedom that comes when we let go of that clinging. This insight hopefully inspires us to look at other ways we cling and other ways we need to let go.

We learn that clinging to the material world as a source of happiness is a myth, and we begin to let go on that level.

We see how clinging to self, to ego, is another trap, and we work to let go there as well.

We see how resisting change, clinging to the way things are right now, inevitably brings grief, as everything must change. Thus, we begin to let go of the very idea of permanence itself.

Eventually we realize, just as the Buddha said, that any clinging whatsoever will cause suffering.

Today, reflect on what you still cling to. Probably none of us will ever let go completely, but it helps for us to be honest about where we resist this path to awakening.

# December 2

*"As the Result"*

While some Steps suggest that certain things will happen, "restored to sanity," and "remove our shortcomings," for example, in Step Twelve we're told that something *will* happen—in fact, something *already has happened*—"as the result" of the Steps. This is a striking claim and one worth examining.

In contrast to the way the Steps are depicted in this book, most people understand spiritual awakening to be solely associated with Step Twelve. The suggestion is that there is some cumulative effect of working the Steps that blossoms at this point in the process, although the language of Step Twelve is somewhat ambiguous—"having had," suggests the spiritual awakening happened *before* Step Twelve, but we're not told exactly when.

But the point, nonetheless, holds that something happens when we work the Steps. This means that each of us in recovery who has genuinely worked the Twelve Steps has had some sort of transformation, a spiritual awakening. Whether you feel this has happened or not, it's important to take in this idea. This might require another sort of inventory, a spiritual awakening inventory.

In doing this, we might look at our relationship to each Step, whether things like powerlessness, turning it over, inventory, and amends (among many others) have changed us. For most people, it's obvious that we have changed. Perhaps the term "spiritual awakening" sounds too lofty, but that's what it is.

Today, reflect on the various forms of spiritual awakening you have already experienced in your recovery.

# December 3

*"Carrying the Message"*

A key moment in the Steps is the connection between "spiritual awakening" and "carrying the message." That connection suggests that if you've awakened, you've essentially solved your problems, so now the natural thing to do is pass it on, to help others. More specifically, we can say that the nature of this transformative experience is the transcendence of self.

One key element of spiritual awakening in Buddhist teachings is seeing through the illusion of self. In recovery, we don't put it in quite such dramatic terms, but the reference to self-centeredness as our big problem, as well as the Tradition that says we trust in "principles before personalities," points to how freedom from ego and self are at the root of our recovery. And if focusing on ourselves isn't the way to freedom, then helping others must be.

The description of the Buddha's awakening tells a similar story. It's said that right after his enlightenment he considered just enjoying being free. He thought that it might actually be annoying to try to communicate the profound and subtle nature of his experience. Then, however, he was visited by a Brahma god who told him he should teach out of compassion for those who were ready to hear his message. In our contemporary view of psychology, we might figure that this idea actually came to him from his own mind, but in any case, he decided to "carry the message," and spent the next forty-five years of his life teaching.

Like a recovering addict who works the Steps and then starts to do service, the Buddha carried his own message. This example is a key one for each of us. Whatever awakening or recovery we have experienced, we can share. That's what makes our life meaningful. That's the perfect expression of spiritual awakening.

Today, reflect on how you can carry the message of Dharma and recovery.

# December 4

## *"Carrying the Dharma"*

Many people who engage deeply with Buddhist practice feel drawn to sharing that practice with others. This longing to teach is a natural outgrowth of spiritual awakening. There are many ways we can do this.

You might simply share with friends about your experience practicing mindfulness. This might lead to explaining the basics of meditation. Hopefully this will inspire them to pursue their own practice.

The ability to carry the dharma in a meaningful way depends primarily on deepening your own experience. You can't share what you don't have. And, because students of meditation have widely varying experiences, you also need to have broad experience if you want to guide and support them. This experience can really only come by sitting meditation retreats.

Carrying the message in Buddhism is, then, different from that of the Twelve Steps. While anyone with more experience in recovery might help and support another person, in Buddhism there is a higher bar to clear in order to be an effective guide. Because of the subtleties of Buddhist teachings and the complex challenges of Buddhist meditation, teachers are typically trained and then authorized by other experienced teachers.

Today there are increasing opportunities to get such training. You should always be careful that someone offering such a program is truly qualified to train other teachers. Only a master teacher should be training others in this way.

Again, though, the primary qualification for teaching is your own meditation experience. If this becomes a goal for you, it's good to first go on a few ten-day retreats, and then try something longer, a month or more. Along with this, you should study both contemporary and traditional Buddhist teachings. All this will give you the beginnings of a foundation for being a teacher. Any teacher will also want to continue to deepen their practice even—and maybe *especially*—after they begin their own teaching.

Today, reflect on your own ambitions or lack thereof to teach.

# December 5

*"Principles: Honesty"*

Step Twelve says we tried to "practice these principles in all our affairs." The principles this refers to are, presumably, the Twelve Steps themselves. But it might not immediately be apparent what those principles are. Various efforts have been made to define them, and in the coming days we'll look at some of these.

Honesty is certainly one key principle, as it's something referred to a great deal in the *Big Book*, and is required for working the Steps in any kind of meaningful way. As addicts, we often lied or deceived others and ourselves in significant ways. We concealed our behavior from others and convinced ourselves we didn't have a problem. Taking Step One requires that we come clean with ourselves and to some extent, with others as well. This is only the beginning, though.

Step Four requires a new level of honesty, reflecting deeply on our past and the harm we have done. Step Five demands that we share this inventory.

Steps Eight and Nine force us to specifically admit who we have harmed and face them honestly. For most of us, this may stretch us beyond what we even thought we were capable of.

What we discover through these radical steps is the freedom that comes from hiding nothing. This is the Bliss of Blamelessness, the lightness we feel when there are no shadows, no ghosts, no shame, or secrets.

Honesty is the foundation for all the work we do in the Twelve Steps.

Today reflect on your commitment and behavior around honesty.

# December 6

*"Principles: Faith"*

After the initial challenge of honestly facing our addiction, the next roadblock the Steps set up is the demand that we trust in the process. Step Two's statement that we "came to believe," puts many non-believers in a bind. This is where some people turn to Buddhism for a less doctrinaire approach. While Buddhism requires faith, it's not blind faith, but one built on experience and logic.

Nonetheless, there is always going to be a need for trust and faith on a spiritual path. In the case of the Steps, you can't know for certain that they are going to work, so you're going to have to take them on faith at first. With Buddhism, the same applies. You sit down to meditate not knowing what the results will be, but you have some trust that it will be beneficial.

Faith is a powerful force. It gives us energy and confidence. It gives us the strength to carry on through challenges, failures, and resistance. To sustain ourselves through the ups and downs of recovery, we need to believe that it's worthwhile and that our path is a wise one. To sustain ourselves on the ups and downs of Buddhist practice, we need the same kind of trust.

In Buddhist teachings, faith is balanced with wisdom. This means that faith isn't thoughtless or irrational. While we understand that we must trust the process, we don't accept everything we hear blindly. The Buddha's advice is to test out any teaching and see if it works, if it brings beneficial results. Only then should we trust it completely. While skeptical doubt is seen as a hindrance, discriminating wisdom is a vital guide.

Today reflect on your relationship to faith both in the Steps and in Buddhism. Do you have too little or too much faith in either?

# December 7

*"Principles: Willingness"*

Resistance to change, to anything new, and to looking honestly at ourselves was one of the biggest blocks to our recovery. As long as we stayed stuck in our behavior and our self-view, there was no possibility of growth and healing. A willingness to step into this process was essential.

As addicts we were set in our ways. We had struggled with life and finally found a way to survive, however destructive that might have been. It was our escape, our solution to the unmanageability of life. And yet it was killing us, both figuratively and sometimes literally. Nonetheless, we were still afraid to try anything different.

Our initial willingness didn't come easily. It was more or less forced on us by coming to a bottom in our addiction. However, once we had opened that door, once we had seen the benefit of trying something new, we got an inkling that such an attitude might actually be worth fostering.

With time, we became even more willing. Everything from our work life, our education, our relationships, our spiritual practice, and more, became fair game for willingness. A whole new sense of possibility opened up. We saw how our formerly closed mind had limited and crippled our life in myriad ways. And we were no longer willing to live in that shuttered world.

Willingness brings freedom from fear. Instead of asking "why?" we ask, "why not?" What will we lose by trying something new, by being open to fresh experiences and ideas? We can always try it, like a new flavor, and if we don't like it, we don't have to eat the whole thing.

Today reflect on your own willingness. Are you getting the full benefits from willingness or do you still hold back?

# December 8

### *"Principles: Humility"*

Arrogance is certainly one of the common character defects of addicts. The belief that we are special, or perhaps that others are less than special, allows us to justify acting in harmful ways. When we learn to be right-sized, when we become comfortable with the idea of being wrong or not knowing, we actually free ourselves from a painful burden.

Humility is the realization that we are limited in our knowledge and power. How could we have all the answers? How could we handle every challenging situation in life perfectly? That's not realistic, but then in our addiction, realism wasn't one of our strengths.

Humility frees us from painting ourselves into corners. We don't find ourselves defending the indefensible or fighting pointless battles. Instead, we're guided by kindness, by curiosity, by openness. We are willing to learn, to listen to others, to grow. Without humility there is little opportunity for growth or change. We stay stuck in one belief system no matter what new information we receive.

In relationships of all kinds, from the personal to the professional, humility brings harmony. No one likes the braggart or the bully. While such personalities might acquire power, they rarely make real connections or develop loyal friends. Humility doesn't mean debasement or lowering oneself, but rather avoiding attempts at domination and respecting others equally.

Perhaps the word "humility" has something to do with being "human." Humility is seeing yourself as human, with all the flaws and fine qualities that implies.

Today reflect on your relationship with humility. Are you humble enough to admit you're wrong or don't know the answer to something? Proud enough to believe in yourself when you deserve it?

# December 9

*"Principles: Service"*

Step Twelve brings service to the forefront of the program. Like many elements of the Steps, it introduces a broadly impactful tool through a simple suggestion. "Carrying the message," is just a recommendation for sharing your recovery, your "experience, strength, and hope." Ultimately it becomes much more than that.

What we learn when we engage in this act of sharing is the great joy that comes from helping others and from being helpful. Within the program, carrying the message has broadened to mean not just helping the newcomer or sponsoring people, but doing service within the program, such as taking a role as secretary, treasurer, or some other position in a meeting.

Anyone who has taken this part of the Step seriously soon learned that they could take this idea further by being of service in the broader world. We bring the spirit of service to our family life, our friendships, our work life, and volunteer work. Because we've seen the happiness that comes from helping others, we now seek out opportunities that we might have avoided in the past.

Service is an act of humility. In that act we put aside ego and discover the freedom of selflessness. From a Buddhist perspective, which sees ego as both a construction and an obstruction, this is a wise stance to take. When we focus on others, we forget ourselves. It is our obsession with self that causes us some of our deepest suffering.

Service then functions both on the practical level to help the world and on the spiritual level to help us escape the trap of ego.

Today reflect on the ways you are of service in the world. Is there more you could do to help others and to free yourself?

# December 10

### *"Meditation Ritual"*

Sometimes when we sit down to meditate it can take a little while even to begin. If you are busy, stressed, or the mind is active, just taking the posture might not be quite enough to engage the attention. This is why it can be helpful to have a ritual or structured way to start each sitting.

You might begin by ringing a bell or lighting some incense. You can also start with a standard focus like a body scan or taking the time to set your posture. You might look for any tension in the body and relax that.

If you decide to focus on the breath, do it very intentionally. Make sure you are getting close to the breath, not just vaguely aware that you are breathing, but attuned to the details and subtleties of sensation. That will tend to focus and ground the attention. The same applies to any other meditation subject.

Further elements of a meditation ritual might be using a loving-kindness practice at the beginning or end. These meditations are very structured and oriented toward arousing positive states. That makes them helpful at any point in your practice.

Some prayer or acknowledgment at the end of practice also helps to give a sense of closure.

Although it's fine to simply use a clock or watch to time your meditation, some people prefer to set a time. This can easily be done with a meditation app that provides a pleasant bell sound rather than a jolting alarm.

Many people bow at the end of meditation, a traditional form of respect, appreciation, and humility.

Using consistent or ritualized forms in meditation helps you to stay on track. It gives structure to the formless realm of meditation and brings a sense of the sacred to your practice.

Today consider how you might ritualize your practice. Is there something you could do that would help in the structure of your meditation?

# December 11

*"All Our Affairs"*

The culmination of the Steps tells us we should bring our commitment to living by spiritual principles into every aspect of our lives. If these values are only applied to special situations, they lack real meaning. Step Twelve challenges us to be wholehearted in our integrity.

As we've seen, the Buddha gives similar guidance in the *Satipatthana Sutta*, The Four Foundations of Mindfulness, when he lists the situations in which we should practice mindfulness: whether standing, walking, seated, or lying down; in all our movements; when eating or drinking; when falling asleep or waking up; when talking or keeping silent. That's pretty thorough. Clearly, like Step Twelve, he wants us to practice mindfulness in all our affairs.

These directions from the Steps and from Buddhism give us a lifetime's worth of opportunities to grow. When we first come into recovery we're just focused on our primary addiction. Later, secondary addictions might become more problematic and give us more work to do. Over time, many people realize they have emotional sobriety issues around relationships that might take many years to resolve. Then there's the question of education and career, with a lot of other possible avenues to explore. Finally (perhaps), there's our relationship to the world—to social, political, and cultural concerns.

While this might seem like a lot, we don't take all of this on at once. Over time we address each of these challenges. Eventually, though, we come to appreciate how this pervasive engagement is actually an opportunity. It gives us a focus in every situation and every moment. We have a lens through which to look at our experience. And, perhaps most important, the different elements of our life are all tied together by these consistent values.

Today reflect on any areas of your life in which you are not practicing these principles. Rather than trying to solve all of them at once, pick one that you can begin to work on.

# December 12

## *"The Allure of Pleasure"*

While our drinking and drugging eventually took us to a place of pain and suffering, originally they were a source of pleasure. To be high felt good, at least for a while. When we become abstinent, we lose that source of pleasure, and we can feel grief at that loss. This is one reason we relapse.

The Buddha acknowledges that there are many kinds of sensual pleasure. However, he points out two limitations: first, that there are better forms of pleasure found in meditation and insight; second, that sense pleasure can't satisfy us because it's bound to change, leaving us longing to get back what we've lost.

Nonetheless, if we're not monks or nuns, we're still going to want a certain amount of pleasure in our lives, and there's nothing wrong with that. In fact, it's probably healthy. How to find non-harming forms of pleasure is one of the puzzles of recovery. As addicts we got used to pretty extreme forms of pleasure, and now we have to become attuned to more subtle joys, and moments of comfort and serenity.

An important part of recovery is finding what can bring us pleasure without hurting ourselves or others. Walking in the woods, biking, and all kinds of exercise can be gratifying. Music, literature, theater, and all the arts can bring great joy. Making our own art of any form can be a wonderful source of happiness. Spending time with friends or in community can be uplifting. These are just a few ways we can find pleasure in the world. We need to be creative and open-minded in exploring things we might enjoy. As addicts we tended to be pretty closed-minded, so now we need to be willing to try things and consider possibilities we never have before.

Today consider what brings—or *might* bring—more pleasure into your life without harming you or others.

# December 13

*"Unworthy"*

Many people in recovery speak of feeling unworthy of love. What does this mean? The sense of unworthiness comes from what Buddhists call "the comparing mind." We don't think we are as good as other people, and therefore, we deem ourselves unworthy.

Buddhists view every being as worthy of love. It's not something we have to earn; it is our birthright. If we base our sense of worthiness on a comparison, there's always going to be someone "better" than us. In fact, our worth isn't based on our accomplishments or even on our behavior.

In pure meditation there is no comparing, there is only being. When we are present and awake, alive to the moment, we sense the preciousness and frailty of this life. We sense our innate wish to give and receive love. We sense that there is no separation, no meaningful difference between us and any other living being. Worth or lack of worth have no relevance to this knowing.

The world determines value by wealth, power, and fame. Likewise, social status, physical looks, and other superficial measures supposedly help determine our worth. But as we deepen our spiritual life and get closer to a more essential truth, these false markers fall away. In their place comes something simple and beautiful, life itself.

Letting go of these false measures of value doesn't mean we stop engaging in the world. In fact, without the burden of comparing and judging ourselves, we are able to be more functional, more creative, and more efficient, not wasting emotional energy on constantly struggling for status. We can see where we stand in comparison to others, but we don't determine our worth through that lens. Our happiness doesn't depend on being the best, the richest, or the most anything. Our true worth is inside.

Today reflect on your sense of self-worth. What false measures do you use to determine your own value? Can you sense your own worth simply in being?

# December 14

*"The Spiritual Foundation"*

The Twelfth Tradition of the Twelve Step program calls anonymity the "spiritual foundation" of the Traditions. All Twelve Step programs have *anonymity* in their name, and yet the true spiritual value of this word is often misunderstood.

The founders of AA, the first Twelve Step program, remained anonymous for practical reasons. At the time, alcoholism was seen as a moral failing and anyone who admitted to such a condition could become a pariah. They felt they needed to remain undercover to protect themselves professionally and personally. But soon they realized that by not focusing on who they were in the outside world, they could connect on a deeper level. Anyone who walked into a meeting was just another alcoholic, no better and no worse than anyone else. In letting go of professional and social status, they were letting go of ego supports that ultimately caused more stress than satisfaction.

The Buddhist idea of "not-self" reflects the same insight. When we simply see ourselves as living beings, we let go of a burden we don't realize we are carrying. Trying to gain and hold onto position in the world, whether financial, professional, social, or otherwise, can be a constant strain. We're always having to check where we stand. Is our position, power, and wealth safe, or we are losing ground?

Anonymity, then, gives us a way of letting go of all that. We are simply one member of a community. Although some people think that saying, "I am an alcoholic" (or any kind of addict), is taking on a negative identity, it might also be seen as stripping away all the other elements of identity that we cling to. When we walk into a meeting, we are simply another addict, nobody special, free of the markers of status or value. This is a way of living out the idea of "not-self."

Today reflect on your relationship to anonymity. What is most important to you about it?

# December 15

## *"Morality and Compassion"*

The Buddhist monastic scholar, Bhikkhu Analayo, says that, "moral conduct is an expression of compassion." He explains that by intentionally not harming others, we are expressing our wish for them to be free from suffering, and therefore we are acting compassionately.

It's worth reviewing the Five Precepts from this perspective.

When we don't kill any living beings, we are most obviously being compassionate. This Precept, when interpreted more broadly, means that we refrain from violence or any form of harm: again, a way of living that is kind and caring.

When we refrain from stealing or taking what isn't offered, we are protecting other people's possessions, which is another way of being thoughtful and kind. This Precept can expand to include not abusing or wasting resources, which expresses a broader compassion to all beings on the planet and the earth itself.

When we refrain from sexual misconduct, we help people to feel safe. With this Precept we are respecting the sanctity of each person's body and sexuality. This Precept expands to include any interaction, not just physical. The ways we speak, dress, or look at others can be invasive. Respecting those boundaries is an act of kindness.

When we refrain from lying or harsh speech, we help to create a peaceful environment. Speaking the truth in useful and timely ways brings harmony, yet another expression of compassion. We expand this to include written communication, especially things like social media.

With the Fifth Precept, not using intoxicants, we continue to protect others and ourselves by remaining clear-headed. We expand this Precept to include all the ways we detach from reality through entertainment or distraction. Staying present, mindful, and attentive brings connection with others.

Today reflect on the ways your commitment to the Five Precepts is an act of compassion.

# December 16

## *"The Effort of Showing Up"*

How to make Right Effort is one of the great challenges and ongoing questions for any meditator. When we learn to meditate and get the instruction to pay attention to the breath, we might get consumed with the idea that if we can somehow just stay with the breath and stop our thoughts, we will have it all figured out.

What happens most of the time is that we can't stay with the breath or stop our thoughts. The mind keeps wandering off. So, we renew our effort. We ask teachers what to do. We read books on meditation to get tips. And we keep failing. After a while we might get discouraged about the whole project. We simply can't figure out how to make Right Effort.

The fact is, most of the effort of meditation is the showing up—over and over. Yes, there is some effort involved in trying to stay present, but if we show up in our meditation place and stay there for the allotted time, that's probably ninety percent of Right Effort. That's the important part.

This might be particularly true about meditation retreats, where the question of effort becomes even more pressing as the schedule has us meditating over and over throughout the day, as well as trying to be mindful in walking, eating, and every other activity. Just like at home, on retreat the mind wanders a lot. To avoid frustration around our lack of control of the mind, it's helpful to remember that just by showing up we've done a whole lot of the work. If you don't believe that, look around and see how many people *aren't* at the retreat, or *aren't* meditating at home. That's most of the people in the world. There are very few of us who even attempt to meditate.

By all means, keep making effort to be present, to develop concentration, and to cultivate open-heartedness. But don't make that effort another reason to blame yourself for being imperfect. We're all imperfect.

Today reflect on how much you are showing up for your meditation practice. If you are already doing that, take a moment to appreciate your effort. If you aren't, make the commitment to show up and cultivate Right Effort.

# December 17

## *"Mental Purification"*

*Sila*, the moral aspect of the Noble Eightfold Path, is often viewed as mostly about cultivating good karma, living wisely and compassionately in the world. This is certainly a significant reason to follow these principles. However, Bhikkhu Bodhi, the Buddhist scholar and translator, says that in the context of the Eightfold Path, even that ethical purpose takes a backseat to the more essential purpose of aiding "mental purification."

What he means by this is that if we, for instance, break the precepts by killing and stealing, our minds become poisoned with hatred and greed. We become habitually driven by those qualities, lost in a cloud of delusion, unconsciously driven by these destructive tendencies. Any spiritual development becomes impossible in these states.

If we follow the Precepts and *sila*, practicing Right Action, Right Speech, and Right Livelihood, we live unburdened by such negativity. These outward actions then have an inward effect. We condition ourselves, not toward greed, hatred, and delusion, but toward generosity, kindness, and mindfulness. The heart and mind become unburdened of guilt, remorse, and shame. That lightness gives clarity to the mind, and thus, "mental purification."

Today reflect on your relationship to *sila* and mental purification. How could you cultivate greater clarity through these practices?

# December 18

*"Holiday Relapse"*

The holiday season is one of high risk for relapse. What with office parties, family gatherings, and social expectations, it's a time when we can easily get triggered. For many of us, this was a time of year when we upped our consumption, whether of alcohol, drugs, food, or shopping. That last can be a big trigger, as we overspend on gifts trying to compensate for our low self-esteem. Furthermore, the "Ghost of Christmas Past" can rear its ugly head with memories that evoke grief and trauma.

All of this can create a toxic mix that results in us taking "just one drink," and spiraling back into relapse. That's why it's so important during this time of year to stay close to our program and our spiritual practice. It's a great time to up your meeting attendance and schedule clean and sober activities. The recovery community is very sensitive to the risks at this time of year, so you'll find lots of opportunities for connecting. That can make this season not just tolerable, but actually joyful as you rediscover some meaning and purpose in coming together. It's a great time to do service, perhaps volunteering at a food bank, homeless center, or treatment center. Generosity starts to take on another meaning.

This is also a great time for retreat. Many centers offer retreats over New Year's or daylong events throughout the month. Again, connecting on the spiritual level reminds us of something positive about the holidays. Instead of focusing on shopping, partying, and our dysfunctional family, we discover the beauty of going inside to find peace and of sharing that journey with like-minded folks.

Today make a plan for getting through the holidays clean, sober, and happy.

# December 19

*"All Those Thoughts"*

The persistent challenge of meditation is all those thoughts. No matter how hard we try, they keep on coming. In fact, trying to stop them can make the situation worse. Recognizing that we aren't actually in control of our thinking is the starting point. Then we need to develop some distance, some sense of separation from the thoughts so that we don't take them personally. This is one of the key projects of mindfulness meditation.

When we first try to meditate, most of us think what we're going to learn is how to stop our thoughts, so we go through a period of trying and failing to do that. Some people just give up on meditating during this phase, figuring that either they are no good at meditating or maybe they need to try a different practice.

If we get through this phase and get some clarity about how mindfulness meditation actually works, we start to see that it's not about controlling the thoughts, but changing our relationship to them. We learn to observe thoughts impersonally, to view them as conditioned output of the mind. We find we can distinguish between skillful and unskillful thoughts. We get curious and start to see patterns, whether we are caught in planning the future, reviewing the past, obsessing about money or work or relationships. All of this moves our practice into new and different territory.

This is the point when we can transition to another phase, where we might give up trying to control thoughts, and instead turn our attention to the breath, the mood, and emotions. We realize that there is another life going on right here in our body, a felt experience separate from the life of the mind. In seeing that mind is separate from (though interconnected with) body, we get the first window into the possibility of unhooking from the mental habits that keep us cycling through these habitual thought patterns.

Today, notice where you are in this process. Are you able to disconnect enough with thoughts that they don't completely capture you and trigger stress?

# December 20

*"Decisions, Decisions"*

One of the things that causes the most stress for people is making decisions. Having to decide means that right now you don't know, and not knowing is something that causes people a lot of anxiety. The unfortunate result is that people make decisions quickly that they later come to regret.

Applying mindfulness to the anxiety about decisions helps you to hold the unknown. Our training reminds us of the uncertainty inherent to life and helps us to become comfortable with that truth.

The first question to ask about decisions is, "When do I have to decide?" The longer we have to make a decision, the more information will come in. Oftentimes conditions and situations change, making it unnecessary to actually make a decision. Or we learn something that clarifies the decision. Time also allows us to mull over an issue. Time means that ideas get explored and considered, allowing past experiences and preferences to be recalled.

When you feel pressure to decide something, your mind tends to close down. Your thinking becomes more narrow and constricted. Taking time to meditate and even do activities that take the mind off the decision allows the subconscious to process the situation. Even a good night's sleep can help clarify things.

We can also fall into the mistaken belief that we need to figure everything out for ourselves. Friends, mentors, and sponsors, not to mention teachers, partners, and therapists, can all be valuable people to bounce ideas off. Sometimes simply voicing the issues to another person clarifies things that thoughts alone can't. Speech activates different parts of the brain than silent thoughts, so talking is an important part of decision making.

Today make a commitment to a decision-making process that allows for time, reflection, and discussion in any decision you have to make.

# December 21

*"Principles before Personalities"*

The final words of the Twelfth Tradition bring home a vital concept: "principles before personalities." Again, focusing on anonymity, they point us to the importance of living by spiritual values rather than self-centered goals. From a Buddhist view, we are seeking to follow the Dharma instead of our habitual craving and aversion.

In our interactions with others, we also want to avoid being swayed by domineering personalities and stick to clearly articulated principles. It's easy to lose our way when forceful people push us to follow them. In community, in business, in politics, and in personal relationships, maintaining integrity protects us from the destructive effects of egos.

In our own lives, we may have to bring to mind what we really believe when we find ourselves driven by grasping or self-seeking. This comes down to the karmic consequences of actions. When we act out of greed, hatred, or delusion, the karmic results will inevitably be negative, even if the initial effect seems positive. It's not always easy to stick to this principle, especially when some bright, shiny object is hanging in front of us, triggering our grasping impulses. In the short run, perhaps we'll get what we want. In the long run, we're likely to regret it.

Acting out of greed means trying to get something no matter the cost; acting out of hatred means getting rid of something or someone no matter the cost; acting out of delusion means believing that acting out of greed or hatred will actually bring lasting satisfaction. This could be said to be the underlying principle of all Buddhist teachings.

Today reflect on your own commitment and intention to live by your principles. Recollect how it turned out when you chose to act out of greed, hatred, and delusion instead of your highest values. This will help you to affirm your commitment to acting wisely.

# December 22

*"Ghosts"*

Although the holiday season is meant to be festive and joyful, it's not that way for everyone. As we've talked about, this is a high-risk time for relapse. What often comes up is memories of loss, ghosts from the past. In the simplest version of this, the holiday simply reminds us of past times and people that are gone. Since many of us had family events at this time of year, when family members have passed away, those memories of loss tend to be strong.

What can make this particularly difficult is if someone close to you died at this time of year. Those anniversaries are difficult anyway, but when combined with the emotional charge of the holidays it can trigger grief and depression. The contrast between those feelings and the festive atmosphere of the season can become particularly poignant, if not painful.

Once again, this should make for a strong impetus to work our program and take care of ourselves. As we get older, these ghosts become more and more prevalent. Inevitably we lose loved ones over the years. Learning to live with those losses is critical to any hope for happiness. The community of a Twelve Step group or a meditation group can be an important support for those losses, especially when the feelings are raw and triggered.

The Buddha frequently speaks about the importance of remembering impermanence, that everything changes, and everyone dies. In fact, he makes this one of his suggested Daily Contemplations. The recollection that everything is always in the process of change is a powerful reflection that helps us to not only accept loss, but to appreciate what we have in this moment. Knowing that whatever is happening right now will soon pass gives us more impetus to be awake and aware in the fleeting present.

Today reflect on holidays past, acknowledging any loss or grief you have related to this season. Then remind yourself of what is beautiful in your life right now, and how your recovery makes everything better.

# December 23

*"The Good News"*

There's a tendency to think of the truth of impermanence as bad news: everyone gets old and dies; all your possessions wear out or get lost; you yourself are in the process of aging, heading inevitably toward death.

But the fact of impermanence isn't all bad news. Change is what makes life dynamic and exciting. Imagine if everything stayed the same. Every day the same weather, the same conversations, the same work, the same entertainment. Okay, so you might never get older, but at some point the boredom would kill you. No, like many other truths, the truth of impermanence isn't good or bad. It all depends on how you relate to it.

If you are trying to hold on to something—your looks, your children, your possessions—certainly you're going to struggle, because these things are all going to change. You'll get older, your children will grow up and leave (hopefully), and your possessions will fall apart. If you want those things to stay the same, you'll be frustrated. It's worth asking, though, do you really want them not to change? Do you want to stay one age forever? Keep taking care of your children for all eternity?

When looked at this way, we see that impermanence is what makes life exciting. It's the very unpredictability of life, the unknown possibilities, that get us out of bed in the morning.

Awareness of impermanence stimulates interest in this very moment. Knowing that the present moment will never come again motivates us to pay attention. Life only exists here and now, not in the past, not in the future. If we want to be truly alive, we must pay attention to this impermanent experience.

Today reflect on the positive aspects of impermanence. Notice the things that will only happen once and take time to enjoy them.

# December 24

## *"Holy Days"*

The various celebrations at this time of year all have their roots in religion and spiritual practices. These are times of celebration, of community, of remembrance, and ritual. While the secular nature of our culture tends to commodify all these events, their essence is something much more important and profound. If we want to be in tune with that essence, we need to go inside, to touch our own connection to these rituals. Different traditions offer us a variety of ways to do this. It's not so important what choice of celebration we make, but just that we do so sincerely.

Buddhist meditation is a daily ritual of life. It trains us to be more fully present to our inner life, the outer world, and the joy and suffering of those around us. Buddhism tries to make every day holy through the practice of mindfulness. All actions are sacred when undertaken with this spirit of open-heartedness, awareness, and wisdom. Likewise, recovery reawakens our capacity to find meaning in the sacred and the mundane.

With this training, we can more deeply appreciate traditional holy days (aka, "holidays"). Now the rituals, songs, prayers, and reflections performed on these days come alive as we tap into their essential meaning. No longer just empty gestures, such rituals express a deep longing of the human spirit to find meaning in this short life. Each religion has its own path to this meaning, but they all ultimately converge. Love, ethics, generosity, and wisdom are shared across traditions. And each of these traditions is enhanced by the practice of mindfulness, which is why people of many faiths turn to Buddhist practice to deepen their connection to their own tradition.

Today, if you have a spiritual tradition, reflect on its holy nature. If you don't have such a connection, simply reflect on the holiness of life itself. Notice how bringing mindfulness to any tradition enhances its meaning.

# December 25

*"Generosity"*

The pervasiveness of Christmas as a cultural event means that even non-Christians wind up participating in at least peripheral ways. And, of course, the most common form of participation is in gift-giving. What began as a remembrance of the birth of a religious leader has become an excuse for commercial excess. But the spirit behind this materialism is a positive one. Generosity is an essential spiritual quality.

The Buddha taught lay people to be generous even before he taught other elements of the dharma. He wanted them to feel on the most basic level the joy of letting go and the gratification in helping others. The way he set up his monastic sangha in relation to the lay community institutionalized generosity. The monks and nuns were banned from growing or storing food. Initially they could only get fed by going on "alms round," walking slowly through a village with their bowl and waiting for someone to offer food. Over time the lay followers started to build monasteries and bring food to the monks, as is usually done today. In both cases, though, the lay community was practicing giving, supporting the practice of the monks and nuns.

Learning the joy of giving on the material level becomes a stepping-stone into giving in other ways. Giving time is one of the greatest gifts we give others. Giving attention is perhaps the essence of love. Giving care heals. Understanding, forgiveness, compassion, and patience are all gifts we can give.

In one sutta, a monk says to the Buddha that the way he expresses loving-kindness is that he thinks, "Why not put aside what I wish to do, and do what these venerable ones wish to do." This is the essence of the generous heart, to think of others before ourselves.

For addicts, perhaps the greatest gift we can give ourselves is the gift of recovery.

Today reflect on how you can act with more generosity in your life.

# December 26

## *"Staying on Track"*

The holidays tend to break our routines, which can be refreshing. But that break can also undermine our efforts at meditating consistently. While it may not be possible to fit in our usual time for meditation over these days, if you can just take a couple of minutes to sit even in a busy, unstructured day, it will help you stay on track.

We have to be creative at such times and look for a little window of time. Perhaps you are waiting for someone to get ready or to arrive? You realize you don't have to do anything for the next couple of minutes. Instead of pulling out your phone and checking your social media feed, sit down and breathe for a few minutes.

In those moments, we'll often find that the body and mind are very stimulated and unfocused. Instead of immediately trying to force the attention onto the breath, do a short body scan with a particular focus on energetic sensations. Stimulation is felt as both physical and emotional. Scan over the different places where this energy appears, and breathe with that.

Let the breath naturally deepen and slow to hold and release that energy. Then, if you still have a few minutes free, gently bring the attention to the breath. At this point you might notice the contrast between the excitement and energy of the holiday, and the natural calm of the breath. You can see how artificial the stimulation is and that there is always this calm center to draw from.

In a few minutes you might even find yourself veering toward fatigue. The holiday stimulation exhausts the body—even without booze and drugs to push it along—and when we simply stop and settle, that fatigue can quickly catch up with us. Taking these few minutes of meditation will help restore your natural energy.

This approach to practice can be used anytime in our busy lives. Whenever we are over-stimulated, stressed, or even elated a few minutes of focus can help us to reset and bring mindfulness back front and center.

# December 27

## *"Mood Swings"*

In our addiction, our moods could be volatile. Some of us grew manic and elated when intoxicated, while others might become moody and hostile. There's nothing quite as scary as an angry drunk. And when hungover or in withdrawal, we could turn dark, surly, and cold. While we're not nearly so likely to go to these extremes in recovery, we're not free of emotions just because we've renounced intoxicants. And during holiday times, with routines thrown off, and social and family obligations putting us under unusual strains, we can find ourselves getting tossed back and forth by mood swings.

This calls for self-care whenever we can find time for it. When traveling, visiting relatives, or receiving visitors, it can be hard to make time for yourself. Sometimes just taking a walk around the block, going to the gym, or taking a nap is all it takes to break out of a difficult emotional spiral. When we lose our center and find ourselves in unfamiliar territory, we need to get grounded, back to a sense of who we are. Just returning to the body is a good start.

For people in Twelve Step programs, this is, of course, the perfect time to go to a meeting. If you are with family, hopefully they know enough to support you in that. The holidays are a time when addicts need to huddle together, and it can be a great respite from all the busyness to sit with a group of fellow addicts and talk about what's going on. We bring compassion and understanding to each other. And most of all, we remind each other of our priority: don't drink or use no matter what. Ordinary people drink more around the holidays, so there may be more times we face alcohol. If our mood is disturbed and we let ourselves get lost in feelings of depression or alienation, we are at risk of relapse. Now is the time for self-care.

Today make some plans for self-care. Make sure your schedule leaves room for exercise, meditation, and a meeting.

# December 28

*"Having Fun"*

While there are probably going to be moments of temptation or stress over the holidays, there's also the possibility of some authentic fun. In recovery we can lose sight of the fact that just because we're not drinking or using doesn't mean life has to be drab and boring. In fact, having clarity, health, and energy makes it all the easier to enjoy playful activities. Whether dancing, going to a concert or show, ice skating or any other pleasurable pursuit, we can feel free to let loose.

Part of recovery is regaining the capacity to enjoy the simple things. At the point in our life when we started using heavily, we began to lose touch with true joy. We came to depend on being loaded for our entertainment and fun. In fact, soon enough, we couldn't even imagine enjoying anything that didn't involve drinking or using. Those activities in and of themselves became our sole form of pleasure. When you think about what it means to go to a bar and keep consuming alcohol to the point of complete intoxication, it hardly even makes sense as an activity that someone would do voluntarily, much less one that would be seen as enjoyable. Yet, this is the state of alcoholism. And drug addiction was much the same. Simply being loaded was the whole point of our existence. We didn't have to do anything else. What a sad and diminished version of life.

So now, in recovery, we have to rediscover what real joy is. You may have to dig way back into your past to remember a time when you enjoyed something like throwing a ball or bouncing on a trampoline. Perhaps you are drawn to art, painting or throwing pots. There are hobbies galore, book clubs, and hiking groups. There are plays, symphonies, and films. As we emerge from the miasma of addiction, we may be amazed to see that the rest of the world has been having a jolly time without intoxicants, and that they've figured out a lot of great activities. Now is the time for us to join in.

Today, if you haven't already, start to think about how you might discover some joy and fun in your life of recovery. If you already have explored this, then recommit to keeping up those activities in your life. Don't miss out! A full life is available if you are willing to participate.

# December 29

*"No Matter What"*

One of the enduring sayings in the Twelve Step world is, "Don't drink or use, no matter what." It's the bottom line, the starting point, and the key to the whole program. If we can't follow this maxim, we simply can't reap the rewards of recovery.

There are going to be days, and maybe even weeks or months, when it doesn't seem worth it. Perhaps you suffer from depression and fall into one of those pits where nothing seems to help. You try therapy, antidepressants, exercise, working the Steps, and nothing seems to work. What's the point? Why not just get loaded? But that question answers itself because what could possibly get better in your life if you start drinking or using again? Perhaps there would be a brief span—hours at most—of feeling good, followed by what? More of the same? Guilt, shame, or regret? A depleted body? An emotional crash? How could this actually make things better? No, the truth is that sooner or later everything passes, including depression. The program reminds us that we just have to get through one day at a time.

Then there are the other times, the good times, when everything seems great, when you're happy and feel that you've overcome your addiction. There you are at your relative's wedding and the champagne is flowing, and everyone else is drinking—even the kids—and you think, why not? If you take that drink, you'll know. But the truth is, if you've been sober for a while and gone to enough meetings, you already know. One drink is too much and a thousand won't be enough. You aren't like those people who have a glass of champagne and say, "That made me sleepy. I better stop." No, it's not going to be just one glass of champagne. Even if you manage to control your drinking that day, the spell of recovery is broken. Now it becomes harder and harder to avoid more relapses.

We simply can't drink or use. That's our condition. If we forget that, even for a day, we risk everything. The best policy is to simply say that you don't drink or use, no matter what.

# December 30

*"Looking Back"*

The end of the year can be a time to look back at how things are going. What were the high points? The low points? What did you learn? What mistakes did you make? This can become a helpful year-end inventory. Our lives pass so quickly, one day blending into the next, that we lose sight of the arc and purpose. Every once in a while we need to step back and consider how it's progressing.

We don't do this review as self-criticism. That's just another way to beat ourselves up. Rather, we want to take time to appreciate ourselves and our opportunities. And, yes, it's also important to consider where there could be some improvement. This consideration isn't a judgment of our behavior, but an opportunity for course correction.

As we look back, we might also remember things that are incomplete. Maybe we started a project and got distracted. Maybe we made some plans that we never followed through on because we got too busy. This is a great time to revive such plans.

Mindfulness, of course, is about being present, so it can seem like looking back is a distraction from true spiritual work. And looking back with longing or regret is not the point. In fact, we learn from the past. When we observe historical patterns, detect habits, and see the results of different behaviors, we are able to make better choices going forward. This is the ultimate value of inventory.

Today consider what lessons you have learned in the past year, either from things that went well or from things that could have gone better.

# December 31

## *"Looking Ahead"*

The end of one year and the beginning of another is a traditional time to look to the future. Where do we want to go with our lives? How can we make things better? And, of course, what resolutions would we like to make to improve ourselves?

As with looking back, we don't want looking ahead to be an escape from the present or from reality. Rather, it is a way of setting a new course. The daily grind of life can make it difficult to check the progress of our larger goals and direction, so it's important from time to time to step back and ask ourselves if we're moving in the way we want.

Now is a good time to consider your Twelve Step program. Is it time to go through the Steps again with a sponsor? Do you need a sponsor, or is your relationship with your current sponsor satisfactory? And how about meeting attendance? Time to step it up? Also, this is a good time to consider giving more service and perhaps offering yourself more as a sponsor. This kind of reckoning is vital to keeping your program alive.

The same can be done with your mindfulness practice. Are you putting enough time into your daily meditation? Do you have a regular sitting group that you join? And what about study? There is so much great material for increasing your knowledge of Buddhism. Meditation alone isn't enough. We need to understand the dharma if we are going to gain the most benefit from our practice. And finally, this is a good time to commit to a retreat in the coming year. Going away for a week or more of meditation can be hard to fit into a busy schedule, but most serious practitioners consider a yearly retreat to be vital to their progress on the path.

There are many other things we consider when looking ahead. Keeping an eye on our recovery program and our meditation practice are at the heart of any progress we hope to attain in our lives.

Today take some time to reflect on these ideas and how you want to move ahead with your program and your practice.

# Acknowledgments

I want to express my deep gratitude to Walt Opie who did the mammoth job of editing this book. During a pandemic, while balancing his duties as a new father and teacher-in-training, he managed to give vital and insightful notes on a challenging project.

Mike Campbell has designed a cover and layout that I love. I appreciate his generosity, skill, and imagination.

I am so fortunate to have encountered two spiritual traditions that transformed my life. I will be forever grateful to my Buddhist teachers and Twelve Step guides. The opportunity to be a part of carrying on these traditions is a great gift.

Buddhism & the 12 Steps

Printed in Great Britain
by Amazon

43548455R00215